THE DEATH OF MANAGEMENT

THE DEATH OF MANAGEMENT

Restoring Value to the U.S. Economy

JACK BUFFINGTON

Pʀᴀᴇɢᴇʀ

An Imprint of ABC-CLIO, LLC

A B C 🦥 C L I O

Santa Barbara, California • Denver, Colorado • Oxford, England

Library of Congress Cataloging-in-Publication Data
Buffington, Jack
  The death of management : restoring value to the U.S. economy / Jack Buffington.
    p. cm.
  Includes bibliographical references and index. 7047814
  ISBN 978-0-313-36212-5 (alk. paper)—ISBN 978-0-313-36213-2 (eBook)
  1. Management—United States. 2. United States—Economic conditions—2001-3. Competiton, International. 4. Recessions—United States. I. Title.
  HD70.U5B84 2009
  338.60973—dc22
                    2009015916

13   12   11   10   09   1   2   3   4   5

This book is also available on the World Wide Web as an eBook.
Visit www.abc-clio.com for details.

ABC-CLIO, LLC
130 Cremona Drive, P.O. Box 1911
Santa Barbara, California 93116-1911

This book is printed on acid-free paper. ∞
Manufactured in the United States of America

Contents

Acknowledgments

Sometimes, I can hardly fathom how I've been able to write and publish two non-fiction business books on current events within an 18-month period when I also have a very demanding corporate job and family responsibilities, among other activities. I certainly feel very passionate about these topics, but that alone isn't sufficient to get the job done. Only through having a fairy-tale-like loving and supportive family structure was this effort possible. My father has played two roles: one as my role model and the other as my copyeditor for this book! My mother has always been my biggest fan and has given me the compassion that I need to understand the world (understand and then be understood). My sisters, Kim and Karen, have been important to my development and are still my closest friends. Most important of all, my wife, Kari, is the rock of my family and the best mate that I could ever ask for. Finally, my daughters, Kate and Marin, are my eyes to the future and my motivation to write about our collective future. Only through the support of a loving family has such an effort been possible, and I'm forever grateful!

1

Management as the Solution

My drive to work on a cold, snowy late-December day was different than usual. Instead of being in reflective solitude in my car, I was taking on a constant stream of questions from my two little daughters, who were joining me for the day. It is typical for me to take them to work with me for one day during the period between Christmas and New Year's, because activities are generally slower around the plant at that time, and they were out of school. They wanted to know everything about what I do as a manager: Was I nice or mean? Did I do work or just talk to people? Did people like me? I did my best to answer almost every question, but, after a while, I could tell that my answers weren't resonating with Kate and Marin. They really didn't understand what it meant to be a professional manager at a large public corporation. I started to wonder if this was because my daughters were only six and four at the time, or was it that nobody can articulate clearly just what a professional manager really does on a day-to-day basis, with any consistency? In today's chaotic, frenetic business environment, just what a manager is supposed to do is an important question that needs to be asked and studied.

Back in the days of my father and grandfather, it was easier to explain what a manager did and what contributions that he made (yes, it was almost always "he"). Fresh from the battlefields of World War II, the "organization man" was supposed to run the public corporation in a similar manner to a military division. Key decisions came from the executives, and planning was a critical element of strategy. A coterie of middle managers took the orders from above, each one with only a limited span of control over the operational execution. And decisions were filtered on down to lower-level managers, supervisors, and clerks, hundreds of clerks; each time, the process was done consistently and predictably. By his job title, everyone understood what an individual did. The requirements for what it took to become a middle manager were fairly generic (at least in today's terms), relative to years of experience, level of education, and nights out drinking with the guys. Most managers worked for the same company for life; a 1952 survey showed that two-thirds of executives worked for the same company for 20 years.[1] It was a tradition for middle managers, supervisors, clerks, and production personnel to work for the same company—from high school to gold watch.

Corporate executives sought to balance the claims of investors, employees, and consumers optimally. Compensation standards were established by larger companies, and these standards percolated through the rest of the economy, providing decent pay and benefits, but without much incentive. Had the United States solved the problem of market inequities through a beloved relationship between workers, owners, managers, and consumers, or was it a temporary historical anomaly? Today, many economists believe that it was an anomaly, the result of a lack of market pressures that would eventually catch up to the U.S. economy. But there is more to the story than that: the U.S. economy has followed an era of balance, between capitalist and democratic forces of a type that hasn't been seen before because of the presence of classical management and real productivity. This book explains the role of classical management in this economic miracle.

THE CLASSICAL DEFINITION OF MANAGEMENT

What is the definition of classical management, and why is it so important to restoring value to the U.S. economy? Figure 1.1 illustrates the evolution of the discipline of management and the place of classical management in this timeline. This book identifies for the reader the classical era of management—before the mid-1950s—that drove productivity, competitiveness, and innovation for the U.S. economy. It retraces the process, over more than four decades, of how management fell from grace and how it has essentially become useless as a discipline today. Back then, this classical definition of management at the turn of the 20th century tied together the input variables of labor, capital, and technology within economic activity and was itself tied to manufacturing; it was like nothing ever seen before. The classical definition of management was neither the drab and boring "asleep at the wheel" approach of the bloated "corpocracy" (corporate bureaucracy) of the 1950s and 1960s, nor the "anything goes," unadulterated style of the 1990s and 2000s. Instead, it was a rational, balanced, scientific approach that enabled the U.S. economy to become the centerpiece of the world's industrial power after World War I, the U.S. industrial production process to outperform the German economy vastly during World War II, and the U.S. economy to reign over global production during the post–World War II period as had never been seen before in the Industrial Age. Many factors have contributed to the rise and fall of U.S. private sector productivity, but this book demonstrates that management as a discipline made the primary difference within the private U.S. economy.

Management Era	Description
Pre-Classical Management (late 19th century–early 20th century)	This era was defined by the robber barons who viewed themselves as the "captains of industry," with little concern over other factors in the economy, including the public sector.
Classical Management (1908–mid-1950s)	Classical management began in 1908 with Henry Ford's covenant between the company and its consumers and workers. This "golden era" of management, defined as the balance of the labor, capital, and technology, including the balance of the needs of the private and public sector. Classical management is a function of a rational system rather than an individual presence. This was the era when the American Dream really took hold.
Post-Classical Management, Phase One (mid-1950s–late 1970s)	Established as the era of "bloated corpocracy" and a lack of competition and innovation. During this era, the U.S. economy and its management was lulled into a false sense of security as a result of the rest of the world rebuilding from the decimation of World War II. This phase began the process of the "death of management."
Post-Classical Management, Phase Two (early 1980s–present)	Defined by "economic limitlessness," the achievement of endless economic growth and profit rather than optimizing the variables of labor, capital, and technology. Began as an overcompensation resulting from the first phase of post-classical management, and the stinging effects of the emerging global economy. Management's perception that *economic limitlessness* existed in the economy led to the complete destruction of the definition of management. Led by powerful individual personalities (e.g., Jack Welch) rather than management as a rational system.

Figure 1.1 Management's Timeline

As is illustrated in Figure 1.1, classical management started around 1908, developed strongly in the 1920s and 1930s, flourished in the 1940s, and then started to slack off during the 1950s and 1960s. It went completely sideways into the 1970s and even 1980s and then was cut loose for good in the 1990s and 2000s, as companies became unregulated, global, and unrestrained. Said differently, management at the turn of the 20th century was a novel concept; it had started in the United States and then transformed into an optimization tool that balanced labor (workers), capital (owners), and technology (invention). It became the greatest optimization scheme in economic history, through the middle class, but became complacent as a function of economic prosperity and lost control in the 1960s and 1970s. In the last part of the 20th century, it became a useless appendage. By the 1980s, U.S. business operations were largely incapable of taking on the newly emerging foreign competition that was entering the lucrative U.S. consumer market, after decades of no competition in a planned national economy. By 1990, the United States no longer manufactured items such as televisions, radios, steel, or textiles, after decades of being the world's manufacturing center. And all this has led to where we are today: a failing economic power—with no manufacturing base to build on—in a ruinous financial collapse. This book shows how this slow train wreck happened in our economy and how we can regain our economic prowess.

Anecdotal and superficial evidence incorrectly suggests that the current decline in the U.S. economy is the direct result of globalization, as though the world were supposed to stand still for U.S. business interests. Although globalization provides a very convenient and sanitary explanation for the problems in the U.S. economy and our business operations, it is a disappointingly inaccurate explanation. Today, China is the biggest scapegoat of all, yet 406 out of 426 U.S. House of Representative districts clocked triple-digit export growth with China between 2000 and 2007, so globalization is not without its possibilities.[2] To assume that economic progress in the developing world is the reason for U.S. economic decline is to assume that evolution is bad—when it is neither good nor bad, just inevitable. We can't change the rules of the game when they no longer suit us. Instead, we must change our institutions to focus on how we can compete under these new market paradigms (that aren't really very new anymore). In the past, management was this effective change agent for the economy.

POSTCLASSICAL MANAGEMENT DISCIPLINE

Today's postclassical version of management is a wildly out-of-control minimization and maximization tool that doesn't understand optimization, has the "dis-organization man" as its leader, is focused on financial engineering (i.e., achieving business results through financial and accounting transactions rather than ongoing operations) rather than true business value, and has a fear of true technological change. All of this is explained in this book. If you believe that the role of a manager is to thrive in and perpetuate a state of constant business chaos, as Tom Peters and other management gurus suggest, or if you believe that the manager must help bring back the "good old days" of the uncompetitive, bloated corpocracy, you probably are a creature of this postclassical management discipline and have likely never experienced true classical management. You and I may call ourselves managers as we stand amid this chaos, just as our fathers and grandfathers called themselves managers as they handled their administrative roles as organization men. But it doesn't mean that any of us really played the role—not the role that built the foundation of the U.S. economy.

In my career, I have been a corporate manager, studying and applying what I believed to be management for almost 20 years. I have been asked to direct financial engineering efforts, lead perpetual change that has been never ending and virtually never fulfilled, and led teams within this state of "destructive destruction" (a term that I frame as the opposite of Schumpeter's "creative destruction") for as long as I can remember. Sometimes, I have been asked to become somewhat of an organization man of the past, memorizing the *Successful Manager's Handbook* (the manager's bible) and trying to memorize and harmonize sets of rules of security and stability that put me at odds with my chaotic financial engineering objectives. On one hand, I am asked to thrive in chaos, to slice and dice the organization—reorganizing and restructuring continuously, if for no other reason than to present an environment of change and transformation. On the other hand, I am sometimes asked to be a stabilizing force as a leader, to build an environment of tradition, culture, and trust, as was the case during the stable period of an earlier era. Suggesting that this dichotomy is reflective of the classical management discipline is a misunderstanding of how management used to be practiced and how it saved the U.S. economy from a dangerous time in our economic history. But a corporate manager in the 21st century must operate in this chaotic environment, and it scarcely matters what company he or she works for. It's a function of the U.S. operating environment, no matter where you work.

The postmanagement discipline of today uses concepts such as short-term cost savings, minimization, maximization, as well as abstract and outdated econometric measurement techniques that have had an adverse impact on the corporation's real value. As a result, today's definition of the term *productivity* (as is shown in Figure 1.2) has dramatically changed from its true inception in the 1930s. That's why productivity has, until recently, been viewed as very strong in U.S. business operations—when it is not. Under great pressures to achieve this pseudo definition of productivity, today's corporate managers have little choice but to pursue short-term profits relentlessly in order to appease the investment community, which is now solely focused on short-term technical gains in surplus value for the investor. Today's pseudo definition of productivity at the U.S. corporation is so destructive and conflictive (as shown in chapter six) that it has become an oddity stripped right out of a *Dilbert* cartoon strip, something that ordinary Americans are finally starting to realize as they watched the U.S. economy spiral into a significant recession starting in 2008. In the past 20 to 30 years, wages have stayed flat or fallen (accounting for inflation) while this pseudoproductivity has surged. Even noted economists who were fans of the downsizing approach of the 1990s (like Morgan Stanley's Stephen Roach) are questioning whether our corporate strategies make any sense. Today, you might be asking yourself the same question, especially when you think about your 401(k) or your job security (or lack thereof). Those of us who are corporate managers must also ask ourselves what's happening in our economy to allow for such obvious discrepancies and lack of boundaries.

I think that it's a fascinating phenomenon that my role as a corporate manager is the alter ego of what my father's role was. Mine is chaotic, destructive, and focused on the short-term financial, whereas his was stable, boring, harmonious, and bureaucratic. Back in the 1950s, business schools taught students about the world of organization structure and how to be a good administrator. In the 1990s, I was taught something much different—creative, out-of-the box thinking and disruption, leading me to become an independent and transformational management consultant. The

Classical Definition (Past)	Post-Classical Definition (Today)
The achievement of surplus value from a corporation, using the tools of labor, capital, and technology, and the fair allocation of this surplus to workers, consumers, owners, and the public sector. Used primarily by managers of a corporation.	An econometric measurement of output from the production process. An abstract and/or nebulous concept that is predominately used by government economists.

Figure 1.2 Classical Versus Post-Classical Definitions of *Productivity*

world of the earlier generation's organization man is strange and unsettling to me, just as my trained world of chaos is strange to organization men. Both as a management consultant and as a corporate manager, those of us from trained chaos have been at odds with the organization man, just as he has been at odds with us. There has been much written on this topic of conflict within management, yet my premise is that it's a topic that's knocking on the wrong door. It scarcely matters today whether the postclassical management approach is that of the organization man or that of trained chaos: neither one is the true definition of the classical manager that was originally put into place to restore value within U.S. business operations and the U.S. economy. Thus, my contention in this book is that management is dead.

THE MODEL T AND THE ORIGINS OF CLASSICAL MANAGEMENT

Classical management used to be a function of a system, not an individual. Management in this classical sense was defined as a business system to optimize the inputs of labor, capital, and technology. As the U.S. business environment evolved decades after World War II, management remained a system, and this system changed through the use of organizational structure and hierarchy. Today, management as a discipline has come full circle, back to the days of the robber barons, and it is barely a system at all. Instead, management has become a function of the individual, a philosophy of personal experience and subjectivity rather than a rational systematic science. What was lost in this evolving process was a transformation from a system of management as a stabilizing, optimizing force in the U.S. economy, to a system more about organizations and structure than about competition, innovation, productivity, and balance, and, finally, to chaos and individualism. With classical management attributes no longer in place, it became up to an individual in management to set the tone for the rules of engagement without having a system, much like what happened during the robber baron era.

I have been at the forefront of this postclassical management era of whim and individualism, an era out of control and chaotic, which has led in part to numerous cases of "cult of personality" (whimsical individualist management) management leaders, both good (Jack Welch) and bad ("Chainsaw" Al Dunlap). When a management discipline is without structure, it is without limits. It becomes a laboratory for economic limitlessness, of growth without end. It's not a balance between the business variables of labor, capital, and technology, nor a balance of the private and public sectors. In our economy today, we are beginning to see the inherent dangers and repercussions that come along with a lack of balance that has been brought forth by management, particularly when it comes to a company chasing economic limitlessness. To the contrary, the wide openness of a global economy is a reason for the system of management, the need for optimization within a global economy that could become dangerous if left unchecked. Today, our economy is unchecked because management is dead.

There are differing opinions as to the specific origins of modern, classical management. I suggest that the logical starting point was in 1908, 100 years before the writing of this book. On September 27, 1908, the first Model T rolled off a production line at the Piquette Plant of the Ford Motor Company in Detroit, Michigan. Before the Model T, the company had produced and prototyped many versions of the automobile since the company's founding in 1903. The following is Henry Ford's rationale behind the Model T:

> I will build a car for the great multitude. It will be large enough for the family, but small enough for the individual to run and care for. It will be constructed of the best materials, by the best men to be hired, after the simplest designs that modern engineering can devise. But it will be low in price so that no man making a good salary will be unable to own one—and enjoy with his family the blessing of hours of pleasure in God's great open spaces.[3]

This statement reflects the spirit in which management was born. As a result of Henry Ford's production methods, the Model T could be purchased in 1908 for $850, for $550 in 1913, and for $440 in 1915.[4] This type of management baffled Henry Ford's competitors, who couldn't understand his refusal to take in maximum profits from a sale, to which Ford replied, "Every time I lower the price a dollar, we gain a thousand new buyers."[5] He was most certainly correct: sales of the Model T went from 69,762 in 1911 to 501,462 in 1915![6] Unlike most of the business owners during the early stage of the U.S. industrial era, Ford wasn't an aristocrat. He was a mechanic first, but he clearly understood how creating a balance between workers and owners could improve the plight of both. He proclaimed early on that his company would "initiate the greatest revolution in the matter of rewards for its workers ever known to the industrial world," and he delivered on that promise: in 1914, he doubled his workers' pay from an average of $2.34 to $5 per day and shortened the work day from nine hours to eight. To the masses who later suffered during the Great Depression, he was a hero. To many of his colleagues in the owner's class, he was classified as a traitor who misapplied biblical and spiritual principles. Truly, Henry Ford was on to something: that a discipline, a system of management, could be used to optimize welfare for both the owner and worker classes in order to create a win-win situation. There was less need for class struggle and violence or for a political solution. The solution was to be provided by management principles that were tied to the optimization of labor, capital, and technology in a production function. The likes of such an effort to inspire both the owners of capital and the workers of society had not been seen before 1908 and would greatly assist in helping the United States become the greatest economic power of the 20th century.

Management enabled the American Dream and economic limits defined it. Today, our postclassical management ethos is at least partially responsible for disassembling it and for creating the false utopia of economic limitlessness. Starting in 1908, the rise of the middle class had begun in the United States. Henry Ford laid out his vision for how members of the workforce would be rewarded for their efforts in ways that were unfathomed even a few years earlier. These same workers would then have an adequate level of disposable income, as well as available consumer products that were affordable and desirable. As a rise in disposable income was paired with efficient production and the lowering of prices for items previously considered beyond reach, workers would enable economic growth through their pocketbooks, money that would go right back to them in this shared covenant between workers and owners. The mercantilist theory (draconian government control over economic policy) of driving production away from the workforce and building a surplus for government from it (by precluding middle class consumption) was not a part of the American Dream. The lack of competitive spirit and bureaucracy within corporations during the middle of the 20th century in the United States wasn't the American Dream either. Nor is today's out-of-control "casino capitalism" and poor management-worker relations. The steady growth of the middle class was the American Dream. It was the story of multiple generations of steelworkers, each having a standard of living better than their old man's. It was the legacy of Henry Ford, never losing sight of how owners and workers could prosper together. Today, this covenant has been lost once again: the role of the professional manager was put in charge of it, but he or she lost control of it after the 1950s, when the U.S. economy was no longer based on the principles of free market enterprise. The exploding middle class of the 1930s through 1970s is being lost. Although the definition of middle class widely varies, the relative percentage of individuals who believe that they are better off is declining rapidly. The American people are losing their faith in the American Dream, because they no longer see it as possible through skill and hard work, in jobs that add value to the U.S. economy. Real hourly wages for most workers have risen only 1 percent since 1979, even as those workers' officially measured productivity has increased by 60 percent.[7] (See Figure 1.3.)

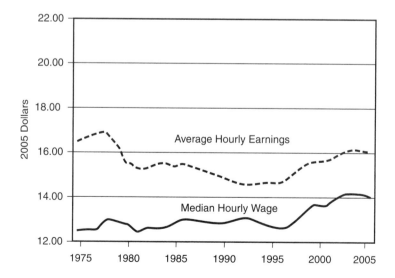

Figure 1.3 Stagnant American Wages

MANAGEMENT AND THE "BLAME GAME"

Today, we have the opposite effect to what happened during the days of Henry Ford: instead of rising wages leading to a higher standard of living for middle-class Americans, with resulting discretionary income to spend, falling wages are leading to a weakening of demand, spiraling true consumer confidence in the wrong direction. The paperboys from the Horatio Alger novels became managers, and now those managers are being laid off and are becoming paperboys once again.

The current popular response to pressures on wages, demand, and consumer confidence is to blame the perceived unfair nature of the global economy. Certainly, adding 1.5 billion new entrants from the developing world into the labor pool has had a negative impact on U.S. wages. But it isn't something that our policy makers can or should try to control. In February 2008, Senators Bryon Dorgan of North Dakota and Sherrod Brown of Ohio announced a "2008 Trade Reform Agenda" that spoke to the fear of globalization but offered protectionist kinds of solutions that won't succeed in a global economy (as discussed in chapter three). Filled with grandiose plans for how benchmarks will be established and measured to determine whether trade is fair, this is the bizarre story of the world's superpower economy feeling victimized by its less-developed upstart competitors. In his own words, Sherrod Brown goes on the defensive in an article in the *Wall Street Journal* titled "Don't Call Me a Protectionist":

> Let's stop accusing one another of being protectionists. And let us agree that U.S. trade policy—writing the rules of globalization to protect our national interests and our communities—is worthy of a vigorous national debate.[8]

It would be amusing if it weren't so pathetic: U.S. policy makers seem to think that writing the rules of globalization is up to us as Americans! Desperate times may lead to desperate measures, but it doesn't necessarily mean that these desperate measures will work. As millions of Americans seek greater financial security, often letting their anger lead to blame, what we must do is to look to our past. We must polish up on our history and understand how, in 1908, a covenant was born between workers and owners that led to our magnificent economic story, the American Dream. This real solution to today's problems can be found by revisiting the covenant of classical management, not through political protectionist efforts. We must understand that an economic model that promotes an optimization of win-win relationships between the owners of capital and the workers can truly lead to success in our expanding global economy, but not through political means. However, if U.S. managers continue to feel boxed in by corporate rules and the systematic rules of the financial markets, they will have no choice but to make absurd decisions to outsource both manufacturing and services, which in turn can potentially falsify measures of surplus value and productivity. The fact that many corporate managers feel compelled to make absurd short-term corporate decisions or to accept meddling government intervention over win-win relationships is testament to the death of management. Starting trade wars and grandiose government policy plans to manage Asian and Middle Eastern influences on our economy will accomplish very little. According to leaked figures, China's foreign exchange reserves swelled by $269 billion in the first five months of 2008, 20 percent more than in the same period of last year.[9] This is an issue of $1.8 trillion that China won't allow us to ignore when policy makers start talking trade wars. Right now, China and other nations are funding our red ink, both in trade and government expenditures, and it's only getting worse. We must solve these problems through private-sector management ingenuity and productivity instead of government-inspired antagonist policies.

Multinational corporations (MNCs) are achieving pseudoproductivity that is bad both for their long-time viability and for that of the U.S. economy. Many outsourcing efforts by MNCs will achieve pseudoproductivity through labor-cost reductions alone, and, although such measurements appear as positive in U.S. economic statistics today, it will be viewed as anything but productive in the future—for our business environment or to the company. The classical management approach that was founded in the United States can be a solution to reversing this rapid erosion of U.S. productivity, and it can bring manufacturing multinationals back into the United States as a place to operate. But we must first realize that we've lost our competitiveness, instead of feeling victimized by globalization. We must take control of our own destiny by reminding ourselves of what has worked in our past.

In this age of consolidation, the U.S. manager typically works for an MNC and must, as a matter of survival, show little to no sense of loyalty to the interests of his or her home country. When managers makes an offshoring decision—to use non-U.S. labor—they aren't committing an act of treason; rather, they are doing their job as it is required to be done, following financial engineering rules, no matter how wrong they are. If they choose to take a path different from the one to maximize short-term financial surplus, they risk putting their career and family welfare at risk. Their task is not to optimize capital, labor, and technology, as it once was: they have no system of management. They understand the rules of the U.S. financial system, which seek short-term financial results over all else, even at the expense of productivity, value, and innovation. With enormous compensation opportunities, such as stock options, given to corporate managers, should the leaders in this role be responsible for changing the system, or should they look after their best interest? Furthermore, managers in training have been taught at business school to optimize shareholder's wealth as the rule, first and foremost. And with a financial market driven by a faceless, international, mutual fund money market manager rather than by more passive individual investors of the past, an increase of shareholder's wealth is a short-term, unregulated exercise. The institutional money manager is encouraged to care little about the going concern of the company or the livelihood of its workers compared to the market fundamentals that lead to buy-and-sell decisions. If the job of today's corporate managers can be defined in one universal sentence, it is for them to maximize the short-term wealth of the shareholder, pretty much at all costs. It is not to balance the needs of the shareholder and worker, the long-term and the short-term. Today, we are paying the ultimate price for this short-sightedness. Having lived in this caustic environment for the past 20 years of my career as a corporate manager, consultant, professor, and author, the choice is clear to me: learn how to maximize short-term profit and minimize short-term cost or look for a career other than professional management. This approach, which I call financial engineering, has caused the slow train wreck that is affecting our economy today.

What about the management consultant? In the 1980s and 1990s, the consulting industry showed growth rates exceeding 20 percent.[10] The death of classical management and the rise of the management consultant are two events that aren't coincidental. Rising from the sacred check-and-balance relationship between the corporation and the public accounting firm of the past, management consulting had an inside track to being involved in the corporation's strategic development. In the late 1980s, Corporate America was full of organization men (and women) whose companies didn't possess the levels of innovation and real productivity growth necessary for U.S. corporations to compete in an emerging global economy. With Tom Peters and other management gurus in the news coming from the consulting sector, corporations looked to these firms to provide them with the thinking that they needed to compete in the new economy.

As revenues started to grow—from consulting at greater levels than their public accounting relatives—the lines blurred between audit or consulting firm self-interest and independent regulatory audit advising. With the financial markets going through a period of deregulation, the Big Five consulting firms used this as an opportunity to turn thinking in terms of management by individual into a moneymaking venture. And grow it did: as the best and the brightest from the top business schools poured into Big Five consulting, the industry was fueled by young thinkers who could quickly offer up firm strategies of all sorts. No longer was consulting the work of a handful of legendary thinkers. It was now the driver of growth in the U.S. service industry that sought to improve the short-term financial results of our corporations. The one helping you with your strategy wasn't the well-known thinker like Tom Peters, but young corporate consultants such as myself, fresh from business school. The principles of classical management were gone, and the cookie-cutter consultants of chaos and change were doing the thinking for the largest U.S. corporations.

What about U.S. business schools? In the early part of the 20th century, some of the legendary thinkers of management (many of them from the private sector) were associated in some way with our business schools, and many of these schools bear their names as testament. Today, as we face a crisis of the lack of true leadership at our corporations, where is this beacon of light coming from our learning institutions to guide us in the right path? If management consultants were the paid thinkers who covered for the incompetence of the organization men, perhaps the business schools were the ones who should have held the management consultants in check and redirected the discipline of management back to its classical methodology of the past. Our business schools should have kept this real discipline of management alive, and they should have been teaching our future business leaders how management can and should restore value at our corporations and economy.

Instead, big business reigned at business schools during the 1950s, and stale theories of organization and finance were taught. There were some practical concepts that trickled from out of the hallowed halls during the 1950s and the 1960s, but these institutions seemed to mirror the culture of staleness that prevailed over the big corporations of the day. In the 1980s, as it became obvious that U.S. businesses were incapable of competing in a more global economy, the business schools searched for the comfortableness of best practices. For example, some leading lights proposed to improve U.S. competitiveness by replicating Japan's Ministry of International Trade and Industry (MITI) as a *prima facie* answer to the question of how to improve productivity in a global economy during the 1980s. Such a suggestion is laughable, particularly in light of Japan's disastrous 21st-century economy, and few innovative management solutions originated from academia.

Despite their stellar reputations, U.S. business schools have failed in their responsibility to ensure that sound management principles are integrated into U.S. economic policies in a competitive global economy. If the curriculum of the 1950s and 1960s was stodgy and academic, today's pedagogy is rhetorical and self-serving. I believe that an MBA program should not only teach the student how to operate within a chaotic and global environment but, more important, how to stabilize the chaos in the direction of true strategy. Instead, our universities have primarily become learning centers on how to cope in a corporate environment. Students are taught that an economic model of unrestrained, economic limitlessness is not only possible but mandatory. Working as a manager in a world of no limits is an outdated economic paradigm. Teaching future managers how to optimize within an economic model of limits is perhaps the greatest tool that a classical manager can possess.

FOUNDERS OF MANAGEMENT: SPINNING IN THEIR GRAVES

Business leadership in the early 20th century was a glorious mixture of corporate leaders, policy analysts, government servants, professors, and management thinkers who created a great discipline that drove economic growth. One of the great roles of management was to balance the interests and abilities of both the public and private sectors. However, some critics today contend that a cozier working relationship between the public and private sectors represents a conspiracy of a military-industrial complex sort, more conspiratorial than productive. In fairness to these critics, the balancing process between government and business has been suboptimal of late, not to be confused with the approach of classic management, in which the leaders included both private obligation and civic duty within their business role.

Famous business leaders and theorists of the classical era, such as Henry Ford, Henry Gantt, Frederick Taylor, Alfred P. Sloan, and W. Edwards Deming, played a role in balancing the needs of society with that of their business operations. Lesser-known corporate leaders understood this role as well, and these individuals played a formative role in building the great bridges between workers and consumers and, more important, between workers and owners. These leaders laid the building blocks for management and this new covenant and, in the process, built the U.S. economy into the greatest success story of economic times. Today, our corporate executives view the public interest as completely off limits from their preoccupation with their own corporate objectives; they become detached from the society as a corporate mercenary. That's not to say that today's corporate leaders aren't involved in local charities and causes—most are—but the covenant of public-private partnership that worked so well in the past is viewed by leaders as taboo. Even in business school, future managers are taught to focus on private sector matters only, as if anything related to the public sector is unproductive by definition.

Not only were the management thinkers of the classical era those who took both private and public positions in support of productivity and growth, they were often controversial figures, not afraid of stepping out. Henry Ford was certainly a controversial figure for many reasons. Beyond challenging the well-established notion that consumer prices shouldn't be lowered and workers wages should be raised, Ford thought that consumerism across the globe could be a key to world peace, at a time when such thoughts were not in fashion. He opened plants all over the world, built a plant in Germany in 1920 (with Herbert Hoover's blessing), and even accepted Joseph Stalin's invitation to build an auto plant in Gorky. He was also a right-wing political extremist who, it was alleged, was too friendly with Nazi Germany, putting a lot of his philanthropic efforts into question. Nevertheless, Ford was an example of management leadership that sought change within the collective business community instead of shying away from such a role (despite political transgressions).

Frederick Taylor was also a controversial figure and one of the undisputed founders of modern management. According to Peter Drucker, the Germans were far better military strategists in World War II, but the Allied victory was achieved through management.[11] He attributed these efficiencies to Frederick Taylor's *Principles of Scientific Management,* published in 1911. Trade unions and workers' rights groups looked down on Taylor's views as degrading the talents of the workforce. But what was often lost in such views was that Taylor refused to take a factory as a client unless the owners first substantially increased wages, sometimes tripling them. Clearly, Frederick Taylor was a systems thinker, and he instilled this discipline in the new definition of management for the 20th century.

Another controversial pioneer of classical management was Henry Gantt, one of the first management consultants. Gantt established the "man's record," which noted what the worker should do and did do.[12] This was the beginning of the field of project management, leading to the development of the now famous

Gantt Chart as a way of tracking progress. Although developed in 1910, the Gantt Chart wasn't used for megaprojects until much later. The first significant use of the record was in the construction of the Hoover Dam in the early 1930s and the U.S. Interstate Highway system in the mid-1950s. Much as with the efforts of Ford and Taylor, critics sneered at Henry Gantt's measurement and tracking tools as heavy-handed and charged that they dehumanized the process. However, Gantt's legacy includes the Task and Bonus System, which linked the bonus paid to managers—based on whether they had adequately trained their employees properly to improve performance. Gantt also strongly believed that businesses have the social responsibility to improve the welfare of the society in which they operate.

Each of these founding fathers of management believed in the need to improve productivity as a function of the optimization of workers and owners and an improvement in the welfare of society. But the sentiment of the next generation of practitioners and theorists, who promoted an organizational approach to management, was that such efforts were dehumanizing.

W. Edwards Deming was another controversial, early pioneer of classical management. Deming was credited for improving production in the U.S. during World War II, and he went on to become a hero in Japan for improving its postwar manufacturing industry. His brilliance was recognized in the United States only at the very end of his career. During World War II, Deming was one of a small team of statisticians who taught Statistical Process Control (SPC) techniques (monitoring processes to improve efficiency and quality through the use of control charts) to workers engaged in wartime production. After World War II, with mass-produced U.S. goods in strong demand, these techniques started to fall by the wayside. During the postwar period, Deming was invited by the Japanese to teach statistical control to workers in their industries. This is where Deming's ideas on quality began to take shape: by implementing certain rules of management, companies can improve quality and reduce cost.

Furthermore, this method of continuous improvement was a systems approach, with two large factors being the absolute improvement in both customer and worker satisfaction. The adoption and implementation of these management techniques led the Japanese manufacturing industry to reach levels of quality not seen before in the United States. After losing significant ground to Japanese imports, Ford finally reached out to Deming in 1981 to improve the quality levels of the Ford automobiles. To the surprise of those at the Ford Motor Company, Deming focused on the company's management, not on its quality per se. As a result of the work done with Deming, Ford rolled out a profitable line of cars, and a few years later became the most profitable car company in the United States. As was the case with the other founders of management, Deming had balanced the needs of the worker with the productivity of the company.

Deming's classical management definition of continuous improvement is much different from how we define the term today. In his speeches, he continued to emphasize that "the problem is at the top, management is the problem," which rankled many leaders who wanted to look into the depths of the organization to lay a finger on what was wrong. Deming also was quite fond of systems, emphasizing their importance in corporations but also noting that "systems must be managed" and that "left to themselves, components become selfish." He also chastised managers and academics alike for thinking that copying the Japanese model would work, noting that "they don't even know what to copy!" Deming was perhaps the first classical management thinker to try to wake a whole economy from its sleep.

WAS IT BECAUSE OF MANAGEMENT OR DEMOCRACY?

Without question, the 20th century was the greatest period in U.S. history, and the management system is certainly a primary reason for this success. According to the Cato Institute, there was "more material progress in the United States in the 20th century than there was in the entire world in all the previous centuries combined."[13] This is a phenomenal statement whose importance should not be underestimated. During this period, life expectancy rose by 30 years, agricultural productivity improved five- to tenfold, real wages quadrupled, and many major diseases became statistically insignificant. From a material standpoint, even poorer Americans have luxury items today that the richest Americans in 1908 could never have possessed. So how does the Cato Institute explain this unprecedented explosion of U.S. prosperity during the 20th century? The answer from the Cato Institute is that "freedom works":

> The unique American formula of individual liberty and free enterprise has encouraged risk taking, experimentation, innovation, and scientific exploration of a magnitude that is unprecedented in human history.[14]

Robert Reich, who was President Clinton's labor secretary, questions the correlation between economic growth and democracy. In his book, *Supercapitalism*, Reich opines that business and politics events shouldn't be correlated and, therefore, must be kept distinct. He provides examples for how nations such as China aren't moving toward democracy at all, but rather represent an authoritarian form of capitalism. Of the four fastest-growing economies in the world today—Brazil, Russia, India, and China (BRIC)—none has a high political freedom rating, and some (China and Russia in particular) could be seen as moving backward, not forward. Figure 1.4 provides a list of the world's largest economies. The list doesn't show a strong positive correlation between democracy and economic power. Certainly, in today's global economy, it is possible and even viable for capitalist growth to happen without democracy. With a flow of wealth from the United States and Europe to the BRIC countries (and to the Middle East, with even more repressive regimes), there's a case to be made that economic liberalism is on the ropes, particularly given what's happening in the current global economy. In

Rank	Country	GDP (millions of USD)
—	**World**	**54,311,608**
—	European Union	16,830,100
1	United States	13,843,825
2	Japan	4,383,762
3	Germany	3,322,147
4	China	3,250,827
5	United Kingdom	2,772,570
6	France	2,560,255
7	Italy	2,104,666
8	Spain	1,438,959
9	Canada	1,432,140
10	Brazil	1,313,590
11	Russia	1,289,582
12	India	1,098,945
13	South Korea	957,053
14	Australia	908,826
15	Mexico	893,365

Figure 1.4 World's Largest Economies, Measured by Nominal GDP, 2007
Source: International Monetary Fund

China, there are significant human rights violations and distrust of the government in an economy that has created 200 million millionaires. Russia is becoming increasingly repressive at home and abroad, yet Moscow is the most expensive city in the world to live in. It appears as though economic liberalism is in trouble around the world, and yet it remains the best future weapon for the United States to become competitive amid of these growing, developing nations. And economic liberalism is only made possible through the use of classical management, as shown in this book.

Another frequent explanation for the American Dream is related to the "sum of the parts" idea: that the United States possesses, relative to its geographical and societal resources, an abundance of natural resources, an almost infinite stretch of untamed land, a steady stream of hardworking immigrants, and a geographically competitive advantage of location. Oil, immigrants, freedom, and a vast expanse of undeveloped land were essential for our nation's growth, as material inputs into a production function.

As the data show, these critical variables existed in the United States well before 1908, as did the possibilities of mechanization, but our economic growth explosion didn't take off until the early decades of the 20th century. Certainly, economic growth happened once mechanization had enabled the improvement in production methods, but it wasn't sufficient for optimal growth. It wasn't until classical management thinkers like Henry Ford had thought through how to improve the lots of workers, owners, and consumers collectively that the American Dream took off. It is the only explanation that makes sense. Even the effect of globalization won't change this. Therefore, the sum of the parts was important for economic growth, but it wasn't until the advent of classical management that the American Dream flourished. Classical management was the glue that brought it all together.

Today, a reversal of course has happened from the tenets of classical management. In 1908, management was originated and developed; today, it has been displaced and disaggregated from its original purpose. We have no pioneers, no protectors of the sacred covenant between the owners of the company, the workers, and the consumers. If management is defined by its pioneers from the 20th century, how do we define what's happening today? In the 20th century, Henry Ford and Frederick Taylor defined the covenant and passed it on to leaders like Deming and Drucker. Today, there are few if any leading thinkers who are promoting these covenants as the key to our economic growth. Have men such as Jack Welch and Ken Lay been protectors of the covenant? How about the corporate raiders from the 1980s to the present? Are these individuals successful managers because of their adherence to the covenant as were Henry Ford and W. Edwards Deming? Or are Welch, Lay, Carl Icahn, and T. Boone Pickens admired for their abilities to become millionaires or billionaires by understanding the path to success in the postclassical management world? Where are our leaders, our innovators who will bring an environment back in which classical management can thrive? Where are our Henry Fords, our W. Edwards Demings?

WHAT THE "DEATH OF MANAGEMENT" MEANS

The "Death of Management" is not a marketing cliché. It instead refers to a reality—our dismissal of a balance that used to work, knowledge that we have chosen to ignore, a discipline that hasn't evolved, and all that was once known about management that we now fail to understand. In my experiences as a corporate leader, management consultant, and business school professor, I have seen the slow death of classical management up close: I have been involved in it, studied it, spoken about it, and even contributed to the perpetuation of it. Between then and now, there have been many leaders who have profited from its demise and numerous Americans who have been on the short end of the stick.

In my opinion, those who have profited in a postclassical management era should be commended and questioned at the same time: commended for being successful business people but questioned for not asking why the system isn't working. As a corporate leader, I have enjoyed the fruits of rich compensation plans and been a regular player by the rules of the corporate dance that we call management. All of these stories tell a tale that reveals why management is now dead and why there's a correlation between its demise and the fallen state of the U.S. economy on the global stage. This book tells this tale.

Whatever we wish to call this postclassical management era, it is clearly out of control, blaming its unpredictable nature on the global economy. With our deregulated financial system of too many or too few rules, our short-term perspective clouds our view of economic value as a result. Therefore, we don't understand how to grow productivity through technological change (tangible and intangible investments) as well as we did in the past, partially because we measure it differently. We don't understand clearly the role of the decentralized owner in the corporate governance process (including the Board of Directors), as well as how to allocate company surplus value properly. We don't understand how to improve productivity through capital infusions, pure process improvements, and reengineering exercises with the workers, as opposed to trying to achieve all improvements solely through the blind use of technology. We don't understand the importance of manufacturing to our economy and its link to classical management.

Such is the environment: in dire need of what management as a discipline can bring to our economy. In lacking the discipline of management to clean up problems, we consider our environment to be in a disruptive state that will inevitably work itself out within a global economy. But work itself out for whom? When our corporate leaders make short-term decisions at the expense of a productivity equation of capital, labor, and technology optimization, there are unintended consequences. When retailers like Wal-Mart squeeze suppliers and workers for improved financial results, they suboptimize our economy. When workers ignore their role in productivity, innovation, and value, they enable postmanagement-era decisions that disregard and disrespect the way workers helped management in the 20th century. And even when the MNCs create an impact on their own profitability through poor decisions, it is clear that the whole situation is out of control and that everyone is looking for someone else to blame for what's happening. Management as a discipline should not be enabling chaos—it should be containing it.

If our business institutions have allowed management to become infected and die, what can the rest of us do about it? With an out-of-control sense of economic limitlessness facing us, can the genie ever go back into the bottle? Can we revisit concepts within our institutional structures as they existed in 1908 and during the 40 years that followed, or must we create something new that is responsive to the dynamic, global economy? And who will decide? We cannot respond to these questions through the condemnation of those who are profiting from the new economy paradigm, because they are just playing by the rules of the game. It is not entirely the fault of managers who are profiting from the bastardized version of management in the short-term financial system. It is also not entirely the fault of workers who understand the rules of the game of management and enable this system to provide profit for them—whether they are consultants, Wall Street traders, or otherwise. Those in the private sector, like myself, are simply responding within the system, good or bad: our livelihoods depend on our being able to do so. We are not being asked to protect the covenant; this is wrong, but it is also the reality in the present corporate environment. This is not an alibi, but simply the straight truth within our corporations and private sector. We shouldn't make victims and villains out of this—doing so is an unprofitable exercise. We must enable a corporate business system that brings the covenant back, but this can only be done through pioneers of thought.

Much as in the beginning of the 20th century, we have two choices at our disposal: the first is a political solution, perhaps one of bitter mercantilism, playing "Rock 'em Sock 'em Robots" between governments. With China becoming increasingly mercantile in nature, there is a coalition of those who want our government to fight trade wars with them. This solution will solve nothing: members of the middle class, which used to make up such a large contingency of management, is losing its American Dream and is upset. Right now, as they seek political answers, they get nothing but empty promises that ignore global realities.

The second option, of course, isn't political, but economic—the only language that is spoken right now within the borderless, global economy—and the best option for the U.S. MNCs will not stop or reduce outsourcing to Asia based on either trade sanctions or presidential elections. Classical management is the economic solution because it enabled the American Dream: it was allowed to evolve through social strife in the early 20th century, through two World Wars, and into the post-World War II recovery. And in doing so, it enabled our middle class to resonate with Horatio Alger lore. Given the past of classical management, it's a worthwhile exercise to reexamine our history and how we salvage our economic future through dusting off the discipline of classical management. And then U.S. managers must work on building a business environment that attracts, not loses, business opportunities with the MNC. I believe that the classical management of the past can be transformed into 21st-century management and can provide the solution.

I have explained the idea of the "Death of Management" to many, and almost everyone understands the relevance and urgency, given what's happening today: employment instability, a loss of wage stability, financial markets collapsing, crises in housing and consumer goods, lack of manufacturing base, and so on. But many question whether there is anything that we can do about it—in an increasingly global economy in which management itself seems to be a mesmerized global routine. Management was the enabler of the American Dream, and the success of the American Dream is the improvements and proliferation of the middle class. Middle-class economics is the "make or break" factor in who's winning in the world economy. If our middle class is eroding, we have nobody to blame but ourselves. We shouldn't and can't blame the Chinese and Indians for what's happening. And yet, for the past couple of decades, as the air is slowly seeping out of the American Dream, the assessment of blame has been our reaction. A quick examination of this strategy in our past will lead the reader to conclude that this is a strategy of futility.

The period from 1908 to 2008 has been fascinating, perhaps one of the most remarkable periods in U.S. history. How we choose to respond in the next 100 years will be just as important as that fork in the road that Henry Ford and Frederick Taylor faced in those earlier years. We can learn from these and other pioneers about how Americans must respond; this is the reason for this book. Our current response has been one of no response, just expecting things to get better, keeping our fantasy of economic limitlessness alive, and deflecting blame to others. These responses are as unhealthy as the response of social theorists like Karl Marx to incite class struggle in the early 20th century. The United States took a different road, a revolution of a different sort: a thinking person's revolution. That is what we need today—and fast. This thinking person's revolution is needed to replace what we think is management today with a 21st-century management, comprising a new covenant between owners, workers, and consumers. There is nothing philanthropic about it; it's just good business practice to do so. By acknowledging the need and developing this covenant, we will have decided that this new (yet old) discipline of management will enable us to succeed in response to our next challenge, the challenge of a hypercompetitive global economy.

The Rise of the Corporate Manager

Five hundred years ago, something was stirring in Medieval Europe. Nation-states were replacing the isolated feudal estates that were spread across the countryside, and urban centers and shipping lanes were enabling commerce to flourish. At a time when warfare and chaos still reigned over new European capitals, the leaders of these nation-states were starting to use commerce as a way of stabilizing their newly forming central governments. The hoarding of gold was seen as a way of securing an uncertain future on a violent and unstable continent. Commerce was seen as a battle in itself between governments in a zero-sum game, with each nation-state's government seeking to control production and consumption carefully, as a way of achieving superiority over other nations.

There was no such thing as a market economy, no economic liberalism, and the principles of economics as we know them today were yet to be formulated. Consumption, for all intents and purposes, was widely discouraged and, broadly, not even feasible, given the relative wealth levels and crude production methods. Education, free time, and money were kept from most of society, and the lives of the working class were categorized by Thomas Hobbes as "nasty, brutish, and short."

As shown in Figure 2.1, the relative gross domestic product (GDP) growth of Western Europe had shown just marginal progress as a function of 16th-century mercantilism. There was wealth growth through imperialism, yet very little through improvement in production. Not until a few centuries later would real production growth occur in Europe through the tenets of economic liberalism. The understanding of a production equation, win-win trade between nations, freedom from government intervention, and the use of the private sector for providing gain—to the owners of capital, the workers (to some extent), and even the

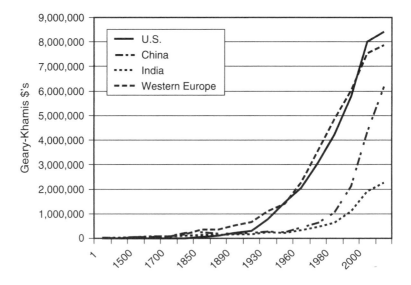

Figure 2.1 Historical GDP

Source: Adapted from Angus Maddison Data, 2006

consumers—were radical thoughts. In *The Wealth of Nations* (1776), Adam Smith said:

> The uniform and uninterrupted effort to better his condition, the principle from which (both) public and private opulence is originally derived, is frequently powerful enough to maintain the natural progress of things toward improvement.[1]

It's hard for us today to imagine how radical this thinking was in 1776. For hundreds of years beforehand, commerce was tightly controlled for the benefit of the state, not the individual. The very notion that an individual should have the right to better his or her lot through competition and commerce was heresy in the hierarchical caste systems of Europe. From Smith's writings, the seeds were being sown for the upcoming Industrial Revolution, which would really begin to turn Western civilization on its head.

There isn't anything definitive to identify exactly when the discipline of management began, and some scholars suggest that its origins go back as far as the Renaissance, with thinkers such as Niccolò Machiavelli and his famous work *The Prince* (1531). The difference between management as a social philosophy, rather than a rational science, as defined in chapter one, is an important distinction that is discussed throughout this book. Nevertheless, the "social philosophy of administration," as explained by Machiavelli, demonstrated how a prince of his day should manage his power within his jurisdiction, when alliances were constantly shifting and governments rose and fell without warning in a matter of weeks. In the 16th century, governments and well-connected merchants gained their riches via the collection of tariffs and the banning of foreign competition.

Machiavelli wasn't the only social philosopher who sought to explain and control the irrational nature of human beings in a commercial setting. During his life in the 19th century, Karl Marx saw free-market economics as out of control and heading for a crash. Marx's view was that technological change and capital were being used by the bourgeoisie in a manner antagonistic to the workers. Although the application of his theories were proven wrong by the end of the 20th century with the collapse of communism, Marx was correct in noticing that the free markets of his day were a horrible disfigurement of their intended purpose.

Certainly, the sociopolitical theorists Adam Smith and David Ricardo never intended their theories to be carried out in the manner in which they were by the industrial nations during the 19th and early 20th centuries. The advent of the Industrial Revolution may have appeared to be the coronation of Smith's free-market economics, but, in application, it was not. The average person was no better off materially in 1800 than in the times before the birth of Christ. The economic growth that followed was numerically impressive but socially repressive, therefore not optimal.

Put simply, Adam Smith's economic liberalism wasn't possible without the advent of classical management. The wild, untamed growth that the United States experienced from 1870 to 1913 was unprecedented, yet it remained linked to the work processes of the past. During the disruptive period of the Industrial Revolution in the United States, industry remained greatly dependent on skilled craftspeople, who commanded substantial wages and controlled the pace of work in a less than rational manner. These craftspeople would train their assistants and pass on the craft to their relatives through a closed society. These fraternal unions maintained a monopoly on production and defined a reasonable day's work, to ensure that no worker could ever exceed it.

At the same time, the owners of these operations were seeking to implement technological improvements that would increase profits through reducing and dehumanizing labor, which were a train wreck waiting to happen. The rapid introduction of mechanization to the U.S. economy led to GDP growth, but it was missing a connection between the human workflow element and the machines that prohibited an optimized economic environment.

Workers viewed themselves as becoming commoditized as the engine of economic growth pushed forward. The GDP growth in the United States was 63 percent from 1870 to 1880, 34 percent from 1880 to 1890, and 48 percent from 1890 to 1900.[2] Immigrants may have been disappointed that the streets weren't paved with gold, but they had escaped famine in the Old World for a new life. And the owners were achieving growth and becoming richer and richer as a result. But the missing element to both growth and productivity of classical management wasn't tapped until a decade or so later, by Henry Ford.

Below the surface of what appears to be a success story of a burgeoning young nation comes an unhealthy situation in the making. The craftspeople felt as though they were being marginalized through the exploitation of labor and mechanization. The immigrant workforce was being mauled, exhausted, and exploited by these machines and their owners, in many cases at a very early age. Technological inventions of great promise, such as the internal combustion engine and electricity, weren't being utilized to any extent in society. And even many from the aristocratic ownership class were disappointed as a result of the monopolies that were putting them out of business as a function of continued consolidation and antitrust activity.

There was clearly a lack of understanding of how important it was to allocate the surplus value of the company equitably between these critical stakeholders. This boil simmered in some of the most extreme ways. In 1886, the Haymarket Affair, which had started as a peaceful rally in support of an eight-hour day, turned deadly, with seven police officers and numerous civilians killed. In 1907, 500,000 Americans were killed, maimed, or otherwise injured on the job.[3] At a speech before a Ruskin Club banquet in 1903, Jack London, author of *The Call of the Wild,* stated his belief that class struggle would ensue:

> Man being man and a great deal short of the angels, the quarrel over the division of the joint product is irreconcilable. For the last twenty years in the United States, there has been an average of over a thousand strikes per year; and year by year these strikes increase in magnitude, and the front of the labor army grows more imposing. And it is a class struggle, pure and simple. Labor as a class is fighting with capital as a class.[4]

HOW THE UNITED STATES PROVED MARX WRONG AND CLASSICAL MANAGEMENT RIGHT

Ideologies are a funny thing: the sweet sound and smell of a classless social utopia of socialism or communism proved to be the greatest failure of the 20th century. As a result of the Industrial Revolution, workers were flooding into the cities, and cheap labor was easy to exploit, much like what is happening in Asia today. At the same time, labor became specialized through the division of labor, and it became essentially a cog in the machine. Before the onset of management, Karl Marx suggested that this division of labor was dehumanizing, the means of production were in place to exploit the worker, and technological change was an enemy of the worker as well. Marx was wrong in his inability to understand technological change in a production process. But who can blame him for getting it wrong in the 19th century? From the farm to the factory, it appeared as though the same win-lose proposition existed, with the worker always getting the short end of the stick. To Marx, this was a societal issue that had to be fixed—through the public sector owning the means of production. He couldn't fathom that a new class of worker could be introduced into the private market setting to optimize the distribution of the surplus value to all parties (workers, owners, consumers), allowing for a multiplier for growth. What Marx also couldn't comprehend is how the petite bourgeoisie (the working middle class, for all practical purposes) could drive the capitalist process through the role of the professional manager. And part of why he couldn't understand this is that he never understood the culture of the place where it originated, the United States.

It was not an accident that Marx was proven wrong in the United States. In the second half of the 19th century, the United States was just recovering from the devastating impact of the Civil War. In monetary terms alone, the Civil War had subtracted an estimated $6 billion from the U.S. economy, including $3 billion the two governments spent fighting it, $1 billion in property destroyed, and $2 billion in the human capital that it consumed.[5] Once the war was over, the economy began to flourish, particularly in the North. The railroad, which had never before paid dividends, was profitable. From the war came a class of multi-millionaires, who began to consolidate their holdings in important national industries, as, just a generation before, Marx presupposed would happen.

Survival of the fittest was a tool to justify the massive fortunes amassed by Carnegie, Rockefeller, and others, sometimes at the expense of greater economic growth in the nation. Often, the Gilded Age is seen as an era of much growth and prosperity and even revered as an age of great progress. A missing perspective on this era is the progress that was lost as a result of a disharmony in the business environment, which was skewed toward the controlling owners. It is as debilitating for monopolists to control economic activity as it is for government to do so.

In his autobiography, published after his death in 1919, Andrew Carnegie provided details on the innovations in the iron and steel industry that allowed him to produce more cheaply than his rivals. Beyond an attention to detail and an obsession with reducing costs, Carnegie revolutionized industry by carefully controlling every stage of manufacturing—from the raw materials needed to the distribution of the goods.[6] He also found ways to reduce wages through the use of recent immigrants, bringing wages down to $1.50 to $2.00 per day—below what was necessary for a family in Pittsburgh to live on at that time.

So the United States had its own "dark satanic mills," to use a phrase from William Blake's epic *Milton: a Poem* (1810). To quote Professor Walter Dean Burnham, although "industrialization adds immensely to national power, and may also promote the long-term betterment of the material conditions of the mass of the population . . . it also involves the creation of structures of power, and, indeed, conquest . . . this in turn requires the economic and cultural subordination of the mass of the population and the redefinition of the terms of their social and cultural existence."[7] Said differently, industrialization in the United States led to a period of harsh cruelty for the workforce and unprecedented wealth for the owners.

To Burham, this was a necessary stage of chaos and disruption for industrialization to proceed to a concentration of power within a small group of private owners from the grip of government control. However, for the worker and the economy, the effects of a tight-fisted control, from either a public or private entity, had negative impacts, whether it was necessary for market evolution or not. This period could not last long. During a tour of Carnegie's mills in Homestead, Pennsylvania, in 1893, novelist Hamlin Garland noted:

> I saw other men in the hot yellow glare from the furnaces. I saw men measuring the serpentine rosy beams . . . I saw boys perched high in cages, their shrill voices sounding wild and animal-like in the midst of the uproar; a place into which men went like men going to war for the sake of wives and children, urged on by necessity, blinded and dulled by custom and habit; an inhuman place to spend four-fifths of one's waking hours . . . Upon such toil rests the splendor of American civilization.[8]

Andrew Carnegie was a symbol of all that was right and wrong about preclassical management in the industrial-era United States. Figure 2.2 is an old cartoon describing Carnegie as "the modern baron with ancient methods," perhaps

The Modern Baron With Ancient Methods.

Figure 2.2 Andrew Carnegie: "The Modern Baron with Ancient Methods"

explaining a transition period between robber barons and classical managers. A self-made man who became rich during the Civil War, Carnegie publicly advocated union sympathies, calling them a "sacred right." However, in 1892 when the Homestead Strike began to simmer into a bloody confrontation, Carnegie was off to his native Scotland, leaving the sticky mess of contract negotiations to his ruthless, anti-union lieutenant Henry Clay Frick to handle the sordid mess. And handle it he did: he fortified the property and brought in a private security service, and, in the end, seven workers were killed and numerous others injured. Carnegie's legacy was tarnished, and his reputation as a captain of industry was cemented.

It was an era with a lack of covenant between workers and owners, a distressed capitalist environment that was a powder keg waiting to explode. Was Andrew Carnegie simply an opportunist before the era of management, no monster at all? Andrew Carnegie, the self-professed self-made man and hero of the workers, led a double life, intentional or not. He preached support for the unions and donated $350 million to build 2,509 libraries around the world.[9] In 1892, *The Saturday Globe* said of Carnegie, "as the tight-fisted employer, he reduces wages that he may play philanthropist and give away libraries, etc."

John D. Rockefeller was cut from the same cloth as Carnegie: he started from humble roots, profited from the Civil War, took a harsh stand against the unions, and amassed a fortune that was of a proportion to the overall economy that will never be replicated in our history. According to Michael Chernow, who wrote *Titan: The Life of John D. Rockefeller,* "the most significant revolt against free-market capitalism came not from reformers or zealous ideologues but from businessmen who couldn't control the maddening fluctuations of the marketplace."[10] Rockefeller wanted to control the business cycles and competition for his own self-interest.

Such was the Industrial Era before the discipline of classical management. Certainly, industrialization meant progress, but progress that was stunted by an inability to optimize the variables of labor, capital, and technological progress in the production function. The sum of the parts of industrialization weren't equal to what production levels were possible through classical management. And the captains of industry felt that it was their duty as the winners in Social Darwinism to control market fluctuations, control the means of production, and, at the same time, profit excessively. Rockefeller's fortune of $200 million was obscenely large relative to the size of the U.S. economy at that time ($101 billion). Such an unequal distribution of wealth always leads to sociopolitical problems, as history tells us.

The preclassical management era of the Industrial Revolution proved Karl Marx right about one thing (and only one thing): that the social disruption caused by technological change was not well understood and that the means of production changes much more rapidly than the impact of the production process on labor. Many of his followers in the early 20th century used this as a call for public oversight over the means of production through a communal approach. The tension of these ideas took the United States and other industrial societies to the proverbial fork in the road over how to solve the problem—to adopt a Marxian view, a revolution of the collective versus a free-market revolution of the individual.

The choice wasn't a great one: to choose a utopian theory of communism or socialism or an out-of-control free market, one that couldn't or wouldn't seek a win-win proposition between the workers and the owners. We would learn 50 years later of the failures of the Marxian applications of socialism and communism that could never support economic growth. Thanks to the commencement of classical management as the optimizer for all variables (both public and private) within the production function, the United States has demonstrated more clearly than any society how a free-market economy can work. Marxian thought presupposed that all workers were equal, but in reality (to borrow George Orwell's famous line) some were "more equal than others." The apparatchiks of the communist system, who substituted themselves for managers in a free-market system, proved this to be the case. These individuals were the privileged of the communist society, without having had to earn such a right through hard work and skills.

THE FUNDAMENTALS OF CLASSICAL MANAGEMENT

To the contrary, the idea of the professional manager originated and developed within the role that supports everyone's equal chance of success based on hard work and ability. In communism, such a thought was theoretical, but not practical. With U.S. management, the idea was completely possible and optimal. The professional manager in the United States enabled a free-market economy that built the fastest growth in middle-class prosperity in history versus a party official who enabled the rise of a privileged class, amid a cover of supposed equality. Management was the discipline that ensured that the means of production would (or could) be linked to the relations (people) of production—that, in a sense, the democracy and capitalism of the United States could be in balance. It was the dream of economic liberalism in practice. Clearly, management has had a special role in 20th century U.S. history.

So commerce has progressed from a premercantile environment (in which economic growth was stagnant for thousands of years), to a mercantile environment (growth driven through government control and trade animosity), and finally to a preclassical management capitalist environment (growth driven through improvements in the means of production, little regulation, and little or no improvements in the worker's standard of living). The next phase was the origins of classical management, driving economic growth in a fashion never seen before. Figure 2.3 lists the fundamentals that were needed for this rational science and that created classical management in 1908.

	Organization	Capital	Technological Diffusion
Surplus Value	Strategy and Structure Info and Organization	Investment in Long-Term	Creative Destruction
Share Benefits	Productivity and Wages	Profits in Short-Term	Functional = Social Progress

Figure 2.3 Birth of Management Fundamentals

Figure 2.3 indicates the fundamentals for how classical management was able to optimize the variables within a production function at a corporation. Without attention to these requirements, optimization is not possible among the stakeholders (workers, owners, consumers, managers), and therefore true economic liberalism can't exist. As classical management lost its way, starting in the 1950s, its importance to the economy drastically changed, and therefore the metamorphosis began, to the first postclassical management phase of the bloated corpocracy to the second phase of today's casino capitalism.

The first column of Figure 2.3 lists the two fundamental factors that management must satisfy: to grow economic activity profitably (surplus value) and to share the surplus benefits of economic activity with both private and public interests. Creating surplus value and sharing the benefits are the fundamentals of the production function in an economic liberal environment; they are what a company is in business to do. First, a company must achieve growth—if it doesn't, it will not be in business for long. Second, the growth must be defined as surplus value (profits from operation) to the company, and how to distribute this surplus value must be determined. The very purpose of a management function must be to achieve surplus value for the company and to allocate this benefit optimally across the multiple stakeholders. If the benefits are not optimally allocated across stakeholders, disturbances will be created at the company and within the economy, such as lower or negative growth, stock market bubbles that pop, worker strikes, income inequality, a loss of market competitiveness, and so on. During the robber baron days of preclassical management, we saw many of these circumstances, just as we did during the bloated corpocracy of the 1950s and the casino capitalism of the 1990s and beyond, culminating in our current massive economic problems.

The top row in Figure 2.3 shows the three variables that must be optimized by classical management in an endogenous economic production function: organization, capital, and technological diffusion. The vertical column on the left details the objectives of management; the next three are the inputs at the manager's disposal to accomplish these objectives. Any economic or corporate environment requires an economic equilibrium for these variables, and corporate executives and government economists should adjust factors accordingly to reach this state of equilibrium. The present problem is that there isn't a goal of equilibrium and balance, so today's postclassical manager seeks a definition of productivity that is not optimal, as discussed in this book.

ORGANIZATION AND INFORMATION: MAKING KNOWLEDGE PRODUCTIVE

Organization is an input that takes into account that both the individual worker and the organization are important elements to the production function of a corporation. Both are critical aspects of the labor input in a production equation. According to Peter Drucker, "the function of organization is to make knowledge productive."[11] The Industrial Revolution brought forth a tremendous potential for knowledge to turn into productivity. Instead, growth was driven through the utilization of natural resources (coal and oil, for example) to be matched with technological invention and cheap, exploited labor in a model of unlimited, unsustainable growth. There was no proper organization to take these factors beyond their surface opportunities until the birth of classical management.

With Henry Ford's efforts to organize companies to optimize the lot of the worker have been called "welfare capitalism." Efforts that improved the workplace setting at Ford weren't just in giving higher wages to workers, but also in improving the conditions and the organization to support the worker. Necessity is the mother of invention, and the largely unskilled U.S. workforce was able to organize around process and organization that allowed the U.S. economy to become the most productive economy during the 20th century. This understanding of organization went from being an informal social function to a formal, structural, competitive advantage for businesses, enabled by the use of the professional manager.

Before the advent of the formal business organization, the typical machine shop of the premanagement era was dimly lit, noisy, and disorganized. Workers carried out their tasks in their own way, steeped in tradition and observation, but not in any sort of structured way. Orders came in and were transferred to the shop. In a time standard established by the workers, the finished product was completed. Sometimes, a supervisor appeared, either to quicken the pace or to demand certain behaviors. After a while (with the advent of Frederick Taylor's principles), the efficiency engineers appeared, with clipboards and stopwatches to improve the amount of time that it would take to complete the product. Engineers and supervisors were involved as well, to ensure that the process of work kept up with that of the machinery, as a matter of principle. Routines from Frederick Taylor's *Principles of Scientific Management* were abused and became another tool of owners to increase profit without corresponding benefit to the workers. But the structure within an organization that was developed through these techniques allowed management to formalize procedures and processes and to increase the economic growth of the company.

STRATEGY AND STRUCTURE: THE BIRTH OF AMERICAN INGENUITY

For the company to grow, management needed to incorporate strategy and structure, two innovative concepts of capitalism of the time. Strategy was a new tool for the profession of management: a rational way to manage the destiny of the company, using an end-to-end definition of the product life cycle, without the monopolist control that was no longer possible with antitrust laws. With the turmoil and supply shortages coming out of World War I, Ford devised a strategy of vertical integration that was innovative. As the demand for Ford's autos escalated, many of the company's smaller suppliers weren't able to keep up, from a lead time and a volume basis. The first response of the company was to establish large stockpiles of inventory, but this wasted money put a large burden on the company's capital. As a strategy to smooth these disruptions caused by Ford's suppliers and raw material providers, it built a factory at River Rouge, Michigan, that was structured around vertical integration, a process in which the company owns its upstream suppliers and downstream buyers in order to control the production process.

In this plant, Ford was able to control its raw materials and replace smaller companies that could not keep up with the escalations in demand. Building a factory around the production, assembly, and transportation of its product was truly a competitive advantage that had been established through a management strategy. And without a mind-set that was driven through the qualities listed (in Figure 2.3 as imperative to management), such a strategy could not have been devised. First, Ford established an operational strategy that enabled Model T production to happen eight times faster than before. Then, five years later, the company began construction of the River Rouge plant, enabling it to manage all aspects of production without a monopolist's control of it, per se.

This is a strong example of how the application of management enabled unprecedented economic gains at the company and national levels in the United States, led by pioneers like Ford. In the 21st century, Dell crafted a modern version of Ford's Model T production to innovate the personal computer (PC) business in the United States by fusing just-in-time (JIT) inventory practices with giving customers the ability to build their computers online—even if its supply chain successes have outstripped its sales and marketing practices. Wal-Mart, for all of its human relations flaws, devised a supply chain strategy that revolutionized retailing.

Henry Ford provided the roadmap for how managers should be responsible for developing and implementing successful strategies in their role as corporate manager. However, these managers needed an appropriate structure to succeed; there is perhaps no greater contributor to the development of a strong organizational structure than Max Weber. Like Henry Ford and Frederick Taylor, Weber is often misunderstood in current business lore and portrayed as an advocate of bureaucracy. This is because his theories were bastardized in the United States in the mid-20th century, and they then led to the hierarchical structures that I call the bloated corpocracy. Weber proposed a more rational form of organization, unheard of during his era. He compared and contrasted a bureaucratic organization to much less scientific forms, such as a charismatic one ("cult of personality") and a traditional one. Weber didn't believe that a bureaucratic form of organization was the best approach. He likened the increasing use of bureaucracy as "an iron cage that threatened the human spirit."[12] Instead of bureaucracy, Weber focused on the following features for an organization:

- Official functions bounded by rules
- Specialization—a clear division of labor, and an understanding of what is expected
- A clearly defined authority
- Stable and comprehensive rules
- Impersonality—equality of treatment
- Selection on the basis of qualification, not favoritism
- Full-time, paid officials
- A career structure
- Officials detached from ownership of organization—lessening the possibility of bribery or corruption
- Systematic discipline and control of work.

These disciplines for structure would become critical to the growth path of the modern U.S. corporation and to the success of the corporate manager in this role. None of these principles should be confused with what we define today as bureaucracy, although, if they are not properly executed by a manager, they could easily seem to be the constituents of one. Both the definition of structure and that of the manager must be balanced to be rigid enough for discipline and process, but flexible enough to be adaptive and to serve both the owners and the workers. Finding this balance is the role of classical management. The organizational structures of the 1950s may have served a practical purpose at the time, but the lack of competitiveness and bureaucracy definitely created a suboptimal situation that eventually led to the big problems in U.S. operations that we are facing today.

PRODUCTIVITY AND WAGES: SHARING WEALTH GROWS THE COMPANY

A successful structure organizes around key strategic objectives. The company shares profit and other benefits with the workers. In 1914, Ford introduced a minimum wage of $5 per day, which was double the existing rate. At the same time, Ford reduced the workday from nine hours to eight, enabling the company to operate on three independent shifts of work. This approach, now defined as welfare capitalism, was a radical departure from the past and is an estranged idea in the present. Previously, the target was to maximize the owner's profit while minimizing the worker's wages. Henry Ford thought that the opposite made sense: to maximize the wage opportunity for the worker and to lower the profit margin for the owners. This became the foundation for how classical management chose to treat the workforce and tied that strategy to its marketing strategy. Many of the captains of industry from the preclassical management era depicted Henry

Ford as a socialist and radical because of this change in emphasis, and, in our postclassical management era today, many continue to fight this battle through more contemporary means. Just a few years ago, Costco's chief executive officer (CEO), Jim Senegal, was challenged by investment analysts for paying too much of his workers' employee benefits. When asked why he paid a higher wage and better benefits for his employees, Senegal answered, "it isn't altruism, it's good business." Ford and Senegal understood how to apply classical management principles in achieving greater surplus growth in order to benefit both the private corporation and the public self-interest.

The concept of classical management redefined what it meant to be a worker in an industrial setting. When Frederick Taylor became involved in what was considered industrial management during the latter days of the 19th century and the early 20th century, it was an amateurish, draconian approach for improving work methods. It was frequently used as a way to demean and debase employees, even as Taylor told a congressional committee:

> "I can say, without the slightest hesitation," Taylor told a congressional committee, "that the science of handling pig-iron is so great that the man who is . . . physically able to handle pig-iron and is sufficiently phlegmatic and stupid to choose this for his occupation is rarely able to comprehend the science of handling pig-iron."[13]

Even though Taylor's attitude is construed as condescending toward the workers according to present standards, he truly believed that the best interest of the worker was in the best interest for the company. Peter Drucker noted the following:

> Taylor's motivation was not efficiency. It was not the creation of profits for the owners. To his very death he maintained that the major beneficiary of the fruits of productivity had to be the worker, not the owner. His main motivation was the creation of a society in which owners and workers, capitalists and proletarians, could share a common interest in productivity and could build a harmonious relationship on the application of knowledge to work.[14]

According to Peter Drucker, Taylor, Darwin, and Marx were the three seminal thinkers who shaped our modern world. Both Lenin and Stalin sought to use Taylorism to improve manufacturing in the Soviet Union, but the Marxist-communist ideology didn't lend itself to Taylor's true principles. It's ironic that both robber-baron capitalists and Marxist communists failed in their implementations of this classical management approach. It is no wonder that Henry Ford in the early 20th century and the Costcos of today succeeded while nonclassical management approaches didn't. As Drucker noted so appropriately, the methods used to improve productivity are through benefits to the worker, first and foremost.

This principle of classical management to improve productivity for the company and increasing wages was revolutionary: it enabled the Ford Motor Company to reach levels of success never before achieved. To quote Costco's CEO, this isn't altruism, but good business practice. And it established a role within a company for the corporate manager that created a sacred covenant between management and the workforce. In both the pre-and postclassical management eras of the U.S. economy, this idea of equilibrium and benefits to the workers is neglected. During the bloated corpocracy days in the United States from the 1950s to 1970s, equilibrium was broken as well: both workers and management lost sight of competitiveness and productivity. This sacred covenant doesn't exist today: organizations use capital and labor mobility at the expense of the worker and the public sector.

The covenant for the corporate manager to seek both productivity growth and to allocate surplus value (including fair wages) equitably is a primary objective of management in the way that it was defined as a discipline in 1908. If management protects this covenant, the role of the labor union, as it is currently practiced, will likely be very limited. Frederick Taylor noted, "With the triumph of scientific management, unions would have nothing left to do, and they would have been cleansed of their most evil feature: the restriction of output."[15] However, when management does not safeguard this covenant, the labor union must step forward and protect not only the wages and the benefits of the workers, but the productivity of the company as well. The labor union organization of late has not been focused very much on protecting the productivity of the corporation, and management has also been callous in protecting the wages and benefits of the workforce. The employee-related cost of an additional $2,000 for a Big Three automobile produced in the United States in comparison to other nations is testament to this point.

USE OF CAPITAL AND TECHNOLOGY UNDER CONTROL

During the mercantile period, capital was viewed as a precious commodity to be hoarded and used as a bargaining chip in the best case, as a weapon in the worst case. From an era of government-controlled hegemony to one of crass monopoly, capital remained a tool for control versus one to propel economic growth; wealth was concentrated in the hands of a small few and hoarded to nobody's benefit. When capital is hoarded or controlled instead of invested, the growth potential of the business and economy is stunted.

On the other hand, when capital floods the international market, as is the case today, an equally disruptive circumstance happens. The concept is known as the "Greenspan Put": no matter what happens in the economy, the Federal Reserve will rescue the situation through creating more cheap money to buy us out of our problems. In mid-December of 2008, the Federal Reserve took this to a new level by lowering the federal funds rate to between 0 and 0.25 percent, down from 1 percent.

When the U.S. government slashes interest rates to a point that money is practically free and this money policy is unsustainable through current economic activity, the government is driving economic activity versus steering it. In contrast, William McChesney Martin, the longest serving Federal Reserve chairman in our nation's history (1951–1970) noted that the job of the Fed is to "to take away the punch bowl just as the party gets going," a much different perspective.[16]

In the years following the Great Depression, capital as a variable was greatly controlled, for fear of repeating this event. Facing a backlash from the public, corporations and their capital structures were regulated to control the casino environment driven by J. P. Morgan and other speculators, as well as by robber-baron friendly corporations and trusts. After the Great Depression, the laws and the role of investors were controlled and passive, and this generally led to a point of stabilization; investors and CEO's weren't able to get as rich as before, and a heavily regulated economic climate allowed for everyone to do reasonably well (particularly the middle class) at a time of relatively low global competition. In the ending days of this period in 1975, the Dow Jones Industrial Average for the world's economic superpower was close to 600; by 2007, it was more than 14,000! From 1982 to 2000, the U.S. stock market went on the longest bull run ever, but it wasn't sustainable. It was a case where capital was being used primarily as a tool for financial engineering rather than for the growth of foundation industries, like manufacturing. The classical manager applied the use of capital to increase surplus value through using it as a tool for growth. During the postclassical management era, capital once again became abused, and today we are starting to see the repercussions from abusing it over a 25-year period.

Lastly, the out-of-control implementation of machinery in the late 19th century led to the origination of classical management as an optimizing force. During the early days of the Industrial Revolution, there was no question that the pace of change of mechanical invention and implementation was much faster than the corresponding change of pace for the human side of acceptable business practices, incentives, and organization. Karl Marx noted that this phenomenon was alienating and destructive and without any potential for corrective action by the private sector. He proposed the need to control the means of production by the public sector as the only remedy. Technological diffusion in an economy and corporation needs to be disruptive, and the government will by its very nature seek to control innovation because its citizens don't naturally like this. Instead, the effective discipline of classical management doesn't seek to control initiative and growth, but rather to enable them in a stable environment—through intangible investments in the workforce, consumers, and the public sector to complement the technological disruption. Take the invention of the telephones as an example. It took decades for this technology to be readily available for commercial and personal use after the technology and appropriate infrastructure were in place. When business owners rolled out technology without sufficient human factors (safe work environments, as an example), the results were often injuries, equipment damage, lower productivity, and, in some cases, sabotage and anarchy. The employment of the corporate manager was the one thing that kept the dark philosophies of Marx from continuing to corrupt our innovation and creativity.

Management as a discipline began to pay attention to the work environments, where the factory workers practically lived. Once professional managers were trained in what they were looking to find, they were in utter shock—not only because of the horror of how such dismal and dangerous conditions affected the workforce, but also as a result of the impact of this on the company's productivity and profitability. In 1924, Hawthorne Works was the site of well-known industrial studies, one of which led to the famous Hawthorne effect, a term understood to mean "a short-term improvement caused by observing worker performance."

Such studies showed a dramatic impact: classical management can make a difference in improving productivity by ensuring that human factors are more closely correlated to the workers' environment (especially the technology). Human factors included variables such as the time of the workday, breaks, changing pay rules, lighting, and so forth. They were studied to improve productivity, and most of them were of immaterial cost to the operations. These studies were conducted on factory workers between 1924 and 1932. From them, we learned that management activities to better understand human behavior and performance in a factory setting can improve the productivity of how workers and technological change were able to coexist in a dynamic, high-growth environment. Therefore, ensuring that the social progress of the workforce was equal to the functional process of the equipment was a major productivity boost, enabled by the role of the corporate manager in the process.

GENERAL MOTORS: BEFORE AND AFTER CLASSICAL MANAGEMENT

Creative destruction was the tie-in of functional progress (technology) with social progress (labor), and it played a large role in the development and optimization of classical management in this new era. The term creative destruction originated in the writings of a few in the early days of the 20th century, but it wasn't popularized until Joseph Schumpeter used it later on in the century to describe how innovative entrepreneurs needed to drive economic growth in an economy. Schumpeter's fear was that the success of the capitalist model would lead to corporatism, which would prohibit, not encourage, economic growth; today, this has become a reality. In this model, creative destruction was the end result, with the old ways of doing things being destroyed and replaced with new ones. The role of classical management is to introduce the invention and introduction of technology concurrently with the destruction of dying processes and industries to ensure that capital and labor resources are appropriated efficiently for economic growth. Allowing or promoting old destructive companies to stay in business is a poor allocation of capital. Even today, as it is being debated whether our government should infuse capital into the moribund U.S. automakers, the concept of classical management and creative destruction is lost on us.

These fundamentals of classical management are what define its objectives, how it was born in the United States in 1908, and how it grew the U.S. economy to unprecedented heights in the following decades. The founders of classical management were men like Frederick Taylor, Max Weber, Henry Ford, W. Edwards Deming, Alfred Sloan, and Peter Drucker. These are the men who laid the foundation for the revolution of thought versus the revolution of class struggle and violence that was assumed by social theorists like Karl Marx and Jack London. It was not coincidental that the birth of classical management happened at this point, yet its impact on our culture and economy is largely understated and overlooked. Thus, the death of management and its impact should not be overlooked, as is particularly relative to our current economic predicament. Indeed, a rebirth of classical management can turn the economy around.

In 1920, Alfred P. Sloan took over the leadership of General Motors at a time when it had a 12 percent market share. Although Sloan believed in Taylor's *Principles of Scientific Management* like his competitor Henry Ford, he also believed that more was needed to drive business results. Some would say that Alfred Sloan was the inventor of the modern corporation, enabling General Motors to grow its market share to 56 percent in the year that he retired, 1956. "His ideas were so clearly correct that we have forgotten that they were an invention," noted Dr. Schein of the Massachussets Institute of Technology's Sloan School of Management.[17] Sloan took the best organizational theories and applied them as principles of modern management. He created the first decentralized organization, essentially breaking General Motors into independent divisions with separate sets of assets, management, and structure; they were even allowed to establish their own external business deals. Today, many old General Motors divisions are separate companies, such as EDS and DirecTV. Sloan's view on organizational structure was that it was in place so that people can be more creative and spend their time more wisely. His focus on a management approach to improve the organization, capital, and technology of an automobile company enabled General Motors to become the world's largest company for decades, into the early 1980s.

Today, General Motors is a shell of what it used to be, with its long-term survival under question. The role of organizational structure and strategy went from being a competitive advantage to a detriment, leading to a year-end financial result in 2008 of a loss of $30.9 billion, with hourly labor costs of more than $70 per hour. For decades, the leaders of the company were finance specialists, apparatchiks who led conformity over innovation. The company that founded the modern corporation's definition of organizational structure became a complicated, uncompetitive, and bureaucratic organization structure (entangled with the United Auto Workers) and an accounting system that was to be thumped by the lean manufacturing methods implemented by Toyota, among other competitors.

Through the innovations of leaders like Alfred P. Sloan, the discipline of classical management was in its heyday in the 1930s through the early 1950s, which enabled the greatest growth for a nation in economic history. Between 1940 and 1950, the U.S. GDP grew by 57 percent and had a per capita increase of 36 percent.[18] At first, the discipline of classical management provided the structure and process via managing mechanization, and human factors via scientific management. Next, the structure of the modern corporation was developed, enabling product innovation and growth to occur in unprecedented ways, thanks to an understanding of the importance of product life-cycle management. Corporate managers proliferated, empowered through Sloan's organizational design and the newly defined role of management itself. Senior managers were trained to exercise some level of control over the organization, but not to interfere too much, in order to allow the mid-level manager to make the right decision. Divisionalization became the business paradigm for growth: it allowed companies to explore new and international markets like never before. Management had created the perfect multiplier—improving the choices for the consumer market by, in General Motor's case, "building a car for every purse and purpose." This, along with effective management techniques, allowed workers and the owners of this corporation to prosper collectively. Management as a function had a purpose and was truly the driving factor for the growth engine of the U.S. economic juggernaut of the mid-20th century.

W. EDWARDS DEMING AND THE NEED FOR QUALITY

After a few decades and after years of success, the requirements of classical management started to be neglected in U.S. business. This is easy to understand, because the U.S. economy was far and away the biggest economy and the United States was the world's superpower. Shortcuts started to be taken and complacency set in. Furthermore, the regulatory remnants from the Great Depression and World War II had remained in place, and the business environment in the United States became stale and uncompetitive. After all, implementing the steps shown in Figure 2.3 isn't easy for workers, owners, and managers to understand. To borrow a phrase from my first book, managers were taking the "easy out." "Planned obsolescence" in manufacturing is perhaps one of the greatest examples of a lack of optimization between the managers and production process of the company and its consumers.

Having grown up in the 1970s, I recall this problem specifically, because my Dad was on a first-name basis with his auto mechanic, Sam, in a familiar encounter, fighting planned obsolescence by overspending for auto repair. W. Edwards Deming faced this problem in the United States firsthand, because many U.S. corporations weren't so interested in his lessons on how to improve design, product quality, testing, and sales. These companies believed that improving quality only cost the company more money and led to lost sales. Despite being spurned in the United States, Deming had an eager audience in Japan's manufacturing industry relative to these principles, in this case, as is represented in a letter from Dr. Yoshikasu Tsuda of Rikkyo University in 1980:

> I (Tsuda) just spent a year in the northern hemisphere in 23 countries, in which I visited many industrial plants, and talked with many industrialists. In Europe and in America, people are now more interested in cost of quality and in systems of quality audit. But in Japan, we are keeping very strong interest to improve quality by use of methods which you started . . . when we improve quality we also improve productivity, just as you told us in 1950 would happen.[19]

In the early days of post-World War II manufacturing in Japan, the quality of the product was so bad that some Japanese manufacturers set up factories in Usa, Japan, so the product could be labeled "Made in Usa."[20] The concepts that Deming preached to Japan were ones of importance to its culture: hard work, quality, and craftsmanship—factors very much tied to optimizing the variables in the production function in order to increase surplus value. Deming's approach was the use of statistics—to record product defects, analyze why they happened, institute changes, record how much quality improved, and keep refining the process until it was done correctly.

Deming's message of classical management was simple: employ a formalized focus on the details of a business as a continuous improvement process, always seeking higher levels of quality. This message is demonstrated in what Deming wrote on the blackboard of every meeting with top management in Japan from July 1950 onward:

> Improve Quality → Costs decrease because less rework, fewer mistakes, etc. → Productivity Improves → Capture the market w/better quality & price → Stay in business → Provide jobs and more jobs.[21]

Deming's perspective on why this approach worked in Japan was the following:

> With no lenders nor stockholders to press for dividends, this effort became an undivided bond between management and production workers. An unfriendly takeover or a leveraged buyout does not take place in Japan. Managers are not sensitive to the price:earnings ratio of their stock. The Japanese manager may adopt constancy of purpose.[22]

In the preceding statement, Deming validates the requirements, as listed in Figure 2.3, for classical management. These are the requirements of a management system, a rational science in place to increase surplus value and administer a fair allocation of it. In contrast to Deming's approach, the conventional wisdom of postclassical management gives too much credit and blame to individual managers and not enough to management as a system. Deming was perhaps one of the last management thinkers who was focused on management as a rational, system-approached science versus a personally inspired philosophy.

Through management science, there were some very important considerations that Deming discussed; many of them were completely different from conventional wisdom (of then and of today). One is that low quality means high costs. This is a rather obvious statement when analyzing an economic production function, but not as obvious to Corporate America. For many managers back then, and even today, it may be viewed as sufficient to cut corners on quality in order to reduce costs. It is a mind-set that ignores quality at the expense of price. Deming believed that the opposite is true: that defects aren't free and rework costs a lot of money. Deming also believed that technological change by itself isn't the answer, which is another point supported by the requirements listed in Figure 2.3, and by the optimization of the production function. In other words, mechanization and technology without sufficient design in process is counterproductive.

Next, Deming believed that measures of productivity do not necessarily lead to improvements in productivity. This is important because, even today, many managers spend a lot of their time measuring productivity rather than taking actions to improve it. We discuss this problem in chapter six. You can walk into the office of many Fortune 500 corporate managers and see graphs, charts, and other visuals that demonstrate certain measurements of productivity, but if you ask the same manager about corrective actions, you'll frequently get something other than a definitive response. Productivity is only productivity if it is achieved, not simply measured. Deming believed in statistics as a tool to improve, not as an end in itself. He was a management thinker, who considered management to be a rational science, supporting the principles of economic optimization. Today, we are sorely missing these types of gurus in our discussions of management.

The era of W. Edwards Deming was perhaps the pinnacle of the era of classical management as the driver of the U.S. economy. Even given the successes of the discipline of management during this period, he warned about what can happen that would derail management as a discipline and about the impact of quality and productivity on the U.S. economy. For one, he mentioned the impact that a short-term financial system can have on a quality and productivity program. Without a balance between long-term sustainability and investment and short-term profitability, a successful management program cannot occur, just as a successful quality program cannot. He noted that this was perhaps one of the reasons why his theories were more accepted and implemented in Japan than in the United States.

Second, Deming believed that workers were not hired hands, but rather associates who must be engaged in the overall success of the company. If the employees weren't motivated, he believed, it was a management problem, not that of the workforce. The well-known Quality Circle concept (volunteer group of workers who talk about workplace improvements) was seen as widely important to both the productivity of the company and the quality of the product by involving the workforce in the process. Lastly, Deming said that workers cannot be successful if there is a culture of fear—fear of losing one's job, fear of not being promoted, fear of a new idea, fear of being slapped down by management, fear of not contributing, fear of not having the right answer, and so on. The role of management was never more optimized than it was during the Deming era: he engendered a balance between quality, productivity, profitability, the long-term and the short-term, and manager-worker relations. As was shown in Figure 2.1, economic growth during the era of the 1950s and 1960s was never stronger. The United States was an economic juggernaut, driven by the discipline of classical management, the rise of the corporate manager. But as illustrated in this chapter, the cracks in the facade started to show up. It wasn't the system of management that started to fail, but rather the evolution of the discipline away from its initial principles. As a result, an environment of win-lose and maximum over optimum would begin to redefine how we would view the discipline of management, and we'd eventually enter the postclassical management era that has led us to where we are today.

Since the 1970s, the United States has lost 25 percent of its manufacturing jobs, or perhaps, the MNCs lost them. The business and government environment since then has been a mess. We find an economy that is no longer based on balanced free-market economics (economic liberalism) and an array of taxes or tax reductions, incentives, tariffs, allocations, pricing schemes, price-and-wage controls, and so on.

In his book, *Supercapitalism,* Robert Reich suggests that large corporations of today can no longer worry about distributing wealth in a competitive global economy, because they are forced to bow to the inevitabilities of globalization.[23] He suggests that managers in large corporations can no longer support the most basic reason that management exists at a corporation: the fair distribution of its surplus value within a company and an economy. Reich concludes that a corporation in the post-World War II era didn't have to compete as today's corporation does, and this is most certainly true.

Yet after these years of complacency and neglect, management was called on to compete against upstart economies in Asia and Europe, but it couldn't find a way to do so. What was missing after all of those years was a tie-in between management and productivity, a rational scientific approach. Is it too late to implement a classical management approach within today's global economy?

THE ORGANIZATION MAN AT THE U.S. CORPORATION

The rise of the corporate manager has become so prominent to U.S. culture that it has seeped into our psychosocial framework as a nation. In his classic, *The Organization Man* (1956), William Whyte suggests that managers not only worked for a corporation but sold their psyches to them as well. These men sold their personal goals to conform to their corporation in return for a stable life in exchange. Getting a job out of high school or college determined one's fate, and the manager became what the company wanted him to be. At the beginning of the book, Whyte notes that the masterpiece created by Alfred P. Sloan was beginning to become a dysfunctional organization:

> The older generation may still convince themselves; the younger generation does not. When a young man says that to make a living these days you must do what somebody else wants you to do, he states it not only as a fact of life that must be accepted but as an inherently good proposition. If the American Dream deprecates this for him, it is the American Dream that is going to have to give, whatever its more elderly guardians may think. People grow restive with a mythology that is too distant from the way things actually are, and as more and more lives have been encompassed by the organization way of life, the pressures for an accompanying ideological shift have been mounting. The pressures of the group, the frustrations of individual creativity, the anonymity of achievement: are these defects to struggle against—or are they virtues in disguise? The organization man seeks a redemption of his place on earth—a faith that will satisfy him that what he must endure has a deeper meaning than appears on the surface. He needs, in short, something that will do for him what the Protestant Ethic did once. And slowly, almost imperceptibly, a body of thought has been coalescing that does that.[24]

With the rise of the corporate manager came inherent limitations. The organization that was so critical to enabling the manager to balance the needs for business growth while ensuring benefits to the worker started to change: now the worker and manager needed to conform and serve the organization structure instead of vice versa. Today, the remnants of the organization man remain at many of our largest companies, if they haven't been downsized or outsourced over the years.

During the 1950s, 1960s, and the 1970s, the organization man was a concept that kept the covenant between workers and managers alive in a manner that worked for the times. For a company to succeed in those decades, it needed quite a few organization men. There was little competition from the global markets, and a regulation existed to allow labor, capital, and technology to thrive with little threat of competition. A steel executive in the 1950s bragged, "Our sales people don't sell steel, they allocate it."[25] Today, the competitive pressures are much greater, and deregulation has changed this tenuous covenant between labor, capital, and technology. Today, there are few organization men and there's no covenant.

The next chapters of this book address how the postmanagement discipline that now exists has become a defective discipline in the United States. We are salaciously focused on the short-term, on pleasing the financial markets versus building value of the company, as Deming noted. We adhere to fantasy driven definition of industrialism that seeks unlimited growth, economic limitlessness. What we do is not in the mold of our famous pioneers, such as Taylor, Ford, Sloan, Deming, and Drucker. Our forefathers of management built a discipline that enabled the avoidance of another Civil War, got us through the Great Depression, powered us through World War II and the Cold War, and raised us to levels of economic prosperity that are unmatched in history. Can we reclaim this system of management in time to save us from ourselves in today's crisis?

Fearing The Chinese Bogeyman

The Chinese are basically the same bunch of goons and thugs they have been in the past 50 years.

Jack Cafferty, April 9, 2008 CNN

He [Cafferty] is obviously unhappy with China "holding hundreds of billions of dollars" of U.S. paper deficits, more and more American consumers "buying from (inexpensive) Wal-Mart," and certainly the "changed relationship" with China.

China Daily, editorial response, April, 2008

THE FEAR OF A GLOBAL PLANET

It was October 1957, and all was well in the United States. The U.S. economy had reaped the benefits of a covenant between workers and owners, and middle-class growth and success could be seen everywhere. The American Dream was in full bloom, and there wasn't anything that the United States couldn't do, if it put its mind to it. But on a chilly October 4, some of this euphoria was dampened as a 184-pound tin can was launched into the sky, not by the Americans, but rather by its Cold War rivals, the Soviets. The news from NBC radio was announced:

"Listen now," said the NBC radio network announcer on the night of October 4, 1957, "for the sound that forevermore separates the old from the new." Next came the chirping in the key of A-flat from outer space that the Associated Press called the "deep beep-beep." Emanating from a simple transmitter aboard the Soviet Sputnik satellite, the chirp lasted three-tenths of a second, followed by a three-tenths-of-a-second pause. This was repeated over and over again until it passed out of hearing range of the United States.[1]

Paul Dickson, the author of *Sputnik: The Shock of the Century* said, "It caught us in the middle of a materialistic fascination with toys."[2] This first artificial satellite in the sky could not only be seen, but also heard; a chilling notice was sent to Americans that our national security couldn't be secured by oceans and that our perception of the brutish Russians was ill-conceived. Sure, we had TVs, fancy tailfins on our cars, game shows, an emerging suburban dream, and superhighways, but little of that would protect us when we looked up in the air. Once the shock wore off, the classical management discipline tied to the U.S. public and private sectors realized that a new course of direction needed to be set. And this new strategic directive not only set the tone and direction for the United States in the mid-20th century, it has been the very foundation for much of our present technology and productivity.

Sputnik resulted in the creation of DARPA, the Defense Advance Research Projects Agency, which spent millions of dollars on research to prevent the United States from being surprised like this again when it came to technological innovation. From this research facility came the Internet and the World Wide Web. A group of U.S. scientists monitored the transmission of *Sputnik,* learned from it, and, as a result, the first global positioning system (GPS) was used by the U.S. Navy in 1960. In 1978, the first commercial use of GPS was introduced by Rockwell International, providing yet another example of how the public and private sector were able to implement a successful invention through the use of classical management as the enabler of the product life-cycle process (viewing business as a cycle that begins with research and development and ends with distribution and use). As a twist of fate, now it is the Russians who are chasing us in 2008, as they seek to develop their own GPS system (tested using Vladimir Putin's dog!).

Americans owe a lot to the way in which our leaders in both the public and the private-sectors (managers) responded to what happened on that chilly night in October 1957. At first, the citizens of the United States were shocked and scared. And then we decided to take action, and what followed was an exercise of how management in the United States was able to drive the components of government, research, capital, and labor for the creation and development of technology. The collaboration of public and private sector goals and objectives was accomplished successfully through the leadership of the classical management discipline.

Fear is a wonderful motivator, but it is, by its very nature, anesthetic. If used in the correct dosage, it can be very useful, but when misused or overused, it can be fatal. Having grown up near Washington, D.C. (in Baltimore) at the very last stage of the Cold War, I grew up learning of the frightening stereotypes that existed in our society regarding the Soviets: spies, communists, crude Slavs, who spent their lives trying to destroy the West and our way of life. In high school, I studied the Russian language to learn more about the people and the culture of our Cold War enemy. What I learned in my first lesson on globalization was mesmerizing: for all of the rhetoric of Soviet and U.S. propaganda, there was a great disparity of insecurity; one nation had been devastated in World War II (23 million, or 14 percent, of the population killed, whereas the United States had lost 450,000, or 0.32 percent). As we look closer at a culture and a people, what do we see—what do we want to see? And how we respond to what we see can make a world of difference, as was shown in the U.S. reaction to the *Sputnik* scare. Our response to globalization must be rational and measured, rather than knee jerk and emotional, as was proven effectively in the 1950s.

Around the same time that the United States was dealing with this scare, the Japanese economy was being rebuilt from the ruins of World War II. Back then, not much attention was paid to Japan as an economic competitor, even though much of its assets (of which 40 percent were destroyed in World War II) were being built from scratch, using the newest technologies as a competitive advantage. Out of the ashes rose a Japanese economic juggernaut, with damaging consequences to the U.S. economy, or so it seemed in an article written by Japanese author Masao Miyoshi in 1991:

> The trade imbalance stands at 50 billion dollars annually in Japan's favor; Japan's per capita income is higher than that of the United States; eight of the world's largest banks are Japanese; a single Japanese corporation, Nippon Telegraph and Telephone, is worth more than IBM, AT&T, General Motors, General Electric, and Exxon combined; nearly a third of the U.S. budget deficit is now shouldered by Japanese investors; Japan's share in the global financial and capital market stands at 40 percent.[3]

I wasn't born when the *Sputnik* scare happened, but I was in high school during the period of the fear of Japan, which finally came to fruition in the late 1970s and early 1980s. It's funny how there are so few of us who appear to remember those days, or at least admit to remembering them. Donald Trump reflected what many Americans were thinking:

> We should have a tax decrease. We should have Japan and we should have Saudi Arabia and we should have all of these countries who are literally ripping us off left and right . . . They should pay for our $200-billion deficit . . . We are supporting—we are literally supporting—Japan, which is the greatest money machine ever created, and we created it to a large extent.

By the middle of the following year, Trump had warmed to the topic, telling *Times* reporter Nina J. Easton, "There is going to be a tremendous backlash against what Japan is doing in this *country*—sucking the lifeblood out of it because of our stupid policies. Our policy is to have free trade, but Japan is not reciprocating."[4]

The bloated U.S. corpocracy was scared of Japan and scared of economic liberalism, the very science that we made operational through the use of classical management. The 10-year period from 1973 to 1982 was the lowest of lows, economically, with one of the worst periods of inflation in our history, foreign investors fleeing the dollar, our corporations lacking competitiveness, and the Organization of Petroleum Exporting Countries (OPEC) increasing oil prices tenfold. The solution to these problems was a dose of Keynesian economics, an attempt by our federal government to jump-start economic activity through excessive government spending, leading to a limited amount of domestic savings to finance the government debt, and to invest in infrastructure and retooling. Interest rates rose and U.S. investments all of a sudden became attractive to the world, particularly to Japan. In order to purchase those investments, the Japanese, Saudis, and others needed to acquire dollars, which caused an appreciation of the value of the dollar on the open market. And when the value of the dollar rose as a result, our products became more expensive, exacerbating the problems that had already been brewing: the decline in U.S. manufacturing and the ascension of Japanese capabilities.

Americans began to buy Toyotas instead of Fords. Some Toyotas were physically sliced in half in protest in Washington, D.C.. When the Japanese purchased Radio City Music Hall, the late Art Buchwald called it "Radio City Tojo Hall." Sony Chairman Akio Morita wrote an essay titled "The Japan That Can Say No" in 1989, asserting Japan's economic might and rights, and many U.S. leaders thought that this was the escalation of mercantilist policies from Japan that would promulgate the weakening of U.S. economic dominance in the world. Charges of price fixing, the use of cartels, government-corporate protectionist tactics, and sheer arrogance were the allegations.

Most of these allegations were with merit, but, ultimately, the Japanese bubble economy burst, and the threat of Japanese world dominance went away, or so it seemed. From this, we saw that the first U.S. response to an emerging global economy had revealed our shortcomings and exposed how our bloated corpocracy, without a true management function, was a competitive disadvantage for us. The U.S. response to the Japanese bogeyman wasn't as rational and measured as the response to the Russian one, and the competitive challenges of the United States were the first signal that its corpocracy model of business couldn't keep up with an emerging global economy.

More than 20 years after this bashing of Japan, Toyota is the largest auto manufacturer in the world; purchasing a product labeled "made in Japan" is now associated with a high-quality good at a reasonable price. Toyota is also a responsible corporate citizen in the United States, with more than 36,000 employees, not including its domestic suppliers. When the U.S. dot-com economy took off, right after the decline of the Japanese economy, all of the bluster associated with Japanese bashing went away and was essentially forgotten.

Today, the Japanese economy is a mess, and it's a barely functioning political democracy, with the same party in power for decades. Alex Emery of Permira

Advisers (a large British private equity firm) says, "Japan is not just closed to foreigners—it's closed to everyone."[5] But the drumbeat of protectionism continues. Lee Iacocca, in his recent book *Where Have All the Leaders Gone?,* said that Japan is a little island with a big ego that does everything in its power to keep its trade imbalance great. Japan is no longer the threat that everyone once thought that it would be, and yet some of our greatest leaders of past and present still focus on protectionism over our lack of management leadership and productivity to face new global challenges.

THE ASIAN CENTURY

In the 1950s through the 1980s, the U.S. obsession with the Soviet Union came and went, and the Soviet Empire disbanded from its Marxist ideologies. As a result of the partnership of the U.S. public and private sectors in math and science during the 1950s, led by classical management, our high technology industry was reengaged, and its effects are helping our economy to the present. In the 1980s and the 1990s, the concerns over Japan came and went, and the fears dissipated amid one of the longest economic growth periods in our nation's history, although this growth wasn't driven by manufacturing and classical management (as discussed in the next chapter). The pattern of bashing continues: we now believe that we are being threatened as never before by a vicious, mercantilist, communist rival in China, which is referred to as, potentially, the greatest economic miracle of all time. The points of view for the readers and watchers of popular media regarding the Chinese primarily appear to be binary: we are both infatuated with and in awe of the concept of globalization (Global-is-Asian), and the fears and bashing from the protectionists, represented in the chapter epigraph by Jack Cafferty. Iacocca himself suggests that today's free trade is a win-lose and that today's loser is the United States. A recent *Fortune* magazine survey noted that Americans believe, by a large majority of 68 percent, that our trading partners are benefiting most from free trade, not the United States. The question for this chapter is this: should we be afraid of this Chinese bogeyman and free trade, or should we look more closely at ourselves to understand the problem?

Regardless of whether we believe that China is an economic threat to our well-being (see Figure 3.1), we shouldn't discount the right of those in developing nations to pursue their own version of the American Dream. Kishore Mahbubani, a well-known professor in Singapore, states that the West refuses to accept that the 21st century is the Asian Century.

For centuries, the Asians (Chinese, Indians, Muslims, and others) have been bystanders in world history. Now they are ready to become co-drivers.

Asians have finally understood, absorbed, and implemented Western best practices in many areas: from free-market economics to modern science and technology, from

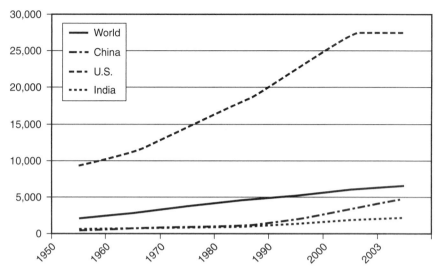

Figure 3.1 GDP per Capita, 1950–2003

meritocracy to rule of law. They have also become innovative in their own way, creating new patterns of cooperation not seen in the West.

Will the West resist the rise of Asia? The good news is that Asia wants to replicate, not dominate, the West. For a happy outcome to emerge, the West must gracefully give up its domination of global institutions, from the IMF to the World Bank, from the G7 to the UN Security Council.

History teaches that tensions and conflicts are more likely when new powers emerge. This, too, may happen. But they can be avoided if the world accepts the key principles for a new global partnership spelled out in The New Asian Hemisphere.[6]

Whether the Asia led by China wants to dominate or coexist, it scarcely matters who is right or wrong in this debate: Asia is already emerging as a primary focus area of global economic growth. With strong winds of discontent in the United States, the prevailing view seems to be a stronger fear of globalization, especially in comparison to the views of the rest of the world, as is shown in Figure 3.2.

FEAR AND FAIR TRADE

Whether it's a poll run by CNN, *Fortune,* AP-Yahoo, *Wall Street Journal,* or NBC, the majority of U.S. respondents are voicing a rising discontent against globalization. Can we blame the U.S. public for being so alarmed about it, when so many of our politicians and experts are beating the negative drum so loudly, without a countervailing view? Stories of China's currency, toxic toys, contaminated

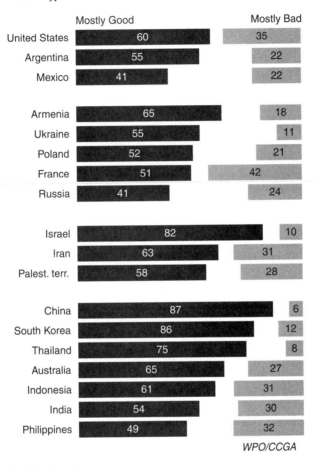

Views of Globalization
...Do you believe that globalization, especially the increasing connections of our economy with others around the world, is mostly good or mostly bad for [survey country]?

Figure 3.2 Globalization Survey
Source: WorldPublicOpinion.com, 2008

food, and the lost jobs of the United States (now documented by some to be almost 2 million jobs since China entered the World Trade Organization seven years ago) are often true statements, but partial truths only. When politicians like Sherrod Brown speak of the "five governments (that) control more than $2 trillion that they use to buy stocks and other assets in America," there is no reasoning as to what these nations are supposed to do with the flood of dollars coming to them from our dependence on foreign oil and cheap imports at the local Wal-Mart.

It's bad enough for them that their surpluses with the United States are tied to a weaker dollar and a collapsing financial market on Wall Street. It's a situation that is almost impossible to believe. Blaming other nations for our obsessive fixation on consumption and poor productivity is a pure deflection of the real problem: an inability to measure and understand what true productivity means and a lack of a classical management discipline in order to achieve these results.

Our displacement of blame hardly matters to the rest of the world, particularly those who are profiting from it. Even the shocking transfer of wealth from the United States to these emerging economies hasn't appeared to have awoken us to the problem. The 2008 trade deficit was $673.3 billion, down from 2007's $731.2 billion, and from 2006's $750 billion, but still a shocking amount. This deficit was broken down for 2007, as follows:[7]

> $293 billion in petroleum-related goods
> $328 billion in consumer goods
> $193 billion in all other goods
> $107 billion in surplus goods

The accumulated trade deficit for the United States in the 21st century is around $5 trillion (not including the public debt), an unheard of transfer of wealth to have happened in such a short time. Prior to becoming Federal Reserve chairman, Ben Bernanke characterized our massive debt to the rest of the world as associated with a "global savings glut," suggesting that our consuming habits appears to be a virtuous balance to Asia's massive saving efforts. The logic of this argument continues to suggest that the United States is a good global citizen because we're accommodating this glut of savings in the world through our consumption. This argument was made in 2005, a few trillion dollars of deficit ago from where the United States is today. But I hardly can imagine that anyone would now admit to such statements. Even after the financial collapse that we're facing, we continue to burrow our heads into the sand and ignore the real problems in our productivity and management ability.

During an earlier era, classical management was a large factor for how the United States responded to the *Sputnik* scare. Many stories can be told of how the practice of classical management pulled U.S. business operations into a balanced solution—among its stakeholders and between the public and private interests. The primary view of so many today is that the MNC supports a policy of corporate globalization that threatens democracy at the national level. Another perspective to the problem is that the U.S. economy is no longer attractive to the MNC because of a lack of management capability and productivity. So, instead of focusing on the ills of our private sector economy, fear is being broadcast to the U.S. public by our leaders, preventing us from trusting globalization. Fair trade anyone? If you poll the world on this term, they will tell you that trade wasn't fair before, shouldn't be equitable (it should be a competition), and is increasingly unbalanced in this growing deregulated, global environment. Mercantilism, the approach of controlling the economy through the government, is in full swing today in the global economy. There is money mercantilism (using currency as a national trade weapon against other nations) where the ballooning accumulation of large U.S. currency reserves is happening in Russia, China, Japan, and other countries. There is energy mercantilism (doing the same with energy, primarily oil) where oil exporting nations (we get more than 70 percent of our oil from other nations) are bypassing the global marketplace and are cutting direct deals with nations, affecting the free market. Food mercantilism may be next, potentially leading to more technocratic battles (perhaps an emerging Brazil in flexing its muscles as a food provider?) versus free-enterprise solutions. The less-than-invisible hand of government intervention will continue to persist, but that shouldn't persuade any economy from doing its best to be more competitive in an increasingly global marketplace. Economic liberalism will make an economy more competitive in the global market, not the use of mercantilism.

U.S. fears of a global economy are shared by our counterparts from all over the world. Even so, few nations can compete with the false bravado of the red, white, and blue protectionists, like Lee Iacocca, who repeat that "America shouldn't be pushed around anymore," leading the public to believe that we've been victimized for almost 30 years now (Iacocca's quote was initially used to introduce the Chrysler K-Car in 1980). As the United States enters 2010, expect such fears to lead to more protectionism and displacement of the economic problem.

The drum beat of fear and mercantilism is growing over our airwaves and at the book superstores. The swords are being drawn, and the chance of a global economy taking shape without a larger role of government intervention is becoming increasingly unlikely. In Gabor Steingart's book *The War for Wealth: The True Story of Globalization, or Why the Flat World is Broken (2008),* he makes clear his fear of the Chinese bogeyman, and he relates his view that the United States and Europe must band together to fight this pending threat, essentially a battle of civilizations.

If this sentiment grows in our world, it is increasingly likely that the solutions will be of the mercantilist versus a free market, putting the responsibility of economic growth into the hands of technocratic politicians over classical management. In the end, this book promotes a different course of action for managers. This is a perspective consistent with that of those leaders who believed that the best chance for a post-World War II era of peace and prosperity was through economic liberalism rather than government intervention. Clearly, we are headed in the wrong direction today.

Facing up to an emerging global economy is scary, but it pales in comparison to the realities of facing up to our own economic performance. When the United States finally got a look behind the Soviet Iron Curtain in the 1990s, what did we see? We saw a failed ideology of communal central planning that was unable to achieve an improvement in the labor, capital, and technology of its closed economy. Soviet workers had little incentive to improve production. There were few consumer goods available to the worker, little chance of making more money, no market-based research and development environment (including public-private partnership), and little understanding of how an economic production function can drive and motivate individual behavior. Without economic liberalism, there was no shared covenant between companies, workers, and society. Political ideology and the nature of the Russian culture prevented that nation from developing and nurturing a tool such as classical management to drive economic growth. Despite the success of *Sputnik* and other accomplishments, the Soviets were little competition to the U.S. economy during the 20th century.

After concerns of Japan overtaking our economy in the 1980s and 1990s, when the curtain was lifted on Japan, what did we see? Despite all of the self-confidence from Japanese leaders about an economy strong enough to say no to the United States, Japan's economy in 2008 is no longer considered first class, even in the words of its own economic minister, Ota Hiroka. With an estimated GDP growth ranking of 185th in the world, a very closed, mercantilist economy, an aging population, and few natural resources and a high dependency on foreign oil, Japan won't be a true challenger to U.S. dominance, as is shown in Figure 3.3. And yet, some 20 years ago, the Donald Trumps of the United States were prophesizing Japanese dominance in the world economy because of unfair trade practices. The moral of this story is that the world economy can be rational, even in the face of mercantilist, protectionist policy among world governments. Macroeconomists and policy analysts must balance the need to protect our industries and workers while, at the same time, not closing ourselves off to the point of becoming irrelevant, as is becoming the case today in Japan. Nations must have a policy of growth through improvements, led by classical managers (as was the case in the United States).

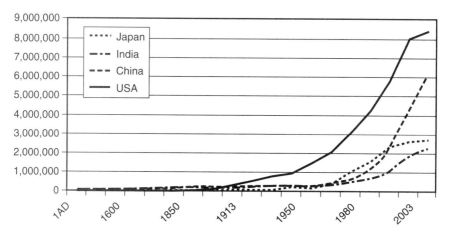

Figure 3.3 U.S. vs. East GDP, 1 A.D. to Present (Estimates and Actual)

THE NEXT BOGEYMAN: CHINA

What will happen when we lift the Chinese curtain? We may view the Chinese government acting unapologetically as an aggressive mercantilist player in the world economy, validating our fears. Or we may see a rising superpower seeking to flex its muscles, perhaps even slightly insecure. We may look and see the fortunate 200 million who have profited from the openness in the Chinese capitalist economy, or the 200 million below the poverty line (higher than the official 10 percent poverty rate). We may see a powerfully modern and seemingly unlimited opportunity for economic growth. Perhaps we'll see a nation hoarding foreign reserves as an insecure sign of economic strength. There is no clear definition of economic growth and productivity for an emerging economic superpower that also has 200 million people in poverty.

China's economy has been introduced to market reforms only since the 1980s, and one-third of this economy remains controlled by the state. It is a vastly immature, albeit fast-growing economic culture. There is no question that China's emergence from the disastrous policies of Mao is one of the most remarkable economic events of our time, but we must temper this exuberance with the reality of what China really is: an emerging, undeveloped nation. And this is what's so confusing about this Chinese bogeyman: it is both a crude and poor nation, but never before in our history has the United States had the potential to become so dependent on another country as is happening with China—a nation with such massive social and infrastructure needs, but one that is willing to allow the United States to borrow from it at such an unbelievable rate. Our trade deficit with this poor Chinese nation is $1.8 trillion dollars and going up by $1 billion per day![8] In 2006, China purchased some 55 percent of new U.S. Treasury bonds and note issues and those purchases (according to the Fed) lowered the 10-year rate by 1.5 points![9] It's a story where the truth is much stranger than one could have ever imagined fiction to be. Perhaps our view of this dichotomy of what China really is tells us more about ourselves than about the Chinese. Perhaps it's time for us to view ourselves as the problem—rather than China, or Japan, or the Soviets. Today, we should learn from our past and present of the dangers of focusing on the wrong problem.

Despite the U.S. obsession with the rapidly growing Chinese economy, there are certain facts that have been discussed less frequently. When looking at the purchasing power of nations, China loses 40 percent of its supposed net economic wealth. In December 2007, the World Bank unveiled a study detailing the purchasing power of 146 nations. When using a new standard of purchasing power (purchasing power parity), the relative size of the Chinese economy fell, and the number of poor (international poverty line) increased dramatically. As China's total income rose sharply between 2001 and 2003, the average income of the poorest 10 percent fell by 2.5 percent (all before consideration of purchasing power).[10] Despite China's economic progress since 2003, this storyline remains surprisingly the same, with the poor of the country making little progress.

Another important question is this: can we evaluate the economic prosperity of a nation based on pure and published economic statistics (such as GDP growth), or must we view other factors as well? Nobel Prize-winning economist Amartya Sen believes that human indicators are a better way to measure economic progress than GDP growth rates, and this philosophy is consistent with my view on classical management and its role in optimizing economic progress within a society as well as the corporation. Many Americans will likely agree with Sen's philosophy: our middle-class prosperity used to speak very favorably about our economic standing. Many Americans today don't feel as financially secure in 2008 as they did in the 1970s, even as our measured GDP tripled over more than 30 years. China's relative strength as an economic superpower is likely overstated today—both by its globalist supporters and its protectionist detractors. This revision doesn't reduce China's growth rate over the past 30 years, the fastest of any large country in history. The nation remains the largest producer and consumer of steel, the second biggest user of energy, and, even in revised terms, the world's second-largest economy. What the alternate view of the effect of purchasing power parities and the view of relative prosperity do is to put into perspective that China's economic ascension is very impressive, but also very early in progress. It begs us to ask the question why a prosperous nation like the United States and its people should create a Chinese bogeyman out of a growing nation with as many significant issues as China has today. The answer to this question, in my mind, is that we're in denial that we are the problem, not China, and we've lost our ability to succeed within the tenets of economic liberalism, as founded by Adam Smith and perfected by classical management.

Management anyone? If we compare and contrast the presence and absence of management in the United States and China over the past century, it'll show an almost impossible contrast of events. Since 1908, classical management in the United States has had a major role in providing an engine of productivity for very significant events, and it has been the most important discipline of economic time. In contrast, China has staggered through some of the most devastating, self-imposed economic disasters (Maoism) in world history over the past century. Just recently, the reforms of the 1980s are taking shape in China, and economic progress is beginning to happen, albeit without a true profession of management within the culture, which instead still relies on Communist Party officials. China's economic growth is a contradiction of terms, of a deregulated, out-of-control, free-market approach run by Communist Party apparatchiks, for the most part.

China's current employment growth is 20 million new jobs per year, which means that it will take 40 years for the nation to restore some level of dignity to the poorest of the massive numbers of peasants in China's countryside.[11] China's professional management pool is largely a combination of party officials, expatriates with a poor understanding of the culture and language, ruthless capitalists, and even some inexperienced, young natives. What exists today in China is not classical management in the form of Henry Ford and W. Edwards Deming in any sense of the term. The thought that Chinese managers or even the expatriates spend any effort purposely optimizing labor, capital, and technology is humorous and questionable, at best. Its unsound banking system, overregulated and at the whim of the privileged and their projects, armies of underpaid and mistreated working poor, and technology unable to be unleashed because of the millions of unemployed hardly reflect classical management. China's published official unemployment rate of 3.5 percent is a complete fantasy, given the millions of transients who travel to find work and the fact that the millions in rural areas are neither shown as employed or unemployed. By some estimates, unemployment may be 20 percent and growing because of the very short-term nature of its economy to focus on low-tech, lost-cost, quick-hit manufacturing. Clearly, a genuine, rational, and scientific form of management in China is decades away, by any estimate.

CAN CLASSICAL MANAGEMENT SUCCEED IN CHINA?

Creating a business environment for classical management to succeed in China will be especially difficult, if not impossible, given its culture and history. During the development phase in the United States, its private and public sectors grew together; in China today, they seem to be at odds with each other. Furthermore, China's history entails an obligation to its ancient traditions and cultures, and, in the words of Mao, involves being "accustomed to misery." China's government inserts itself like a fireproof layer, between the core and the crust, ensuring that nothing can escape from the red-hot core to the perimeters.[12] This private-public sector approach isn't suitable for an environment where classical management can thrive, but it isn't without function (Machiavelli says, "the ends support the means"). Beneath the surface of a China that is glowing in recent success lies the pain of the past and the problems of the present. Who's to say that China's approach to economics won't work? There may be different approaches to achieving sustainable and equitable economic growth to its society and corporations, but the possibility of a classical approach to management working as the optimizer in the Middle Kingdom appears to be very unlikely in the short- and mid-term future. Without classical management, it is my stance that China will never achieve the level of success that the United States achieved during the middle of the 20th century or can even achieve again if it gets back to the right principles of innovation and productivity.

Short-term thinking (or societal realities) from the Chinese government has favored low-tech manufacturing solutions, and government estimates that exports are 50 percent high-tech is a laughable allegation that could never be validated.[13] China is a nation that conceivably has 25 percent of the world's total workforce, or 800 million workers. Labor rights for workers are officially accepted as a social concern, but there is more talk than action in solving the problem. On January 1, 2008, a sweeping piece of legislative reform was enacted that both domestic and foreign business entities have to follow regarding how workers must be treated:

the enforcement of this law has been questionable, at best. Both domestic and foreign corporations fought this landmark bill, suggesting that this type of law would dramatically increase labor costs and thus have a great impact on doing business in China.

There have also been a growing number of disputes since 1987 when China resumed the practice of arbitration. According to the Ministry of Labor and Social Security in China, cases increase by 27.3 percent every year. In 2006, there were 447,000 cases, and this number would be much larger if the cases rejected by the system were included.[14] Such reform should be leading labor relations in China in the proper direction, but it remains to be seen how much impact it will have on the plight of the typical factory worker. One view is that this will lead the nation back to the "iron rice bowl" era of Maoism, when jobs were for life and there was no incentive in the economy. The other fear is that the Chinese government will be unable or uninterested in providing the proper resources to support these types of reforms adequately, rendering them useless. Inflation-adjusted funding and staffing for arbitration committees and other boards have barely increased during the last decade, which is a troubling signal. With a current focus on low-cost manufacturing seeking quick-hit growth, it is unlikely that this sort of labor dispute progress will move too quickly, preventing a fair relationship between the general workforce and corporations to flourish.

Can a nation like China, with such labor and population problems, ever conceivably use classical management as a tool to optimize labor to capital and technology to the extent that was possible in the United States? With an unemployment figure likely to be closer to the unofficial estimate of 20 percent (versus the official estimate of 3.5 percent that the government provides), there is great pressure on this nation to provide jobs to millions of workers, many of whom are either transient or in undeveloped areas of the nation. With public sector pressures on its economy in a communist society and a wild laissez-faire private manufacturing sector that is moving forward, its approach to balancing the private and public sector is much different from the approach used in the United States during the days of classical management. With an official inflation rate easing up to less than 8 percent in the second quarter of 2008 and even less than 6 percent during much of the third quarter (after being more than 8 percent in the beginning of 2008), China's rising prices and oil have been stabilizing with a slowing world economy, but inflationary pressures remain, given the vast spending power of an emerging population.

China's future strategy will be to retain a base of low-tech manufacturing, while gaining access to high-tech manufacturing and the world services sector. High-tech manufacturing and services are a riskier endeavor because they require more capital, less labor, and a more educated workforce, resulting in a slower economic growth payback than low-tech exports. Furthermore, without an educated workforce versed in classical management fundamentals, growth in these industries will be especially difficult for China, giving the developed nations, like the United States, an opportunity for competitive advantage if they choose to seize on it. Therefore, it is not a foregone conclusion that China will gain the footholds necessary to grow its economy in areas other than low-tech manufacturing, for the most part.

Another peek under the curtain reveals more reasons why the United States should be less concerned with China and more focused on its own economic misfortunes. China doesn't possess a logical urban/rural planning model to account for what's happening in its nation today. About 600 million Chinese live in cities; that's only 45 percent of the population.[15] Given the current movement of the population to the large cities, it is clear that this trend of an emigration to the supercities will continue, for employment reasons alone. In a nation whose population will grow by a few hundred million naturally over the next decade or so and a quarter of a billion rural workers trying to move into the cities for work, this influx will likely push the cities to the breaking point, if it hasn't already. If the well-known monuments of modernity in China's big cities are taken out of the equation, what's left from an infrastructure standpoint is very primitive.

Once again, the storyline is one of dichotomy between haves and have-nots: Shanghai is the city known as the "Jewel of the Orient," but also one of insufficient living conditions for millions of people, particularly the new migrants moving in for new opportunities. People spill out into the streets, literally. The low-level smog becomes increasingly ominous, as more and more coal is used to meet the cities' commercial and personal needs, as well as the influx of so many cars. As is the case with so many other issues in China, the problem has gotten so bad that it is unlikely that the government can step in and truly mitigate such an enormous social and environmental problem (much like labor laws and the environment, as is the case with two other problems). And not only is the surge of the peasants from the rural areas into the cities a problem, it's a growing problem for the land that the rural people are leaving behind.

Another major problem facing China today (and precluding it from a rational approach to management) is its inadequate, immature, and overregulated banking system, although the U.S. system certainly shouldn't be viewed as a role model either. With bad lending practices and insufficient capital structure programs, China is outrunning these bad loans only through the constant and heavy stream of capital infusion as a function of its international trade surpluses. The inefficiency of its state-owned and state-run banking system is not without an impact on the economy: According to a McKinsey study on the matter, fixing the inefficiencies in its banking system would save the Chinese about $25 billion per year and raise the GDP by $259 billion per year.[16] This matter is critical to China's economy because it relies on its banking structure for its financial needs more so than other nations that rely on other types of financial institutions (a plus for China in that sense, given the state of today's financial market). When banking rules are enacted according to strict monetary standards and yet the cronies of the Communist Party circumvent the rules to cater to their special interests, it isn't a legitimate financial system for an economic superpower (just as the U.S. system today is unwarranted). Banking reform is a big issue and another example of how classical management is unable to play a serious role in the economy of China.

SCARY U.S. ECONOMIC DEPENDENCY ON CHINA

Beginning at the start the 21st century, the United States had fueled much of its economic growth through the national deficit: estimates assume that more than 50 percent of our growth over the past eight years has been financed by deficits. Every business day, our standard of living is being financed through foreign investors, like the Chinese. According to Brad Setser, a former Treasury Department economist, about 70 percent of China's foreign holdings are in U.S. dollar assets.[17] For those of you keeping score, China is holding more than $1.8 trillion dollars in U.S. holdings, which is, of course, a lot of money. If people in the United States live beyond their means, the country needs funding from foreign governments, and this exposes our economy to being controlled by the government's policies of the lender, if they choose to do so. Our 2006 account current deficit was funded with about 70 percent of the rest of the world's surpluses and was responsible for more than 60 percent of our economic growth, a staggering statistic![18] Americans should find it insulting to their own sense of well-being that a developing nation like China, without a strong private banking system and with mercantilist government tendencies, has the upper hand in our commercial relationship, at a price of nearly $2 trillion and growing! However, Americans seem to be in denial about the true problems and want to focus instead on conjuring up bogeymen from around the world. In 2008, the bogeymen are from China.

Even with an economic relationship with the upper hand, China appears to be acutely aware of its own problems and those of its leading trading partners, like the United States. In November 2008, the Chinese government announced a financial stimulus package of more than $0.5 trillion to shore up its economy. Over a few years, China has slowed on infrastructure spending, fearing inflation. Today, with the rest of the world heading toward a recession, if not there already, China is well positioned to grow its economy, more so from the inside rather than other nations that are hurting. China's leaders "realize this is really about sentiment and confidence, which needs a very fast and strong policy response," said Wang Qing, an economist with Morgan Stanley.[19]

Such a signal from the Chinese government presents the world with a perspective that, even though it remains a developing nation, it possesses the economic strength to respond to weakening global demand through means of it own. However, the signal of strength is also a symbol of weakness, in the extraordinary nature of the Communist Party system to mobilize to allay the fears of a rather fragile economic system. Certainly, all other major economic powers are promoting stimulus packages in order to stabilize their financial systems and economy, but there is probably no major economy as dependent on government intervention as is the Chinese economy. This is something China needs to address if it is to achieve its desire to become the world's most powerful economy.

IS AN EMERGING CHINA A GOOD CHINA?

Things will change economically for both China and the United States in the 21st century. As hard as it may be to believe, China's problems are more massive, complex, and contradictory than are those of the United States. Only 0.4 percent of the Chinese population owns 60 percent of its total personal wealth![20] Party officials are without significant experience and judgment in the conduct of economics and management in facing these problems, and they are overmatched by the magnitude of the challenge. Just to feed the population is a challenge in China: vegetable prices rose by 46 percent from 2007 to 2008, and the price of pork rose by 63 percent (also as a result of disease).[21] From an oil standpoint, Petro-China is selling fuel at state-capped prices because of government subsidies, although this is slowly being phased out. It is clear that the Chinese approach will be to solve economic problems via a next-generation definition of the Communist Party rather than via economic liberalism and classical management, even while it possesses an economy built on few haves and many more have-nots.

Despite its issues, China's emergence is reshaping trade, the world financial system, global manufacturing and supply chains, and services. In many ways, China is opening itself to the world in ways that the West isn't comfortable with and doesn't understand. Amid the financial banking system collapse in the United States in late September, Vice President Zhu Min of the Bank of China noted that his bank was open to making significant investments in Wall Street. Despite the cries of warning that would occur if this came to fruition, the greatest problem of the United States today is that foreign investors are actually diversifying away from investing in the United States. We shouldn't be worried about foreign investments into the United States, particularly if the only other option is government bailouts. Instead, we should be more worried about the saying in the international markets: "Shanghai, Dubai, Mumbai, or good-bye."

In 2008, China has overtaken Germany as the world's second-largest exporter, and it is already the world's largest producer and consumer of steel and the second-largest user of energy. Certainly, China is becoming a serious trading partner for the United States, with an enormous potential in its consumer markets. From mid-2006 to mid-2007, exports from the United States to China grew by 10 percent, whereas imports from China to the United States grew by 4 percent. But this is nothing compared to what's possible in the future: by the year 2011, China will have almost as many middle-class people as the United States will have citizens, and, by 2025, China will have more than half a billion people in the middle class, according to a 2007 McKinsey study.[22]

Spending is growing rapidly in the retail sector of China's economy. Increasingly, exports are becoming a less important aspect of China's growth, particularly given the world recession of 2008. It will be rebalancing domestic demand to focus on carrying more of the necessary consumption to drive its economy, relying less on the outside world. With a growing middle-class market willing and ready to be unleashed, China is a huge retail market opportunity for U.S. exports, and trade wars or regulations would limit those possibilities. China should be viewed more as an opportunity than a threat.

For those viewing China as an opportunity, consider that the ratio of U.S. exports to imports with China has been rising over the past few years (even if it is largely unbalanced in favor of the Chinese). A more protected trade policy with China in the future would be harmful to the United States in a global economy and would place positive export growth trends in jeopardy. Meddling by politicians who don't understand global trade simply makes things worse. These same politicians grandstand over pet food recalls or lead paint on toys, as if such problems haven't happened in the United States. And yet, our fear is our ignorance. Consider the words of Zachary Karabell in an editorial for the *Wall Street Journal,* dated September 5, 2007:

> We have a China problem. It is not, however, a China problem in the way most people think. It is not a problem with safety standards that threaten our children and our pets. It is a problem with the very fact of China as an emerging force on the global economic stage, and it underscores a profound and worrying trend in American political and economic life. For half a century we fought for the creation of a global capitalist system. Now that we have one, we seem to have forgotten one little thing: Capitalism means more competition, and we are acting like we can't handle it.[23]

So, it's our problem, not China's. Whenever issues arise over the safety of tires being produced in China, we should be reminded that 88 deaths happened in the 1990s from tires produced in Mexico and Illinois, a much greater public health issue than what happened in China. Our China problem will hurt us more than it will hurt China, given the future size of it burgeoning domestic consumer market and the likely downturn of ours.

In 2006, Chen Xingdong, chief China economist in Beijing with BNP Paribas Securities, noted that "the United States is no longer a manufacturing economy," and that "If they (the United States) don't import from China, they will have to import from other countries anyway. The only change is that they may not have such a good combination of quality and prices."[24] Sadly, in both cases Mr. Xingdong is correct. Both the United States and Britain have histories of protecting industries for the sake of their own economies. Americans can lose their stomachs for the real truths of globalization when we have reached the top position. But barking up the wrong tree to fix the problem will simply exacerbate it rather than fix it. Again, the solution lies in the lack of classical management in the United States and a manufacturing strategy and base—a pair of problems that go hand in hand.

In 1997, the Bureau of Labor Statistics estimated that U.S. exports would double over the next decade and that this would lead to a boom in well-paying jobs in the United States. We know today that this never happened: real wages increased by 1 percent whereas the measured productivity of our corporations increased by 60 percent, suggesting a clear reallocation of production to overseas operations. The rapid increase of products and services was driven via international markets where U.S. consumers (through lower prices) and investors profited, but not our workforce. Harvard University's Gregory Mankiw notes:

> No issue divides economists and mere Muggles more than the debate over globalization and international trade. Where the high priests of the dismal science see opportunity through the magic of the market's invisible hand, Joe Sixpack sees a threat to his livelihood.[25]

Americans need to understand that a company's domiciled nationality is unimportant relative to its impact on the U.S. economy. Siemens, a German company, is an example of a company that has invested heavily in its U.S. operations because it makes sense for them to do so. An MNC will be drawn to the market that presents to it the greatest production and/or consumption opportunities. In the bloated corpocracy of the past, it was essentially the responsibility of the U.S. corporation to provide well paying jobs to Americans via a covenant, in return for less competition in the marketplace.

Today, a new, wide-open, deregulated, and, some would say, brutal model has burst onto the global economic scene. Poorly run MNCs set rules and ignore laws that they believe are in the best interests of their shareholders, often from a myopic viewpoint. In today's model, it appears that the nation with the most to offer a corporation has to do with lower labor costs and an emerging consumer base, basically ignoring the measurement of real productivity (as discussed in chapter six).

However, it is my hypothesis that changes to the world financial markets in the future will lead to a model that promotes competitiveness and productivity over exploitation and economic limitlessness. With China's rising consumer markets and virtually unlimited source of cheap labor, it is the source location for much of the world's manufacturing. But China is also investing in its physical infrastructure and human capital (via education), whereas the United States is not doing so. The deteriorating U.S. public infrastructure, endangered education system, eroding manufacturing base, failing financial markets, and declining definition of management will not attract as many MNCs as in the past. The U.S. median earnings for all educational levels (high school, some college, and bachelor's only) except advanced degrees fell from 2000 to 2007, according to the Bureau of Labor Statistics. We should be asking ourselves how this happened, as opposed to expecting our corporations (though they aren't ours, really) to bail us out. We must be willing to look closely at ourselves and our management tools rather than at anyone else.

CLASSICAL MANAGEMENT: LEARNING FROM OUR FEAR

Sputnik awoke us to the need to improve our proficiency in science, math, and technology. From the Japan scare, we learned that our manufacturing operations are not competitive, and we haven't yet focused on the real problem. What will we learn as a result of Global-is-Asian, the rise of the Chinese dragon? First, that globalization is here to stay. According to the U.S. Treasury Department, 57 million Americans are employed by companies engaging in international trade. As well, China is adding $1,000 in annual disposable income to each U.S. citizen through economic growth and lower prices, according to the China Business Council. However, poll results suggest that Americans today feel threatened by globalization, even when they understand that it's inevitable. In a late 2007 campaign speech in New Hampshire, then-presidential candidate Barack Obama told an audience that "global trade is not going away, technology is not going away, the Internet is not going away," and the U.S. public understands this. However, the real fear is a lack of options to combating globalization rather than trying to wish it away. I don't believe that many of our politicians understand this nuance.

Second, Americans should learn that the MNCs of today aren't loyal to the United States; they really aren't U.S. entities that should be loyal. In their own dysfunctional manner (that is discussed in the next chapter), MNCs make decisions about what's in the best interest for their stakeholders, and often these decisions are contrary to what's in the best interest for normal Americans. In his book, *The Disposable American, New York Times* writer Louis Uchitelle notes that only 27 percent of laid-off workers make their old salary again, suggesting that global trade isn't working out as originally planned. The good news from this lesson perhaps is that the U.S. public will wake up to the idea that it will take innovation, competitiveness, and productivity for MNCs to want to locate and source jobs in the United States, not loyalty. However, this message doesn't appear to be ready for most Americans to accept in their angry state of mind.

Third, perhaps through our fear of this Chinese bogeyman, we should learn that manufacturing must matter in our economy again. Today, manufacturing comprises a small percentage of our economy (only 12 percent of total private sector jobs), whereas China is the manufacturing center of the world, with more than 100 million workers, compared to only 14 million Americans. The historical relevance of shedding an industrial economy in favor of a predominantly financial (service) sector is chilling; the Dutch, British, and even the Spanish saw their empires fall as a result. With 44 percent of all corporate profits in the United States coming from the collapsing financial sector versus 10 percent from manufacturing, we should all sit up and take notice of who's the bogeyman here.

I've been told frequently in response to my speeches for my first book, *An Easy Out,* that I'm a dinosaur for thinking that the United States can take on China in manufacturing, but this simply isn't the case when the focus concentrated on the proper industries. In a study conducted by John Sun, chief operations officer for Hollysys in Beijing, these universal laws for Cost in China (CIC) are starting to change: in some industries, manufacturing in the United States is starting to become viable in comparison to China. Because of rising costs of labor, Renminbi (RMB) appreciation, and higher logistics costs, it makes sense for some heavy equipment to be sourced in the United States.[26] In this study, Mr. Sun analyzed the cost of supplying a heavy duty commercial valve body between China and the United States: as a function of China's rising costs, it no longer made sense for this item to be sourced in China. Sun told Chinese suppliers to be concerned and to address this by working directly with retailers (cut out the U.S. middlemen), move production facilities into China's inland West, improve efficiencies, and improve legislation.

If China's collective response is to figure out how to become more competitive in manufacturing versus the United States, shouldn't we be focused on industrial competitiveness as well? Sadly, our postclassical management era considers manufacturing not to be worth the attention, in comparison with the emerging sectors of financial services and information technology. How wrong we are!

In a potential twist of fate, the future advantage in manufacturing for the United States (if it chooses to do so) could be its labor pool (yes, I really mean this!). Today, as more people around the world enter the labor pool, the value of labor has become devalued: nobody is special, and labor is a commodity driven by price over real productivity. This is called a "loss of equilibrium," a dysfunctional state of affairs. Lately, the effect of this loss of equilibrium on the U.S. labor pool has been dysfunctional as well, and, in a virtually unlimited world labor pool, the United States would lose and our labor rates would drop as we get drained by these developing Asian economies. However, when taking a classical management approach to the problem, a much different result happens, and the higher-priced, more productive labor will prevail (if it is more productive). If classical management in the United States is to be restored and the U.S. labor market becomes more productive (in real terms), labor could actually become a competitive advantage for the United States! These improvements will not give the United States a competitive labor advantage in sectors such as textiles, but they could do so in critical sectors and emerging sectors of manufacturing. As well, the auto industry in the United States could use a little creative destruction to flush away remnants of old policies that either marginalize labor costs or protect them from market values (the $70 per hour in labor cost is geometrically higher than competitive markets). Improvements through the use of classical management can save the auto industry as well.

On the world stage, the accomplishments by the Chinese Communist Party appear very impressive indeed: Beijing's new airport terminal is 17 percent larger than all of the terminals in London Heathrow combined. The world's largest sea-crossing bridge was just built in China, the second-largest highway network in the world is being constructed, the largest dam in the world (Three Gorges) is being made, and the world's largest railroad capacity project undertaken since the 19th century is being built. On the surface, some believe that a streamlined chain of command of government to make business decisions is an optimal approach to management in the private sector.

But take a closer look behind the curtain and see the 15 villages that were flattened and the more than 10,000 residents who were resettled for a massive project and then received nothing in return for the disruption to their lives. The mother of all relocations is the Three Gorges Dam: an estimated 2.3 million displaced citizens, with charges of corruption preventing a large number of people from getting help in their relocation. Communist-type efficiency may seem to have its advantages over democracy, but how efficient is this approach if economic development is measured in terms of management, the optimization of capital, labor, and technology? Not so good. Capital is sloshed all over the place by draconian banking rules, set by the Communist Party, that, in many cases, aren't being followed by corrupt officials. Citizens are turned into migrants, labor conditions are tough albeit improving, and wages are kept low through a low utilization of technology. This being said, the Chinese are looking hopefully toward their futures and they should be: an amazing degree of progress has been made in a short time. Today, we shouldn't be labeling China as the problem when we really need to look in the mirror and focus our economy on becoming more competitive in the face of such challenges.

When I think about Americans fearing the Chinese bogeymen, I think of the famous Marie Curie quote on fear: "Nothing in life is to be feared. It is only to be understood." Much of what we understand today about the ancient Middle Kingdom of China is from our media and our politicians. However, an understanding of a nation is an understanding of its culture, which is deeply reflected by normal people like us, not by China's party officials, newly minted billionaires, or famous imported athletes. China is on a long path to progress, facing the ghosts of Mao that lurk too frequently in the inner workings of its business operations. While this is happening, Americans should revisit their economic roots and understand how the United States became an economic superpower in the first place. To return to Marie Curie's thoughts, what needs to be understood is more about China and more about us. In doing both, we'll learn that China isn't the primary problem relative to our productivity concerns—we are. The blame needs to be placed squarely where it belongs, as painful as that might be. As illustrated through the *Sputnik* scare, fear can be a powerful motivator when a nation faces its own problems!

The Mismanaged Economy: Greenspan Versus Management

In July 1944, when World War II was still raging, all 44 Allied nations gathered at a hotel in Bretton Woods, New Hampshire, to establish the future of economic security for the free world. With the failures of the Great Depression fresh on the nation's minds, and in the middle of the horrors of war, the Allies were seeking to establish a model for economic liberalism that would promote a lasting postwar peace. U.S. Secretary of State Cordell Hull, referred to by Franklin Delano Roosevelt as the "father of the United Nations," was a believer that economic discrimination and trade warfare were the primary causes of these world wars. He noted:

> Unhampered trade dovetailed with peace; high tariffs, trade barriers, and unfair economic competition, with war . . . if we could get a freer flow of trade, freer in the sense of fewer discriminations and obstructions . . . so that one country would not be deadly jealous of another and the living standards of all countries might rise, thereby eliminating the economic dissatisfaction that breeds war, we might have a reasonable chance of lasting peace.[1]

Hull was referring to the impact that a few of the largest economies were having on the stability of the world, largely as a result of their mercantilist and imperial policies. When the Nazis took over in the aftermath of the Great Depression, German unemployment was at 30 percent, and the government undertook a drastic and bellicose approach to improving its conditions. The British Empire practiced a trade system that offered preferences to those lands under the Crown and abused free-trade principles as a function of its power. Applying the Bretton

Woods system was anticipated to allow for a more optimal approach to currency convertibility, with a benchmark currency (acting as a stabilizer) that would promote free trade—which would lead to economic liberalism across the globe. The architects of Bretton Woods sought both currency rate stability and the need for economic growth that wouldn't be possible with the limits of the gold standard. The U.S. dollar would be used to allow stabilization in world currencies; at the same time, it would enable global economic growth. Keeping the dollar in fixed price to an ounce of gold (at $35) would attempt to be the best of both worlds. In 1944, these measures, as well as the creation of the International Monetary Fund (IMF) and the World Bank, were the plans to restore world peace and order through economic means.

The Bretton Woods agreement was the master strategy for economic liberalism for the 20th century, but it wasn't the only grand vision for the world at this time. Another strategy blueprint for global economics, entitled *Proposals for the Expansion of Trade and Employment,* was put in place in 1945 by the State Department. This treatise was a clear statement that free trade and a global, multinational economy were what was needed to produce stability and peace during a new era. It reasoned that if more citizens of the world were able to experience the unfettered prosperity of the balance of capitalism and democracy, the world would be a safer place for everyone. And indeed, there was no greater example of this than the U.S. economy. During the 20th century in the United States, there was more material progress than in the entire world in all the previous centuries combined.[2] Almost every indicator of health, wealth, safety, nutrition, affordability, and availability of consumer goods and services indicated improvement for Americans compared to the earlier century. Simon Kuznets, the famous economist, once said, "We Americans are so used to sustained economic growth in per-capita product that we tend to take it for granted—not realizing how exceptional growth of this magnitude is on the scale of human history."

For sure, the U.S. economy was the least disrupted major economy from the aftermath of World War II. The United States was also an oil-based economy, at a time when so many economies hadn't evolved to this yet, and one that not only innovated through the use of oil for production, but also had a large production and refining capacity, enough to fuel growth through its own energy source. Lastly, big U.S. companies controlled large percentages of key industrial sectors of the world, such as steel and automobiles, allowing it to be the factory of the world. These special attributes of the U.S. economy were not driven through the economics of a theoretical pipe-smoking academician, but rather through the powerful middle class of the United States (and pro-middle-class policies), the true owners of economic liberalism. Innovation and technological change turned into invention, and these fueled economic growth for both workers and consumers, optimized to support a growing middle class. Carroll Quigley, in his epic book *Tragedy and Hope,* noted, "its (America's) values and aspirations were middle class, and power or influence within it was in the hands of the middle class."[3]

Throughout the previous centuries, other societies had attempted the middle-class concept; the European bourgeoisie who moved into the towns (thus the name *bourg,* or town) without any status did so in an era when status really mattered. Quite differently, the middle-class Americans of the 1950s were the drivers and the beneficiaries of the balance between capitalism and democracy through a management class populated by their own, not by the owners of the capital: it was the first time that this happened in the economic world. Through middle-class management, all of the stakeholders in the economy were rewarded and yet all compromised: labor shared a greater slice of the corporate pie, and it rarely disrupted economic activities with strikes and other work stoppages. Labor was also expected to understand its role within the hierarchy of the organization, and to support corporate initiatives. The ownership of the company shared a larger percentage than before of its profits with labor—in return for a stable, organized workforce. The ownership was also essentially guaranteed little competition in the marketplace through regulation and government intervention to ensure balance, stability, and measured growth. The return on investment for owners was consistent and steady, but not at the astounding rates possible after financial deregulation of the 1980s and 1990s. Consumers' choices were limited in comparison to today, but there was hardly ever an issue with the availability of supply, so consumers were content for the most part.

Management as a function wrapped this up in a tidy bow and proceeded in a growth mode for the United States that was steady yet unprecedented, but also very tenuous, as we would find out just a few decades later. In essence, the Bretton Woods agreement and other grand visions of the world economy were built on the middle-class-driven U.S. economy, fueled by classical managers, and built on balance, not on limitlessness. However, in practice, this concept was only possible in the United States.

With a burgeoning private sector partnering with the public sector in an effort to balance capitalism with democracy, the United States was a special land that was achieving a system of economic liberalism as a first in economic time. But it wasn't always so; the largest housing boom in our nation's history (before the 21st century boom) occurred in 1926 and had spread to the stock market in 1929, triggering a severe banking crisis that affected almost every business. Home prices fell by 30 percent from 1925 to 1933, and unemployment reached 25 percent at its height, during the Great Depression.[4] The presidency of Franklin Delano Roosevelt was considered an unbridled success by those who lived during this period for reasons that would be considered heresy today: government regulation, protection, and controls and the search for a balance between democracy and capitalism (public and private sectors). The National Labor Relations Act of 1935 provided important protective rights for the worker; however, it was also the springboard for the involvement of the federal government in controlling a planned economy (eventually leading to the bloated corpocracy). When the railroads, telephone, utilities, and energy were regulated, it was a popular move, but it also became the foundation for the planned economy. Price subsidies and laws regulated competition, and big business learned to adapt to an approach of economic limits.

U.S. disillusionment with speculation continued, as President Harry Truman castigated speculators and war profiteers and called those on Wall Street "blood suckers." Whereas the Americans of an earlier generation had dreamed of the rags-to-riches story of Andrew Carnegie or the Horatio Alger paperboy hitting it rich, this generation dreamed of something more modest and predictable: peace and stability, a white picket fence, a yard, and a job for life. Most Americans back then and even today would trade in an opportunity to strike it rich in exchange for middle-class financial stability. Classical management was the tool to make this happen, because it was a middle-class-driven role that balanced all of the factors to ensure stability over wild, astronomical growth. It took a Great Depression, followed by regulation and controls, for Americans to understand what they really wanted was stable prosperity, not the chance for unbridled riches.

THE FLAW OF ECONOMETRICS OVER COMMON SENSE ECONOMICS

Many managers in business today don't understand the foundation of past U.S. economic success because the common sense economics of the past has been replaced by the complex and theoretical world of econometrics. The combination of economic theory and statistics leads to a mathematical representation of an event, but one that has little in common with real-life economics. Before econometrics made solutions so complicated, it was a practical application for a manager to understand that all stakeholders (both public and private) involved in a company should gain surplus value from the production function—and to understand the importance of balancing these variables in a production function for economic growth. Back then, economics and management were linked to each other in a rational science that sought to optimize within the world of limits. Manufacturing was the form of production, and it led our companies and economy to productivity.

But as our economy started to grow rapidly in the post-World War II era, as shown in Figure 4.1, economists sought to model real-life events as computer technology became available. What happened was that economic modeling became separated from the real-life events of management and became a theoretical, academic exercise, too complicated for the real-world business environment to understand and apply. These models opened the door to two dangerous propositions: that economic limitlessness was possible and that money could be used as a means of production. Both of these constructs are the opposite of the original assumptions of economics that had been made possible in practice through the use of classical management.

Even though the GDP growth chart in Figure 4.1 shows strong growth in the statistical representation (remember what I said about econometrics!), fundamental business vision, and the shared public/private stewardship over the economy

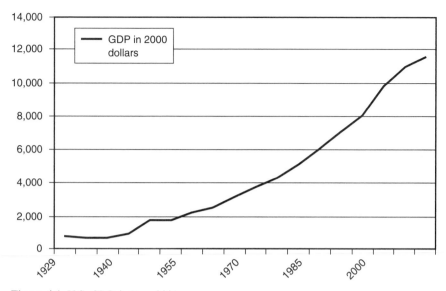

Figure 4.1 U.S. GDP, in Year-2000
Source: BEA Data, 2007

began to wane during the 1950s as the impact of New Deal's governmental controls started to have a detrimental impact on corporate activities. The top U.S. companies from 1910 were still largely in place in the late 1970s, suggesting a lack of
competition and "creative destruction" (the process of transformation that accom-
panies innovation) in both the corporate and economic environments. U.S. Steel,
Bethlehem Steel, Standard Oil, Gulf, General Foods, AT&T, GE, Westinghouse,
Anaconda Copper, Alcoa, Dupont, GM, Ford—all of these companies (or some
close derivations of them) remained largely untouched for most of the 20th
century.[5] U.S. Steel controlled half the world's steel market and noted that it
administered to its customers more than it sold to them. With the predominance of
market innovation in Japan and Europe in the 1970s and 1980s, U.S. Steel continued to lose market share, and today it is less than 10 percent of the U.S. market
(with large operations overseas). Bethlehem Steel filed for bankruptcy and now is
no longer a corporate entity.

Prior to the econometricians and their complicated models of endless growth,
the bloated corpocracy concept from the 1950s ran U.S. competitiveness into the
ground. Instead of driving business improvements, managers found comfort in a
niche through stable employment. Carroll Quigley, in his book *Tragedy and Hope*
(1966), positions what he sees in this newly entitled middle class of America:

> the petty bourgeoisie . . . millions of people who regard themselves as middle class
> and are under all the middle anxieties and pressures . . . [T]hey are often very inse-
> cure, envious, filled with hatreds, and are generally the chief recruits for any radical

right, fascist, or hate campaign . . . and live in an atmosphere of envy, pettiness, insecurity and frustration.[6]

This strength of the U.S. economy, in which big corporations had little competition, started to become a Petrie dish for the study of the individual and the organization, essentially being more important than the company's economic objectives. William Whyte explains this phenomenon in his classic, *The Organization Man,* which treated the growing dysfunction within the corporation, where the worker gets a job for life but trades his personal desires and goals for betterment to the corporation. The corporation, in turn, receives loyalty and less labor strife, but less focus on innovation and quality efforts. Not only was this mentality acceptable within big business, it became proliferated through a whole bevy of management thinkers, human resource professionals, and organizational design experts who were obsessed with it.

MANAGEMENT DECLINE AND THE BEGINNING OF U.S. ECONOMIC MALAISE

Corporations became overly concerned about employee well-being, as though the workplace were a mental health clinic. Management's role became to keep the peace rather than to improve productivity. Big behemoth corporations—with little competition, protected by regulation, and obsessed with the concept of organization—led to a lack of competitiveness. A whole field of study focused on the needs of the worker, and the weighting on the inputs took a 180-degree turn from the days of the robber barons: back then, the owners received a disproportionate share of the surplus value from the company; during the bloated corpocracy days, it was almost the exact opposite. Management became less about optimizing and balancing and more about appeasing and administering. And as a result, much of the middle class in the United States became entitled to a cushy economic way of life.

From the standpoint of balancing private and public interests, the Keynesian economic policies of the U.S. government sought to do it all, eventually fighting three wars at once (the Cold War, the Vietnam War, and the War on Poverty), which stretched the government's ability to fund it all. The largest percentage of increase in postwar public spending occurred in the United States between 1947 and 1973. As a percentage of the total economy, federal outlays peaked in 1983, at around 24 percent, and then declined steadily, to less than 20 percent in a dramatic turn of events.[7] More specifically, social expenditures doubled between 1960 and 1975, reaching 21 percent of the national income, if employer contributions were included. The perfect storm was brewing: poor corporate productivity and competitiveness, an emerging global economy recovering from war, and idealistic technocrats who believed that they could solve U.S. economic woes, world conflict, and domestic social problems at the same time—with a growing trade deficit, as emerging foreign manufacturers and oil economies started to create a balance-of-payments deficit (sound familiar?).

Something needed to be done, and fast. The United States began to experience the downside of globalization for the first time in the late 1960s and 1970s, as agriculture, leather, and shoe imports starting flooding the country. By the late 1960s, it became increasingly difficult for the United States to defend the dollar at a fixed peg of gold at $35 an ounce, particularly when massive government spending was flooding the world with dollars. The value of the dollar plummeted because the market lost faith in U.S. ability to address its government and trade deficits, as the United States ran its first trade deficit in the 20th century.

In response, in 1971, President Nixon implemented wage and price controls, instituted a 10-percent surcharge on imports, and closed the gold window, actions otherwise known as the "Nixon's shock." Just like that, Nixon assisted business, with wages pressures and supplier price increases, and gave the consumer flat prices. This enabled the Federal Reserve to increase money supply to kick-start growth without much concern for inflation.

Perhaps this was the only move that Nixon could have made, because the economy was so anemic at that time. However, such government control over the private sector really began to squash the American Dream and debase our currency. Price controls lasted for years, not months, and the decline of U.S. competitiveness continued throughout the 1970s; government intervention, such as the bailout of Chrysler, was the order of the day. So much for economic liberalism! Government technocracy and monetary policy became the new means of production rather than growth in real production through manufacturing.

Nixon's shock was just the first step in how classical management was disassembled from economic life. No longer was the impetus for economic growth to be driven by Main Street; it was now to be controlled first by the technocrats of the Beltway, the econometric financial wizards, and then the central bankers of Wall Street. Econometric theory and models favored the use of bankers and government policy analysts as the "easy-out" solution—rather than through the middle class, classical corporate managers, and capital investment in manufacturing.

Economic malaise continued through the 1970s into the 1980s. Inflation was consistently higher than at any time in history, and foreign investors fled the dollar as though it had the plague. Meanwhile back at the lab, the technocrats of the U.S. government continued to believe that economic growth could be stimulated by government: the more they tried, the more they failed. Real productivity was falling as well, and the optimistic economist contended that this was due to a falloff in investment, and a rising swell of baby boomers entering into the workforce. No mention was made of past demographical or macroeconomic theory, to suggest that perhaps our woeful corporations were the main culprit for this problem. In the early 1980s, some surveys concluded that a lack of industrial policy was the reason for our competitive woes, yet the solutions continued to focus on unimaginative technocratic solutions.

In 1980, when President Reagan entered office, inflation hit 13.5 percent, output was dropping, and the dollar continued to spiral into the abyss.[8] The free-market monetarists brought with them a plan for financial deregulation and the reduction of central government's involvement in the economy. Even though Federal Reserve chairman Paul Volcker wasn't a dyed-in-the-wool monetarist, he played the lead role, putting an end to inflation by clamping down on the money supply and evangelizing the need for sacrifice. Financial regulations requiring companies to set aside money to fund pensions were imposed, along with the deregulation of how companies could invest, and the market started to take off. Deregulation of the U.S. economy during the 1980s and the radical departure from an industrialized economy to a new age, service-sector-based economy must have been viewed favorably by Wall Street; in 1975, the Dow Jones Industrials Average was around 600, and, by 2007, it had hit 14,000 (and now is back under 8,000)! Today, services make up 60 percent of our GDP, and, in the first four months of 2008, service employment increased by 98,000, while goods producing jobs plunged by a staggering 358,000! [9] Although some of this market growth is surely a result of the benefits of deregulation, the geometric rise also epitomizes the bubble mentality that was created by the financial engineers of Wall Street, who became the self-imposed drivers of economic growth.

NEW ECONOMY IN AND CLASSICAL MANAGEMENT OUT

Since the 1970s, investor power has become further enhanced by the infusion of massive pension and mutual funds, which in turn pushed companies to generate higher returns. And, with an emerging global economy, the proliferation of the personal computer and the Internet, and an aging baby boom population, U.S. services sector became the growth sector within our economy. At the beginning of 2008, the U.S. financial services sector has swollen to an unprecedented 21 percent of our GDP, an unheard of percentage of any national economy. As late as the Nixon era, manufacturing was twice the share of the U.S. GDP, as was financial services; today, it is half of that total.

In the history of modern economics, no economy has been able to thrive predominantly as a financial-services-based economy—not one. Although the alarming rate of private debt that is being accumulated in the United States is staggering ($5 trillion of mortgage debt in 2007, or 40 percent of our GDP!), the biggest problem that this causes is the impact on U.S. business operations, as is noted in Kevin Phillips's book, *Bad Money* (2008):

> The 1980's has been by far the worst period for business investment in physical assets like plant and equipment since World War II. Instead of borrowing to build new facilities or even to build liquidity, the corporate business sector as a whole has mostly used the proceeds of its extraordinary volume of borrowing since 1980 to pay down equity through mergers and acquisitions, leveraged buy-outs and stock repurchases.

This massive substitution of debt for equity, in conjunction with the onset of record high real interest rates, has sharply raised the debt service burden that the average American business faces.[10]

In the 1980s, U.S. corporate operations were in dire need of capital and other sorts of investment in order to improve their ability to compete in a global economy. As globalization and deregulation were beginning to offer U.S. consumers options that they didn't have before, U.S. managers weren't appropriately responsive to the need for change. Quality and capital investments were the type of deep dives into the bowels of a corporation that aren't easy and that had been the focus of the classical manager before easy-out solutions were made practical during the 1980s. With the deregulation of the financial markets, Deming's classical view of management—focused on quality and investment—was less of a required activity for any corporate manager to undertake. Instead, the corporate manager of the 1980s could use money as the means of production via the stock market and associated financial instruments to create shareholder value.

In the 1970s and the 1980s, it was the corporate raiders, not corporate management, who took on the bloated bureaucracies of the U.S. corporations. The Leverage Buyout boom lasted from 1982 to 1989, and, for the first four years, it was a lesson in the power of the free markets. Later on, it just became excessive, as well as a function of financial engineering—the use of financial markets to drive the means of production. In the end, it became a poor substitution for classical management, as the financial engineers who undertook these efforts grabbed a large financial reward for their efforts, often at the expense of the worker. The stories are of legend: Carl Icahn chopping TWA into little pieces and selling it, making $469 million on the deal, and leaving the remains of the company with $540 million in debt. T. Boone Pickens and his greenmailing (selling shares of stock back to company at a higher cost) that led to his massive fortune. A pop culture depiction of these financial engineering exercises was dramatized in the 1987 movie *Wall Street,* starring Charlie Sheen and Michael Douglas, with the famous line, "greed is good."

Over these past three decades, the role of the Federal Reserve and the monetary function has become front and center as a function of a merger and acquisition deal and of an investor buying a stock. Despite the cries from critical academicians and several billionaires—Warren Buffet, George Soros, and Bill Gross—the economy based on speculation and bubbles had won out over that of market fundamentals and solid business strategies. Buffet, Soros, and Gross in particular have been critical of derivatives, bubbles, and the fairy tale of market efficiency that all graduate students were taught in explaining the markets. From these days rose the theory of money versus manufacturing as the means of production. The de facto abandonment in manufacturing and classical management was a disfigurement of economics that has led us to the present financial collapse.

Money as a means of production became the new economy, taking the place once held by classical management. The jubilation of the free-market economy was glorified through CNBC (known as "Bubblevision"), CNNMoney, and the glory of day traders working from their homes, watching five screens at once. The euphoria only fell silent when their king, the maestro of it all, imparted his wisdom as to what the markets meant to us and to the world: yes, when Alan Greenspan spoke, everyone listened!

THE MAESTRO OF THE NEW ECONOMY: ALAN GREENSPAN

Even though the silliness of any politician knows no limits, this one was a real whopper. In a debate with George W. Bush during the 2000 Republican primaries, John McCain replied to the question of whether he would reappoint Alan Greenspan as Fed chairman: "not only would I reappoint him, but if he died we'd prop him up and put sunglasses on him as they did in the movie *Weekend at Bernie's*."[11] Consider the praise from business writer Brett Fromson on what it means to be Alan Greenspan:

> Greenspan has done a superlative job as Fed chairman since taking over in 1987. He has learned the craft of gradualist policy-making so as not to shock the financial markets. He cottoned a good four years ago to the beneficial economic effects of growing globalization, technological progress and market-oriented public policies like deregulation. Unlike many stick-in-the-mud Wall Street strategists who missed the meaning of the "new economy"—you know who you are—Greenspan got it.[12]

Before Greenspan was to be confirmed as chairman of the Federal Reserve in 1987, Senator William Proxmire of Wisconsin studied Greenspan's performance on forecasts that he made from 1976 to 1986 in his role on the Council of Economic Advisors (CEA), and chided Greenspan for his "dismal forecasting record." Proxmire noted that Greenspan was wrong by the biggest margin of any CEA chairman. Here are a few lines from this prophetic dialogue between the chairman of the committee and the candidate:

> Proxmire: "As you know, you put your forecasting to a direct test in the private sector." (As noted in an article that he quoted, Greenspan and O'Neil turned in one of the least impressive records of all pension fund advisors.)

> Greenspan: "All I can say is I acknowledge that did not work out very well, and I take my share of the responsibility."

> Proxmire: "I hope . . . when you get to the Federal Reserve Board everything will come up roses. You can't always be wrong."

> Greenspan: "All I can suggest to you, Senator, is that the rest of my career has been somewhat more successful."[13]

Even today, with the catastrophe that is the situation of our financial markets, Greenspan has as many fans as detractors. The purpose of this discussion isn't to demean the former chairman of the Federal Reserve or even to change your view of him and his work, but rather to present the case that the economic growth over which he officiated for 20 years was more of a mirage than people were led to believe.

For almost 30 years, the U.S. economy was expected to grow without a manufacturing base, through the use of financial engineering, using money as the means of production and productivity. Greenspan was the conduit of the policy makers who chose economic growth based more on financial gimmickry than on how the capital markets could be used to invest in the infrastructure and production facilities for mainstream business growth. In the words of the highly esteemed economist Stephen Roach, Greenspan was a "serial bubbler." Greenspan's continual use of easy money was the preferred approach to be used in Corporate America. Says one economist, "they (the Fed) have basically polluted the world with dollars. It lays the foundation for inflation and an asset bubble."[14] This was the ultimate easy-out: when Reagan was president, the supply of dollars in the market was $1 trillion, and today it is $14 trillion!

Greenspan's track record as a free-wheeling serial bubbler was evident even before he became the Fed chairman. After his questionable record as the CEA chairman, Greenspan was hired by Charles Keating in 1989 as an economic consultant to exempt Lincoln Savings and Loan from certain regulations. Greenspan's favorable ruling noted that Lincoln Savings was "a financially strong institution that presents no foreseeable risk to depositors or the government." Four years later, 21,000 investors (many of them elderly) lost $285 million, for many of them their life savings.[15]

If we put anyone on a pedestal, isn't it possible that they will fall or even slip? The deification of Alan Greenspan as the Federal Reserve chairman is an example of this. Greenspan was the maestro of the idea of the U.S. economy being driven by the concept of a new economy in our rise beyond industrialization. It goes like this: U.S. economy succeeds through industrialization after World War II; the middle class grows and gets prosperous, and the entire U.S. economy gets complacent and no longer wants to do blue-collar work. The U.S. economy reinvents itself and blue-collar labor moves to developing markets while almost everyone in the United States receives a higher-paid, cleaner white-collar job. This was the game plan for the new economy, a concept without historical precedent. And, after a decade or so of stagflation, the new economy was just what the doctor ordered. Alan Greenspan wasn't solely responsible for the idea of this new economy; he was just the maestro of it. And what a maestro he was, particularly for those economists, financial professionals, managers, and pundits who missed the meaning of the new economy. Here is the maestro at work, in August, 1995:

> There is a major statistical problem. We are all acutely aware that there has been a shift towards an increasingly conceptual and impalpable value added that actual GDP in constant dollars is becoming less visible. All of these intellectual services have historically tended to be written off as expenses in income statements, research and

development clearly being the largest and most obvious of these. We are moving towards an economy in which the value added is increasingly software, telecommunications, technologies, and various means of conveying value to people without the transference of a physical good; entertainment is the obvious classical case . . . We have seen, I think you are aware, a number of industries in which the stock market value to book value is much higher than one. In fact, in certain industries it is a huge multiple. The trend of market to book value has been rising dramatically for years, and I suspect we cannot extract all of that from changing market valuations of stocks in general . . . The stock market is basically telling us that there has indeed been an acceleration of productivity if one properly incorporates in output that which the market value as output.[16]

So there you have it: the stock market was higher because productivity was far greater, profits were greater, and stocks were cheaper than was generally understood. About this same time, I decided to undertake doctoral level research on the business value of information technology (IT) because I found it difficult to achieve a positive return on investment on IT projects in my role as a regional controller for a financial services company that invested heavily in it. To Alan Greenspan, the soaring stock prices that began around 1995 weren't a function of low interest rates, the dollar glut, and a dot-com bubble, but rather the inability of market valuation techniques to measure these transformation companies properly in the new economy. Greenspan suggested that myself and others just didn't understand the value that we possessed in these new technologies!

Seeking to understand the difference between what I saw at work and what Greenspan was telling me, I conducted research on this topic and went to work in Big Five consulting (where I studied the bubble intently) and then as a director of e-Business for a brick-and-mortar company. I was being told by my friends, by executive recruiters, and, indirectly, by Greenspan that I was being too cautious in both my investments and my career. Instead of investing in my 401(k), they said I should be investing in dot-com stocks in a once-in-a-lifetime opportunity. And in my career, I was told that I should go work for a dot-com startup or new economy consulting firm and watch my riches pile up.

None of this made sense to me, and, when the bubble burst in 2001, the fears from my practical management experiences were confirmed. I tried to find these productivity improvements that were solely the function of technology, and I couldn't find them, in either research or in Corporate America. Paul Strassmann, a renowned researcher on the very same topic, came to the same conclusion. Corporations spent millions on IT and harvested few benefits: spending on technology without a management optimization scheme leads to limited results. Today, there is much research to support the fact that the stock market gains associated with IT value back then were a mirage and a fantasy. But everyone believed Greenspan when he heralded this misunderstood new economy, even though nobody really knew what this term meant.

Even after the tech bubble burst, Greenspan and the Fed remained committed to the new economy. As long as Greenspan and his crew had the nation focused on it, there would be little focus on the old economy, on the role of management (instead of Wall Street) to solve the problem, and on the importance of manufacturing in our economy. In his book *The Age of Turbulence,* Greenspan acknowledges the threat of a bubble in this new economy, but he wrestled with the question of productivity and how to measure it properly. His focus on productivity, however, was on defining it within the new economy while essentially ignoring it in the old economy (manufacturing). Back then, it was referred to as "clicks (of a mouse) over bricks (a factory)."

At the same time, during the late 1990s, when companies were scrambling to hire software engineers to fix their Y2K problems, the next wave of orchestration was available in the market economy, now perhaps being one of the largest bubbles in history. Right in the middle of the dot-com boom, companies were starting to become worried (particularly in financial services, the industry I was working in at the time) about the Y2K scare and the horror of waking up on January 1, 2000, without a computer system available to run processing systems, etc. Those of us managers in IT at the time had a double-edged problem to face relative to Y2K: on one hand, we needed to get someone who could fix a lot of lines of code, fast, and, on the other hand, we really couldn't afford an army of U.S. software engineers, who were overpriced at the time as a result of the dot-com boom.

Just in the knick of time, the Indian IT sector was open for business! No, you couldn't use them for more complex coding projects yet, but you could use them for the tedious, boring, and rather menial work on Y2K code. Not only were their prices very reasonable for the work that needed to be done, their service was impeccable, and they actually acted as if they wanted my business! Poof, as a result of the Y2K scare came the proliferation of IT outsourcing as a viable service opportunity within the U.S. corporation.

This practice, of course, greatly helped the measured productivity of the U.S. corporation because of the inaccurate manner that outsourcing labor is measured. Globalization during the early period of the 21st century began to become a really viable factor of the U.S. corporation's measurement of productivity: about 40 percent of U.S. measured pseudoproductivity of late is attributable to outsourcing. Using software engineers in India and manufacturers in China came to be seen as good business, as a matter of fact. It became important for the bubble financial markets as well.

Even though Greenspan had made disparaging remarks about irrational exuberance in 1996, he nonetheless increased the provision of credit in 1999 in response to Y2K fears. This rapidly increased the rise in value of the NASDAQ stock exchange, which exacerbated the tech bubble burst of 2000. But Greenspan was asked the question before, and we ask it again today: how is productivity measured, and should productivity for the U.S. economy be measured such that MNCs get lower costs by exporting jobs from the United States? Using poor econometric representations of what optimal means, the answer was yes.

IT BUBBLES, HOUSING BUBBLES, ECONOMIC BUBBLES EVERYWHERE!

Contrary to what many in the media have said, the growing anxiety of investors away from the go-go financial market was already happening before the events of September 11, 2001; the terrorist attack on the United States just exacerbated the situation that was already in play. And, the maestro was beginning to be questioned, although he still had quite a following that would stand to attention and believe in the bubble. And now, with the concepts of technology and productivity on the ropes relative to being a market force, Greenspan changed his tune and noted that globalization was the reason.

So the problems in the market in late 2001 and 2002 were widely perceived to have been due to 9/11 and globalization, with little to do with the irrational exuberance that Greenspan himself had warned about in 1996. It was finally the time for globalization to take hold of the U.S. economy as a result of deregulation in the United States, the Pax Americana from World War II, and from technologies from the Cold War—cargo ships, cargo planes, overseas cables, steel containers, satellites, and the Internet.[17]

As new technologies and innovations in shipping, telecommunications, logistics, and computers came from our national war efforts, the private sector made good use of these emerging opportunities through the public-private partnership. However, in our postclassical management world, any sort of private-public collaboration for partnership (such as the *Sputnik* scare's math and science investment) has fallen on deaf ears, given the unwillingness of both the public and private sectors to spend capital dollars on old-industry investments or to focus on quality, productivity, and innovation. The clear focus was on the new economy, not what was perceived to be the historic one. Forget about the fact that manufacturing workers who were losing their jobs had found new jobs paying 13 percent less, or that 72 percent of them couldn't find a job at the same wage as before. By default or design, the deindustrialization of the U.S. economy was happening during this period. (See Figure 4.2.) And without classical management, it all appeared to make a lot of sense.

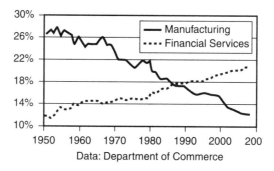

Figure 4.2 Growth of Financial Services Sector. Percentage of GDP, 1950–2007

During the early days of the 21st century, everyone was squeezing the supplier to get better deals for the consumer, cheaper prices at Wal-Mart, higher returns from U.S. pension and mutual funds. The stock market continued to climb to reflect this euphoria. The bubble kept building, and we continued to ignore the warning signs. The impressive array of technology that was so new economy was unprecedented, even if official statistics were unable to measure its real impact. There was the rise of the global economy and the technologies associated with making it possible, the Internet or international logistics. With the proliferation of globalization and technology, consumers would now have product choices that they didn't have before.

The advent of globalization appeared to challenge the notion in Henry Ford's theory that workers and consumers can multiply economic growth, and it even questioned whether this was optimal at all. Although analysts and traders were celebrating the entry of billions of people into the world consumer market and 500 million people into the cheap labor market, the workers of the West were feeling no such euphoria. The sleeping giant of Asian manufacturing had awakened, and Wall Street was reassuring the U.S. worker that everything would be okay and that he or she would become a higher-paid knowledge worker instead.

The corporate manager of the U.S. corporation also had to fall into place, playing this financial engineering game of pseudoproductivity, which had more to do with the stock market valuation of the company than the true value of that corporation as a going concern. Many corporate managers wanting to apply the classical rules of management were kept out of the game and were told that the rules of the game had changed: financial engineering, not good old-fashioned productivity, via the optimization of labor, capital, and technology, was required. And with managers being rewarded with stock options if they conformed, there wasn't any reason to challenge this financial engineering notion.

With the economy a bit on the ropes in the early 21st century, Alan Greenspan delivered the good news for why this downturn in the economy would be softer than ones of other eras:

> [This particular downturn] was significantly milder ... than the long history of business cycles would lead us to expect. The reasons for that, in summary, were technology—real-time information has played a key role—and financial innovation. New financial products—including derivatives, asset-backed securities, collateralized loan obligations, and collateralized mortgage obligations . . . Lenders have the opportunity to be considerably more diversified, and borrowers are far less dependent on specific institutions for funds . . . They have contributed to the development of a far more flexible and efficient financial system.[18]

So the explanation went from the tech bubble, to globalization and its impact on the economy, and then to the housing bubble. The Wizards of Wall Street and the central planning economists directed our economy and business organizations from one speculative bubble to the next, using monetary policy rather than classical management principles to spur economic growth. I saw this in action, as I was being recruited for a leadership position at the company marchFirst, which started off in 2000 as the consulting firm Whitman-Hart. During its heydey, Whitman-Hart was a hot dot-com consulting firm, with its stock trading on the NASDAQ at a high of $52 a share—although much of it was a façade, because it never made a profit. Led by an aggressive CEO named Bob Bernard, who embodied the famous growth term of that period, "large or loss." Bernard dazzled his way through growing this business via acquisitions of smaller dot-coms and sketchy business plans. The firm filed for bankruptcy in 2001, and the dreams of a dot-com windfall by a young entrepreneur were dashed. Still seeking his entrepreneurial dream in 2007, Bob Bernard died of an apparent heart attack, another sad story of an intelligent man chasing the bubble instead of the productivity and substance of management. Back then, the rules of the new economy applied, and many never understood that it was a castle built into the air.

During these early days of the 21st century after the tech bubble, Alan Greenspan and his central bankers only focused on consumer inflation in monitoring the state of the U.S. economy, not on asset inflation (particularly housing and bonds). Housing prices track to inflation over the long run, and yet, because housing prices were rising, the Fed wasn't paying attention to these signals. My wife was in the mortgage lending industry during the crazy years of lending (late 20th to early 21st century) in the subprime market. Her role was to work with the mortgage brokers to attract individuals who wanted to buy a house or, more likely, to refinance an existing loan.

Refinancings jumped from $14 billion in 1995 to nearly a quarter of a trillion dollars in 2005, with a great majority of these individuals seeking to pull money out of their houses for other activities. Money was practically free (and still is today!); lending cost much less than before (because of IT advances and deregulation), and the lenders were told, in effect, to keep lending until there was nobody left. And even then, they kept going. The banks had an unlimited amount of credit, it seemed; mortgages were packaged into mortgage-backed securities and sent from out of the portfolio. The lenders were no longer to "originate to own," but rather "originate to distribute," as they swept clean these loan liabilities through distributing the risk into the securities market, enabling them to lend to even more borrowers. The lender would approve or deny and then package the loan up to some faceless buyer, using some absurdly complex mathematical construct.

One of the few voices from the Federal Reserve circles who spoke out about this early on was the late Edward Gramlich, in 2004, when he warned against the risk of predatory and dangerous lending among vulnerable home owners.[19] Unfortunately, such voices were few and far between when the housing and mortgage lending industry was driving economic growth in the United States! As my wife decided to leave, the industry was being built on a house of cards, yet those involved were making too much money to take notice. Once the bubble burst, it took a lot of people down hard.

Although we know today of all the tragic personal stories associated with the borrowers, there are many stories as well of those who were in the industry: mortgage brokers losing their own homes, divorces, suicide attempts, and every imaginable type of hardship from the people who thought that the good times would never end. These stories are just as tragic, and, in effect, those who made their money and then lost it are all victims as well of the Greenspan Put, the "productivity less growth" story of the 21st century. Of course, the greatest stories of loss are those of the borrowers; today, one of every five subprime loans is in foreclosure according to the Center for Responsible Lending, and the worst is probably still to come. During the first seven years of the 21st century, banks and financial institutions added $8 trillion in new debt, and $6 trillion of that was during the subprime speculative boom of 2003 to 2007. Economic growth created without productivity and optimization isn't growth at all. The housing bubble of the 1920s was the greatest of all time until this 21st-century housing bubble made it blush in comparison. Productivity must prevail.

Remnants from the Great Depression left the concept of debt to be a dirty word among Americans for a few decades. Since 1950, the U.S. consumer installment debt outstanding had soared twelvefold, to roughly $179 billion, omitting mortgage debt, which had risen comparably.[20] In 1977, *Time* magazine hailed us as the "Credit Card Society," and I can remember from my experiences as a boy in the 1970s when families started to get in trouble with credit cards. Although Americans and our government were so concerned over these decades of the public debt that was being accumulated by our government, nobody was talking about the private debt that was escalating (household, corporate, and financial). Why? Because it was fueling our economic growth. During the 1990s, household debt increased by 9.8 percent while household income rose by only 5.2 percent.[21]

During the early 21st century, Americans with stagnant wages began to use their appreciating homes as ATM machines, and now they are paying the consequences. As shown in Figure 4.3, the consolidated debt level in the U.S.

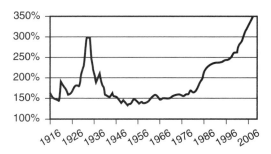

Figure 4.3 Public and Private Debt in the U.S. as a Percent of GDP, 1916–2007

Source: Federal Reserve, Department of Commerce

economy is higher than before the Great Depression, although this may be a misleading statistic, given the differences between our economies then and now. Needless to say, the debt statistics regarding our economy are scary, any way you slice it: U.S. home mortgage debt has increased by $3 trillion in five years, subprime originations were 20 percent of the market in 2006, and public debt has soared to $11 trillion.

But the biggest, scariest statistic of all is the amount of private debt: $36 trillion, an indication of how our economy over the recent years has been built on a bubble of consumerism and bad corporate business practices that have played the game of the financial community versus a solid understanding of strong management principles. This was largely made possible through an exponential increase in credit in the economy through the securitization of debt—and, poof, off the lenders' books it went. This was the Wall Street approach for prodding economic growth in the bubble economy.

Today, it's scary to turn on one of the cable channels for fear of hearing more bad news about the economy or, worse, how some of the pundits explain what's happening and what needs to be fixed. If you watch one of these shows, you'll notice that they always have some guy explaining things in financial jargon versus business rationale; it remains the language of the new economy. The explanation of what needs to happen is articulated in detail in later chapters of this book, but, in summary, it's this: we need to focus our strategies on classical management and manufacturing versus financial engineering and cheap money. To put it another way, we need classical management and manufacturing economy principles versus econometrics and the new economy.

One economist called the bubble bursting on the new economy as one of the slowest train wrecks in recorded history (and we just saw it crash!). Those zealous supporters of Greenspan may spin the answer toward a different definition, just as Greenspan himself has changed his explanation of the stock market rise from being a result of technology, then globalization, and, last, housing. The masters of financial engineering may appear on "Bubblevision" and provide a new reason for what's happening, some explanation that can be fixed with more market corrections. And if Americans and our markets buy into this, we'll just be buying into the next attempt at creating another bubble before the last one pops. Americans should be done with expecting to grow our economy thanks to everyone becoming a sanitary, high-paid service worker and the magic of bubble economics! Think about that when the U.S. government announces its next plan for economic stimulus.

FINANCIAL ENGINEERING AND OTHER GAMES

Financial engineering, a term that I have used throughout this book, has two elements: the first is the bias of the financial markets to attempt to drive economic growth through monetary policy and financial transactions instead of through real production, and the second lies in the use of economic data to reinvent the state of the economy. The first approach has been discussed in detail in this book and is well known, but the second method is just as dangerous. To add to what's already been discussed, the financial engineering of turning asset classes into complex, mathematically abstract new investment products caused problems that we are only beginning to understand today. The complexity of these instruments bordered on the absurd, taking full advantage of the power of computerization and computerized trading to make it all viable. These methods of financial engineering were built on abstract econometric models that practically nobody understood or even understands today. Even after the housing bubble collapsed, most Americans don't clearly understand the role and purpose of Fannie Mae and Freddie Mac, the two companies at the epicenter of this massive financial crisis.

There is nothing new about the use of economic statistics and accounting rules as a way of constructing economic and corporate growth, but the art form to which it has been taken in the 21st century is perhaps the greatest bastardization of economics in the history of commerce. In the 1990s, the Consumer Price Index (CPI) was a simple calculation of the cost of a fixed basket of goods using market prices. But starting in February 1982, Alan Greenspan chaired a presidential commission on Social Security, seeking to find ways in managing its costs. No long-term reform came from this commission, and, given the "sacred cow" nature of this program, no changes were made to it, or even considered in any serious manner, to control its expenditures. Testifying before the Senate in January 1995, Greenspan noted that inflation was probably being overstated by 0.5 to 1.5 percent. If this could be proven to be the case, it would save the government a lot of money on cost of living increases (COLA) on entitlement programs, such as Social Security. So in 1995, the Boskin Commission was to study the validity of the CPI. In December, 1996, the Commission concluded that CPI was being overstated by 1.1 to 1.3 percent, and the burden of this would add $691 billion to Social Security costs by 2002.[22]

To many economists, the objectives of this Commission were to focus on how to decrease the cost of federal entitlement programs versus understanding the true measurement of inflation. When these changes were made and the calculation of inflation was implemented in 1997 to 1999 to the CPI to adjust down the measurement, the country was distracted by a strong stock market and other issues, and this indirect way of managing inflation was implemented without much consideration. But journalist John Williams (ShadowStats. com) has been measuring the way that it used to be measured, as shown in Figure 4.4, and there is around a 3.5-point difference between the two (as of November 2008). This difference has a remarkable effect on the nature of the consumer, worker, and corporation. In this example, economic statistics were used as a means to an end for a problem, rather than just an economic measurement tool.

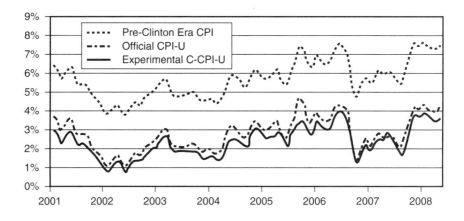

Figure 4.4 The Old and New Ways of Measuring Inflation. Alternate CPI Measures of Year-to-year Change, Not Seasonally Adjusted, to May 2008

Source: ShadowStats.com

The CPI isn't the only questionable statistic: GDP replaced the gross national product as the measure of economic growth in 1991 when rising U.S. international debt costs made the GDP a more viable measurement technique. John Williams is equally skeptical of the measurement of the GDP, calling it the least meaningful of economic statistics being used by investors and the media. He and others believe that the 1991 and 2001 recessions lasted much longer than reported and that downturns in 1986 and 1995 were missed completely.

The fact that the U.S. economy is in a severe recession, with possibilities of an economic depression is a signal of the weak reliability and validity of this statistic. The other measurement that is clouded among economic statistics is that of productivity (discussed in depth in chapter six).

Because of the financial engineering bias in the U.S. business environment, corporate managers are prone to make decisions based on complex mathematical constructs, with accounting rules taking precedence over economic rules. We as corporate managers get paid good salaries, but our real financial incentives are often tied to stock options, which are dependent on share prices. And although most corporate managers won't purposely embellish financial reports for the sake of an improvement of corporate earnings, there is a fine line within the accounting results, and a bias often happens in favor of improving results for personal gain. Although nobody knows for sure to what extent corporate earnings are inflated as a function of wiggle room in the accounting rules, nobody denies that corporate executives have a lot of incentive to inflate results within the constraints of the rules. And the corporate managers' mastery of accounting rules has become much more the focus of their work than true productivity enhancements.

This discussion, both in this book and in the media, about financial engineering is not only difficult for the public to understand, but also for a trained financial professional. After all, how can the concept of a collateralized debt obligation (CDO) be any more complicated? An economy's growth cannot be built on such chicanery and wizardry that even Wall Street doesn't understand—they don't even know today the effects of securitization. Just as they've done over the past 30 years, our politicians and central bankers will likely provide more soundbite solutions to fix what is broken, such as the $700 billion bank bailout.

We've seen them all and continue to digest them, one by one, neglecting what made us successful in the first place. The watchers of Bubblevision will again breathe a sigh of relief, as they did in April 2008 when the boss of Lehman Brothers, Dick Fuld, said, "the worst is behind us." Just five months later, the company filed for bankruptcy, after leveraging their assets by more than 30 times. Also, in mid-September, AIG required a government bailout and was replaced on the Dow Jones Industrial Average with Kraft, in an effort to stabilize investor perception of the stock market! With practically the entire nation blaming AIG and other financial houses for what's happening in our economy today, we need to stop looking to Wall Street for answers, and instead look to our private business operations. And we need to require more from our managers.

THE JOURNEY OF ECONOMIC LIMITLESSNESS OVER CLASSICAL MANAGEMENT

In this journey that we've taken, you've seen that the battle of the corporate manager versus Alan Greenspan (and all that he represented) was won by Alan Greenspan and the theory of economic limitlessness. It really was a battle between, on the one hand, classical management—which seeks to achieve economic growth through real production and a fair allocation of a company's surplus value—against an economic model that seeks growth and prosperity through the illusion of economic limitlessness and a glut of money.

There is no question that Corporate America's business results have been driven by the idea of economic limitlessness for more than 30 years, a concept that emerged as a solution to a previously moribund economy that was losing strength in a growing global economy. The foundation was the supposed limitlessness of everything— limitless wants, growth, wealth, natural resources, debt, and even knowledge—all of which is a fallacy in economics, of course, which is the study of limited resources and how management can best optimize them. As managers, this leads us down the path of efficiency at any cost and of growing revenue at any cost as well. This concept of maximization and minimization without boundaries is a fallacy within the discipline of economics, and it certainly has led to the death of management. I hope that we've learned this, if anything, from the collapse of the 2008 economic conditions.

Today's U.S. middle class has never felt so low. According to the Pew Research Center, more than half of Americans believe that they haven't gotten ahead in the past five years (25 percent) or have fallen behind (31 percent), and 80 percent of them find it hard to maintain middle-class lifestyles. In a 2008 CNN poll, 75 percent of all Americans had a negative view of the economy, and the results appear to be heading downward, if anything. These survey results are the worst on this topic for more than a half a century, and yet things will likely get even worse before they get better. Today, the mood of our nation can hardly get worse.

But perhaps horrible lessons from the financial engineering of our economy can lead to a new day, a truly new economy, with a new covenant. The central planners represented by Greenspan had a strategy, and, in the slowest train wreck in history, the train has finally crashed. The days of the middle class, the middle manager, and an industrialized, driven economy are over—for now. It's time to call classical management back in and see what it can do and how it can reshape our economy into a competition engine that is able to win against the most productive world economies.

Tricks and Treats of Management

If anyone understands the concept of the death of management, it's Scott Adams, the creator of the *Dilbert* cartoon. Since the 1990s, *Dilbert* has been a part of U.S. culture, allowing us to laugh our way through technological change, financial engineering, restructuring, outsourcing, and, of course, the death of management. The lead character, Dilbert, is an introverted engineer and a prototypical organization man. His boss is a nameless character called the Pointy Haired Boss, who has been described as follows:

> He's every employee's worst nightmare. He wasn't born mean and unscrupulous, he worked hard at it. And succeeded. As for stupidity, well, some things are inborn. His top priorities are the bottom line and looking good in front of his subordinates and superiors (not necessarily in that order). Of absolutely no concern to him is the professional or personal well-being of his employees. The Boss is technologically challenged but he stays current on all the latest business trends, even though he rarely understands them.[1]

Unfortunately, what so many find intriguing about *Dilbert* is that the stereotypes that are personified in this cartoon resemble co-workers, managers, and the environment of their workplaces. Besides Dilbert and the Pointy Haired Boss, there is Dogbert, who is Dilbert's pet, and a part-time egotistical management consultant, who cons the Pointy Haired Boss with his schemes. Catbert is the evil director of Human Resources, who was hired to do the downsizing, which he obviously enjoys. The nation of Elbonia is a fourth-world nation that is the source of cheap labor and outsourcing. There are *Dilbert*-related books (more than 3,000 listings on Amazon), calendars, dolls, television shows, blogs, clubs, lectures, and so on. Many who work in Corporate America identify with Dilbert. For a lot of U.S. workers and managers, we're all Dilbert, at least in our minds.

If so many of us believe that we're Dilbert, who in Corporate America is the Pointy Haired Boss? If even the management of the company is feeling victimized by the culture, who's responsible for fixing the culture of the company? I've participated in "culture sessions" for practically every company that I've worked for, the point of which is to answer the question, "What can be done to improve the company's culture?" Typically, these sessions are requested and led by either the head of Human Resources or the CEO of the company. Usually, a group of 10 to 12 leaders informally discuss what can be done to improve the corporate culture. Once the discussion gets going, the issues brought up are the same as those in *Dilbert*. They include bureaucracy, paper pushing, "administrivia," why so many meetings, and so on. Go to any workplace in Corporate America and you'll find the same complaints involving the same topics.

The blame for these problems is typically pointed at the faceless, nameless culture of the company, which is a culprit for which nobody can be held accountable and which nobody can even define. At many companies in the United States, most managers feel overpowered and helpless in the face of this culture. For most workers, management is the culture, and workers get frustrated and apathetic when nothing changes. When management feels victimized by the culture instead of responsible for it, we get the "tricks and treats" of management—substituting games and (legal) sleights of hand for true value and productivity.

Too many in corporate management feel incapable of changing the corporate culture, as if the organization itself is more powerful than its leaders. Maybe it's not that they are intimidated by the culture, per se, but rather that they use that as an excuse for a business environment that they don't understand and can't control. That's certainly understandable, given the confluence of the impact of globalization, the pace of technological change, and the use of financial engineering in an unregulated U.S. business environment. This brings to the forefront the primary question that must be answered about today's discipline of management versus the classical approach used in yesteryear: can the current version of management own the culture of the company as it did in the past, or is it just a helpless victim of the new economy?

WHAT CLASSICAL MANAGEMENT WAS AND WHAT MANAGEMENT IS TODAY

Figure 5.1 was presented in chapter two as a balanced model of what classical management used to be. Although these fundamentals are not perfect, they were important in the development of a balance between capital, labor, and technology; the needs of the individual and the company; and the public and private sectors. Management orchestrated this balance. These fundamentals have been dissolving over the past 50 years into what they have become today, illustrated in Figure 5.2.

	Organization	Capital	Technological Diffusion
Growth	Strategy and Structure Info and Organization	Investment in Long-Term	Creative Destruction
Share Benefits	Productivity and Wages	Profits in Short-Term	Functional = Social Progress

Figure 5.1 Management Fundamentals

As a function of complacency and a lack of competition, the corporate manager of big business of the 1930s and 1940s started to become the organization man in the 1950s and 1960s. The corporate manager described in William Whyte's classic 1957 book is a mixed bag of good and bad. On one hand, the corporate organization man was loyal to a fault and revered the organization, sometimes to the point of an obsession. In return for his unbending loyalty and adoration, the organization took away, in many cases, his hopes and dreams but gave him economic stability and job security. His yearning to become the organization man was struck in a psychological yearning to belong, a need to be a part of a communal setting, something that was bigger than himself.

The corporate organization started to become as much of a societal club as it was an ongoing business. Corporations weren't in place solely to "maximize shareholder's wealth" as they are today, but also to provide a community for the worker and to help develop society. The worker's need for individualism, creativity, real competition, and the hard work on one's own behalf was conflicted inside of him, because his role was, in many cases, more administrative and bureaucratic than leading and transformational.

As Whyte noted in his book, the reining in of the professional manager within the corporation would lead to problems, leading to a drop in the competitiveness and innovation needed for big businesses to succeed, as was the case in the 1970s. For decades, the need for balance was led by the corporate manager and it was successful. But then it became inefficient, as the manager started to worship the organization instead of being focused on the balance between labor, capital, and technology. Whyte noted:

> The fault is not in organization, in short; it is in our worship of it. It is our vain quest for a utopian equilibrium in which society's needs and the needs of the individual are one and the same.[2]

In the late 1950s, Whyte was a management prophet, warning Corporate America of the dangers of a worship of organization over purpose and function.

	Organization	Capital	Technological Diffusion
Growth	The Disorganization Man	Financial Engineering	Destructive Destruction
Share Benefits	Loss of Equilibrium	Post-Management Capitalism	Technological Anxiety

Figure 5.2 Tricks and Treats of Management

The corporate managers were the organization men, but there was also a whole industry that grew around the role of the corporate manager, such as organizational development specialists, industrial-organizational psychologists, management consultants, and others. In Whyte's view, this was the perpetuation of this social ethic. The art of administration, the role of organizational development as a discipline, and the bureaucracy of human relations (as Drucker called it) began to trump classical management and its legacy as a rational science, replacing it more with psychology than economics. This changing dynamic of classical management in the support of the organization man reverberated across the entire corporation, and it began to have an impact on the competitiveness and productivity of the U.S. corporation starting in the 1970s.

CHAOS VERSUS STABILITY IN MANAGEMENT

The 1980s were all about chaos and change. If the 1970s were the lowest point of U.S. economic performance, the 1980s were about disrupting and displacing the poisonous planned economic environment that had made it so. Perhaps there was no greater voice in the United States in helping everyone understand this new economy than Tom Peters, the famous management thinker of the 1980s. After his success with *In Search of Excellence* (1982), he wrote another best-selling book, *Thriving in Chaos,* in 1988. In it, Peters told the readers that "we must learn to love change as much as we hated it," and that the role of a manager was to lead an organization through this chaos and change. Chaos and change, therefore, were something to be expected and inevitable versus something purely destructive and disharmonizing. Certainly, Peters was correct, that disruption and chaos are necessary for change and transformation to occur.

As a graduate student in the late 1980s, I was taught that my future management role was to lead during these turbulent times, to get others to accept turbulence and disruption as a function of the new economy. We were being taught to be "disorganization men" (and women), just as the generations before us were taught to be organization men. They were taught to love the organization, to serve it, and to hold it above everything else. We were taught to destroy the organization in order to rebuild it, perpetually, without end. This is why we are the disorganization managers. We were and are being tasked with a dysfunctional approach to management: to destroy and break the rules and, at the same time, to understand the corporate culture and to respect it. However, what we are doing today isn't the constructive creative destruction of the past, because a continual process of destruction never allows for anything to set, to start anew. Such a conflict is an impossibility for even the best corporate manager to solve.

Many companies don't know what to do with this sort of "psycho change agent" in their operations. On one hand, I was frequently praised for getting to the heart of the matter and implementing change; on the other hand, I was always an outsider, somewhat disenfranchised from the mainstream of the organization.

Typically, the disorganization manager is an outsider, who doesn't fit in well, working within an organization. Fair enough, but it's very difficult for the disorganization manager to balance real change, the culture, and the state of chaos within the corporation. The pressures for results from a corporate manager today can be enormous, and yet the overbearing weight of our worship of organization and tradition remains, to an extent. Corporate rules, traditions, unwritten rules, and cultural do's and don'ts are what the disorganization manager must understand. He or she must understand the landscape: who the decision maker really is, where the land mines are, what and who the sacred cows are, what the unofficial strategy is, and what the real path for how to get things done looks like.

One of the biggest roadblocks that the disorganization manager faces in Corporate America is this obsession with organization. It is the notion that there is something magical about the organizational structure per se, that the organization is even more important than the workers themselves. In this Organizational Development (OD) mind-set, the leaders are supposed to lead the organization instead of leading the people within the organization.

These corporate managers are responsible for servicing a structure more than a balance between labor, capital, and technology. Corporate managers serve the structure by administering the rules. There are even managers today in Corporate America who aren't responsible for managing any people. I guess they manage the organization! Spending a day in meetings versus spending time with the workers is the first sign of such a manager. I've been a leader of people in many different settings (both blue- and white-collar), and I have seen this phenomenon. The disorganization manager of today is in conflict with the remnants of the organization man and his love for organizational structure.

Too many disorganization managers are the moth to the flame: excited and addicted to the rush associated with restructurings and reorganizations and to the praise associated with creating turbulence and constant change. There is an endless list of names of disorganization managers that I have known who got too close to the flame, so to speak. Both the corporation and the managers lost sight of what they were seeking: just as the organization man's psyche became a part of the organization that he belonged to, the disorganization manager's psyche became engaged to this fraternity of change and restructuring.

Once involved, the disorganization manager typically has a financial incentive to lead the department through chaos and change, even if he or she doesn't understand what it means or whether it makes sense. Much as what is shown in the *Dilbert* cartoon, the Pointy Haired Boss is often on record as being in favor of change, even if he or she doesn't understand what it means. After awhile, it doesn't even matter whether the corporate managers understand—so as long as they execute the change, any change.

Today we must really ask ourselves whether this environment of perpetual change and chaos led by postclassical management is an improvement in the corporate business objectives and whether it adds value to the U.S. corporation and economy. Are our corporate managers promulgating an environment of competitiveness, or does a continuous environment of change prevent real change from happening, disguising the problem?

In the companies that I've worked for in the past 20 years, in financial services, consulting, and manufacturing, I don't believe that I've had many solid years without reorganizations, restructurings, reengineering, mergers, acquisitions, or joint ventures. That's right—three different industries and the same environment of constant change. As a college and graduate student, I was taught that this was my purpose, to lead the organization through this change. But barely would one effort end when the other would begin, if the first effort ended at all! And every time that a significant change occurred, my responsibilities from the prior effort were wiped clean, as a function of a completely different operating environment, with little time to set and complete a real strategy.

Few people were held accountable for results as well, because the result objectives would frequently change before the end of the measurement period. We were both the owners of change and the benefactors of chaos. We enabled productivity through chaos, but we really never understood what real productivity meant, as discussed in the next chapter. It was a matter of continuous movement, continuous improvement, and, really, there was no time for strategic execution. How is it possible to change something really if we change the change before it can change anything?

Coming out of the stagnant business environment of the 1970s, the continuous restructurings of the 1980s and 1990s became more illusion than reality. In 1990, I took my first corporate position as a special projects accountant for USF&G, one of the largest and most stable employers of my hometown of Baltimore, Maryland. Getting a job working for USF&G in Baltimore was a sign of success: the financial services company occupied the tallest building in downtown Baltimore, was building a huge campus on the outskirts of the city, and even sponsored the Sugar Bowl for college football (I still don't understand why).

A few months after I started working for this company, the long-standing CEO (an organization man) was abruptly fired and a disorganization manager by the name of Norm Blake was hired. With a nickname of "Pink Slip Norm," Blake laid off 53 percent of the workforce and got rid of 70 percent of the management during his reign, tidying up the company before it was consumed by St. Paul Companies, a larger property and casualty insurer.

Fresh out of graduate school, I not only endured one Black Friday after another (the day when the layoffs happen), I also learned that becoming a disorganization manager could prevent me from being a victim of the restructurings myself. A good disorganization manager was able to reengineer his or her department and financials in such a way as to show change, even if intrinsic longer-term value wasn't being gained for the company. My efforts at this company as a financial analyst and a controller were to reposition our business strategies through a redefinition of a market and labor (consolidation and elimination of branch offices and roles).

Although I wasn't really sure at the time what I was accomplishing by whittling down our business, the stock market seemed to notice: USF&G's market capitalization increased by 320 percent.[3] I was promoted and rewarded early on in my career for having displayed the talents of a disorganization manager in the mold of the turnaround artist, "Pink Slip Norm." In the end, what was left of USF&G was scrap-heaped to St. Paul, and Norm and his coterie of managers went off to the next deal with their financial prizes. Norm moved on to spin Promus Hotels to Hilton and sought to spin Comdisco from out of bankruptcy. Just recently, the man who was my disorganization manager mentor was called to testify on the Enron affair, given his role on its Board of Directors!

Having learned everything that I needed to learn about being a disorganization manager from Norm Blake, in 1998 at the height of the management consulting frenzy, I moved on to work for KPMG, a Big Five consulting firm. There was much to be excited about in management consulting at this time: even though "Pink Slip" Norm Blake and "Chainsaw Al" Dunlap had already made their mark on some of the Fortune 500 in Corporate America, there were many fields to plow, so to speak, and I was well versed in adding my experience as a disorganization manager.

I spent my next few years embodying everything that it meant to be a disorganization manager in management consulting: focusing on the chaos and helping corporations reengineer their organizations in manners that were appealing to the financial markets. Job layoffs, organization redesigns, and other new economy strategies were sought from me by clients, at $300 per hour plus the support staff cost needed for me to advise many organization men who were bewildered during this time of chaos.

Quite a few top executive leaders from many of the Fortune 500 were unable to adapt and needed us as hired guns to get them through what the financial markets wanted to see—not longer-term investments in operations, retraining efforts, or repositions of their business strategies—but, typically, layoffs, selloffs of non-strategic business units, consolidations, and income statement and balance sheet disguises and tricks. Working as dangerously close with the audit side of the business as we did, we likely knew more about the client than what was legitimate for us to know, and business opportunities flowed from the audit work to the management consulting side of the firm. Our brain power and experience in disorganization caused management consulting to grow to levels never before seen: the outsourcing of management-enabled disorganization. Corporate America was using management consulting as a crutch, unable to stand on its own, having armies of organization men in a fog, not knowing what to do to survive in this new economy. Disorganization managers like myself were there to play this role, at a nice price for our firms and ourselves.

DISORGANIZATION IN MANAGEMENT AS A RULE

As the last few years of the 20th century dripped into the beginning of the 21st century, the enablement of information technologies really began to disorganize the role of management and its association with the organization. In theory, technology is supposed to destruct industries and rules (creative destruction), allowing for an improvement in growth and efficiency through the transformation. However, nowhere in economic theory is there any evidence that technology should continue to disrupt capital and labor without allowing for an initiative to be stabilized and rationalized toward success. Quite to the contrary, studies suggest that the use of IT investments can only achieve a positive Return on Investment (ROI) when an adequate corresponding investment is made in the intangible nature of the operation tied to workers, such as training of employees.

There was so much buzz in the late 20th to early 21st centuries about the possibilities, particularly how they related to the dot-com world. Henry Blodget, the infamous Wall Street investment analyst from the dot-com days is known today as the Pied Piper of the dot-com bubble. In contrast to scholarly research from noted economists like John Galbraith and studies on the business value of IT from people like Paul Strassmann, Blodget manufactured the business value of IT through the markets, enabling disorganization managers from all over to sell their wares and to disrupt companies.

When the opportunity presented itself, I sought to test Blodget's notions and, at the same time, get off the road from Big Five consulting. As the first e-business leader for a large financial firm (and one of the first e-business leaders in the industry, in 1998), I had the opportunity to test Blodget's dot-com euphoria. At my new employer, the world of financial services was ready to transform: our "factories" of green-screen computers were ready to be replaced by Windows and Web applications. It was a transformation in the world of insurance that was never seen before. I was to lead this company into this new world of disorganization. I was the ultimate disorganization manager, right out of a Tom Peters book.

In this role as the lead for e-business and in consecutive roles as the leader for e-business at other large companies, I found a strange commonality of disorganization managers who were testing the use of this tool as the new way to manage the chaos and to manage business growth. If only we can automate and broaden our systems out to the World Wide Web, we thought, we will solve our problems of falling sales, brand recognition issues, falling productivity, and even employee performance management concerns: technology to the rescue for chaos! I was the leader of the group, but I was no technologist, and I was skeptical of any manager willing to throw technology at a problem without first understanding the business strategy and underlying issues.

At the time, disorganization managers were blindly tying e-business solutions to everyday problems without understanding the necessary conjunction of labor, capital, and technology, believing Greenspan's notion that the IT problem was in measurement, not in use. And who can blame them for this? Their CEOs were reading all about this e-buzz on the airplanes and in the *Wall Street Journal,* and everyone was making a lot of money. It was almost too good to be true—and it was too good to be true.

At this financial services company and at subsequent employers, I experienced a continuous flow of mergers and acquisitions, joint ventures, outsourcing, reengineering, and restructuring—and for what? The financial services company that I led an e-business strategy for was bought out by a much larger U.K.-based financial services company, which sold off all of its U.S. operations in 2006. In 1999, we created the first online business to business (B2B) portal for personal insurance to be bought through brokers, called AutoLink. The effort was all for naught, because disorganization managers bought and sold various operations of the company until it went off into oblivion. It's difficult to see this as a successful effort of management when everything that was created no longer exists.

MANAGEMENT WITHOUT WELFARE CAPITALISM

The next element of trick-and-treat management is the loss of equilibrium within the labor market. Before the convergence of technology and the deregulation in large, developing nations, starting in the 1990s, the labor market of the West was a stable, comparable market with equilibrium. Prior to this period in the United States, the pay and benefits of the workforce grew by 2.5 percent per year, real income doubled, along with the value of what that workers produced.[4] Pay for everyone, even for the managers at the top, was affected by the bargaining between big business, labor, and even the government, within a planned arrangement. Few got super rich in this system, but most everyone in the United States prospered, especially those in the middle class.

Then it all changed: the IMF calculates that the number of workers on the global labor market has quadrupled since 1980. We're ready for a "flat world," to borrow a phrase from Thomas Friedman. With half of the 3 billion people earning less than $1 per day, labor has been marginalized to practically nothing.[5] Even U.S. workers at a wage of up to $12 per hour (50 percent lower than the average U.S. wage) are under siege as a function of this unlimited amount of cheap foreign labor. There's a loss of equilibrium, indeed.

In a disorganized, chaotic business environment, a loss of equilibrium is a one-time, short-term benefit, at best, for the corporation. On the surface, the proposition of paying $1.50 per hour for a manufacturing worker versus $18.00 plus benefits is an easy cost-benefit analysis to undertake and an easy decision to make. Likewise, if you're an MNC, it appears to make sense to pay $35.00 per hour in India for a software engineer versus $150.00 per hour in the United States. Typically, the approach of trick-and-treat management is to look at these labor costs alone, all else being equal, as an opportunity for continuous improvement. And in evaluating such a decision using our conventional cost accounting and regulatory accounting measurement, the labor cost differential is an attractive option for management to undertake. By compartmentalizing costs, today's management is having an adverse impact on the U.S. social ethic between the public and private sectors. These facts are well understood and accepted. However, what isn't well understood is the harm that the compartmentalization of labor, away from other steps of the product life cycle, is having on the corporation in reality.

Product life-cycle development describes how the functions of a corporation work in conjunction with one another (sales, marketing, manufacturing, etc.). Hacking this product life-cycle process into little pieces has not only harmed U.S. workers—relative to their competition with 1 billion workers in the developing world—but is also harming the MNC in its efforts to be competitive within a dynamic global economy. Most MNCs don't understand this yet. It is my belief that outsourcing through compartmentalization (e.g., taking just a piece of the operation and moving it to China) can be worse for a company's marketing efforts than it if moved the entire company to China. It's not only a matter of protecting the public but also of protecting the corporation and its interests! The truth of this statement will reveal itself over the course of the 21st century.

Through the use of econometrics, financial accounting measurement techniques, and financial engineering through Wall Street, labor markets in the United States have been shown as less productive than they are, and developing markets are perceived as more productive. Productivity has been transformed in definition, and it's easy to make cheap labor look very productive. But when U.S. management moves labor operations to China and India, it is doing more than saving costs in the operation; it is reducing both the productivity of the company, in many cases, and making U.S. labor less productive relative to the rest of the world.

The focus on stagnant or even falling U.S. labor rates isn't in the quality and innovation of the labor, but rather in the nominal cost of what that labor provides. Labor becomes a commodity and is no longer correlated directly to real productivity. The impact of labor on the product life-cycle process, which is critical to innovation and market leadership, is changed because the labor and the product have been disconnected. On the other side of the ocean, the opposite effect is happening: not only are jobs gained by China and India from the United States in this disconnected effort, but these developing nations are able to start connecting the pieces of their industry, in order to understand the product life-cycle process, evolving them from contract manufacturers to gaining key processes within the life cycle, such as research and development (R&D), accounts payable, advertising, and so on.

The commoditization of the U.S. workforce is a trick being played out by managers that isn't just a societal problem, something discussed by academics and politicians. Through the commoditization of a workforce, managers are piecemealing a process in the product life-cycle workflow without clearly understanding the value that it plays in the essence of the product or the service of the firm. Can a manager make a decision to outsource manufacturing without having an impact on quality or productivity? Can this same manager not foresee this short-term solution as having a negative impact on sales and the efficiency of the supply chain, on longer-term value? Can software code be broken down into noncultural factors, simply coded by a software engineer in India who doesn't understand how the United States will use the final service?

I can assure you that most if not all of these questions aren't being asked when compartmental decisions are made. Decisions are sliced up neatly into compartmentalized business cases in search of short-term cost reduction, void of end-to-end strategy discussion. The commoditization of a labor market may be a social question that is discussed by public sector professionals, academics, and those with an eye on the societal effect, but it should be pondered even more so by the managers of the U.S. operations, from both a short-term and a long-term perspective. In the classical management model, labor wasn't objectified because it was an equal variable in the production function. Today, it isn't a matter of societal salvation, but rather good business within a systems view of management, looking at the product life cycle completely from end to end.

Has globalization forced the sacred covenant of Henry Ford into obsolescence? The answer to this question is certainly no, because this covenant was broken well before the advent of globalization in the early 1990s. Perhaps the good old days of the 1950s, 1960s, and 1970s felt good, but it is my contention that the family environment of the corporation from these days was more about the organization structure than it was regarding any sacred covenant between the worker and manager. Back in those days of the organization man, employees were viewed as personally important, but, from a business standpoint, they belonged to the organization. Often, the alcoholic worker often wasn't retained by the corporation not because he was valuable but because he was one of the family. On the other hand, many aspirations and talents of men weren't supported because they didn't fit within the organizational structure. Today's worker is no longer a member of the family and not a strategic asset.

Henry Ford and others described the worker as a strategic asset, defined in terms of welfare capitalism. As is mentioned in chapter three, the workers of developing nations such as India and China are less protected than the ones in the United States, but they are no more or less valued. Without question, in today's cost-accounting system at the typical U.S. corporation, the value of the worker is the output that results from his or her labor for the cost incurred, not taking into consideration any value measurement relative to price. Corporations have lost their ability to measure the intrinsic value of labor in the product life-cycle process, because globalization has pressured operations to consider the price rather than the value of labor within the production process.

MANAGEMENT THROUGH FINANCIAL ENGINEERING

The next category of trick-and-treat management is that of financial engineering at the U.S. corporation. There are two elements to financial engineering in the current definition of management: one is in the manager being able to manage earnings, and the other is in the bottom-line financial approach known as cost cutting. Today, every corporate manager out there does earnings management to some degree. The question is where most corporate managers are on the continuum: on the worst side of manipulating earnings or on the best side of seeking earnings quality in their financial statements.

The pressures from the market are enormous, and fluctuations in a company's quarterly results can have a material impact on the price of the stock, which directly affects the livelihood of the corporate manager. This concept of forecasting is addressed by the leadership of Google:

> Many companies are under pressure to keep their earnings in line with analysts' forecasts. Therefore, they often accept smaller, but predictable, earnings rather than larger and more unpredictable returns. Sergey and I feel this is harmful, and we intend to steer in the opposite direction . . . We will make decisions on the business fundamentals, not accounting considerations, and always with the long term welfare of the company and shareholders in mind.[6]

In a 2005 study, Graham, Harvey, and Rajgopal found that chief financial officers (CFOs) of large U.S. corporations are as keen as ever to beat earnings benchmarks, such as analysts' forecasts, given the stock market's fixation with these numbers, even after the Enron scandal and the ensuing regulatory reforms of Sarbanes-Oxley.[7] Although other studies have shown that the impact of Sarbanes-Oxley regulatory reform has made most companies more conservative, steering away from the manipulation of financial results, it remains very much in question regarding the practice of earnings management. Given the rules of public accounting standards, it is entirely legal and subject to interpretation, in most cases, for corporate managers to determine how to account properly for many transactions. Given the earnings pressures from the analyst community (that haven't decreased materially as a result of accounting reform), professional managers will continue to use earnings management as a tool for them to make their numbers for the quarter and the year.

To summarize, there are three philosophies for how corporate managers report their earnings today:

> Earnings Management: an attempt by management to influence reported earnings by using specific accounting methods (or changing methods), recognizing one-time, nonrecurring items, deferring or accelerating expense or revenue transactions, or using other methods designed to influence short-term earnings.
>
> Earnings Manipulation: an obvious, fraudulent attempt to distort financial results through questionable means.
>
> Earnings Quality: a measure of the ability of reported earnings to reflect the firm's true earnings and to help predict future earnings.[8]

As a financial analyst and controller for USF&G in the 1990s, I was involved in the last days of the CEO Jack Moseley and his crew of organization men, who were accused by the watchdog group Public Citizen of covering up USF&G's poor financial health. Moseley's response was that the National Association of Insurance Commissioners (NAIC) had given USF&G a "clean bill of health" in

1989 and that they were a much better judge of financial condition than was Public Citizen.

Shortly thereafter, Moseley and his crew were fired, and Norm Blake later explained to the employees that, in the early days, "we barely had enough liquidity to keep payroll." Blake instituted a new approach to earnings management—an approach to restructure and reengineer according to the stock market's liking. In the end, there were no special accounting treatments left to pursue, and Blake and crew were left with no other choice than to sell the company.

But in the end, although both leaders may have admitted to establishing good standards for financial reporting, it is in the eye of the beholder as to whether these managers acted with integrity, twisting the rules, or in gross misconduct. This is the nebulous nature of the problem that we face today. As such, quite a few CEOs and CFOs believe that they can present as much of a positive spin on the company's activities from earnings management as they can from making concrete changes in the operation.

Some of the tricks involved in legitimate (not manipulative) earnings management are excluding big expense items from operating statements, including revenues that possibly should be omitted, underfunding or not funding pensions at all, and employing methods of accounting for stock options. All of these treatments are entirely legal, but they may distort the true financial performance of the firm. Today, one of the largest concerns for financially troubled companies is their unfunded pension liabilities. In 2002, when United Airlines filed for bankruptcy, its unfunded liability was an estimated $6.4 billion. It is not overstating the case to suggest that more companies could file for bankruptcy if they can't meet their pension obligations, as yet another way to engineer results financially and to delay facing up to the problems that aren't well represented on their balance sheets.

In mid-2008, I gave a speech at a conference titled "The Cost Savings Death March." In this discussion, I focused on how corporate managers must demonstrate courage and dig deeper into the department and company's financial results to find true productivity—labor, capital, and technology optimization. The message was that much of today's cost cutting doesn't work because costs exist for a reason—and unless you take the reasons away, the costs will return.

This message resonated with many of the attendees of this conference, but, in many cases, they didn't feel as though their CEOs and CFOs will give them a chance. "I'm under such enormous pressure right now to make my numbers given the state of our industry that I don't know what else to do," was a typical response that I got from these attendees. "How can I convince my leaders that true cost savings may take a little more time than immediately?" Many of the corporate managers who attended got the point—now the question is whether their organizations will give them the opportunity to perform like managers instead of thinking like Wall Street analysts? Or will they continue to be asked to thrive in chaos?

For decades, the drumbeat of cost reduction has been the focus of the corporate manager—restructuring, cost cutting, reengineering, rightsizing, downsizing, whatever you wish to call it. In the 1980s, the Fortune 500 industrials shed

3.2 million jobs in the name of downsizing, and the trend continued into the 1990s.[9] Employees are downsized, and the result is the boomerang effect of "cost returning," typically in lower-quality temporary workers or higher-priced consultants, or of "collapsing job descriptions," as it is called, giving more work to one individual without any corresponding business process changes.

As a corporate manager eager to earn my stripes, I participated in some of these downsizings as a good soldier of the strategy. Today, there is very little left within most corporations in creating large staff downsizings, unless there is a change in scope in the business, or a merger, acquisition, or joint venture relationship. But in normal operating circumstances, the new modus operandi of cost reduction involves creating a contingency workforce. Corporate managers found that this boomerang effect (cost returning after being reduced) to be problematic when they were expected to achieve cost reductions for the company to achieve its financial results. If cost boomerangs happen, the next option isn't to eliminate the labor associated with doing a certain job, but rather to reduce the cost of it and/or make it less permanent, so to speak. These are the pressures that the U.S. business operations are under as a function of our financial markets.

Cost cutting and bottom-line thinking by corporate managers doesn't just have an impact on labor but also affects nonlabor-related expenses, such as maintenance, training, product-development schedules (creating delays), and needed capital projects that are delayed or avoided altogether. Maintenance is a good example of how managers try to engineer a budget financially to show cost savings but that ends up being counterproductive. A maintenance budget is typically seen as presenting an opportunity for cuts by financial analysts. But, as is typical when short-term cost decisions are made in order to improve a financial statement, cutting maintenance can be a very poor decision indeed. If a factory's maintenance budget is cut, it may make that department's budget look good, but the actual result can be lower factory efficiency (more unplanned outages because of less preventative maintenance) and even higher maintenance costs (more unplanned versus planned costs). Many of the companies' managers that I have spoken to have told me that their maintenance budget is always up for discussion because it's viewed as an "opportunity," without managers understanding the full impact of cost cutting. It's an example of the "Cost Savings Death March" that is difficult to avoid once it gets started.

At its very worst, the corporate manager's obsession with financial results through misunderstood cost savings can lead to some unanticipated problems. Closing the company gym, cutting off mobile phone service, and canceling Christmas parties are more examples. This "burning the furniture" message has been presented to me as well on line items, such as training and travel, that were materially insignificant to my overall budget.

Having to deliver such messages on cost cuts as a corporate leader has embarrassed me, because it was both annoying to my employees and damaging to their morale. Furthermore, it really screams to the employee base that management doesn't have an appropriate strategy on how to cost cut really and instead focuses on trivialities. The symbolism of the message is much greater than the cost savings itself: it's a trick of the corporate manager to convey that financial results will be met at all costs.

There also have been some high-profile examples of cost cutting blowing up in corporate managers' faces. In March, 2007, Circuit City announced that it was going to lay off 3,400 employees, or 8 percent, of its workforce and replace the workers with lower-paid hires. Forget about the fact that it was 2007 and that the "7 percent rule" (stock goes up 7 percent when layoffs are announced) no longer worked, as it did in the 1990s. Imagine being the manager at Circuit City, who told his higher-paid store employees that they were being terminated immediately (with severance) but could reapply for their jobs—after a 10-week delay. The stock market turned its back on Circuit City, immediately lowering its stock price in opposition to this strategy. Today, the retailer filed for bankruptcy protection, and has shut down all of its retail operations.

What is surprising is that the corporate leaders of this company didn't expect a backlash in service at their stores as a result. But its same-store holiday sales fell by 11.4 percent from the prior year, and its stock price has plummeted rapidly, to a price around $2 today.[10] After six straight quarters of losses, this retail innovator (the first big box electronics store to have a warehouse retail lay-out), which had been founded in 1949, filed for bankruptcy, fueling the perspective that trick-and-treat management will affect even the most successful innovators of the past.

Another almost-impossible cost-cutting strategy to understand is that of the auto industry and its employee buyout plan. In 2006, General Motors announced and implemented a cost-cutting scheme that offered $140,000 to those with more than 10 years of service, $70,000 to those with less, and early retirement to those with at least 26 years of service (versus 30 years). As a result, the company expected to save $5 billion in structural costs. This allowed the company to move ahead faster on its goal to cut 30,000 employees of its 113,000 member U.S. workforce by 2008. The stock market heralded the move, increasing the company's stock price as a result.

CEO Rick Wagoner was pleasantly surprised when more workers came forward than expected for these options. But maybe it worked out too well: as a result, General Motors was forced to recall laid-off workers, make transfers from other plants, and hire temporary workers, all at a time when its market share was under siege from Toyota. Today, the stock is worth around $3 a share under continual fears of bankruptcy.

For 30 years, the entire U.S. auto industry was in denial, it was slow to take on cost pressures and unions, and it failed to invest in new products and innovations. The trick-and-treat management has come home to roost for the U.S. auto industry, and even another bailout won't do much to fix this problem. At the time of this writing, the Big Three are asking the U.S. government for a $25 billion bailout, noting that they can't borrow money from their normal sources. "Would you buy a car from a bankrupt automaker?" asked United Auto Workers President

Ron Gettelfinger, who suggested that workers will make no concessions amid these problems. Maybe the question that should be asked is, "Would you buy a car from an automaker who charges an extra $2,000 for labor costs?" Apparently, neither the leadership of the Big Three (recently quoted as noting that leadership isn't the problem) nor the labor unions can look at themselves in the mirror.

CHECKS AND BALANCES OVER MANAGEMENT SELF-INTEREST?

The next trick is what I call postclassical management capitalism, a play on Vanguard founder John Bogle's term, "manager's capitalism." In his view,

> The corporation came to be run to profit its managers, in complicity if not conspiracy with accountants and the managers of other corporations . . . the markets had so diffused corporate ownership that no responsible owner exists. This is morally unacceptable, but also a corruption of capitalism itself.[11]

Today's manager may be self-serving, as Bogle and others suggest, and the manager is without a doubt filling a hole left as a result of an ineffective corporate governance (including audit firms) and a nameless ownership role of these companies from big financial funds that look at it as a financial commodity, as opposed to a going concern. I agree with Bogle that this is a failure of our capitalism. Postclassical management capitalism thus describes the self-interest of the manager over that of the workers, investors, and even consumers through the absence of gatekeepers (auditors, regulators, legislators, and Board of Directors), enabling management to become rotten to the core.

There is no conspiracy here, and I certainly don't agree with Bogle on the point that the single largest reason for this problem can be attributed to the compensation of the executive in the form of stock options. The stock option is simply the carrot for an improper incentive—an effect, not a cause. Of course, corporate managers will jump through hoops to meet their financial objectives to be rewarded, but if they do so in the pursuit of the wrong objectives, are the corporate leaders the ones who are at fault? It's too simple an explanation to assume that this is the case.

Instead, postclassical management capitalism is the disfigurement of management that is perpetuated by a lack of a gatekeeper. Yes, in its proper format, management should naturally seek to optimize the variables of labor, capital, and technology, but if a very lucrative reward system is in place that enables leaders to make more money by taking shortcuts, the wrong behaviors will be supported more often than not. There is something entirely dysfunctional about the leadership role of management that has no gatekeeper holding it accountable for optimization and balance versus out-of-control economic limitlessness.

As an effect, but not a cause, for the dysfunctional nature of management via postclassical management capitalism, the leaders of the large companies are making a lot of money on equity incentives, at a time when members of the rank-and-file workforce are facing layoffs or wage reductions or concessions. In the 1980s, the multiplier for the compensation of a CEO versus the average worker was a factor of 42. By the year 2000, it was a factor of 531. Today's Wal-Mart CEO takes home 900 times the pay of an average worker! Every two weeks, former Wal-Mart CEO Lee Scott made what his average worker would make in a lifetime.[12]

Another classic example of postclassical management capitalism is that of the legendary past CEO of General Electric, Mr. Jack Welch. Even seven years after his retirement as the CEO, he is still viewed as a legendary thinker, who turned General Electric around through his vibrant and no-nonsense management style. As a result, he made hundreds of millions of dollars at General Electric and a lot on top of that by selling books and doing speeches about what he did. He has accumulated a personal fortune today of more than $700 million. With a stock price today hovering around $10 a share, worth 100 percent less than what it was during Welch's day, the question is whether Welch and his leaders actually created long-term value in the company or just short-term earnings management. This statement is not to vilify Welch (or to praise him, for that matter), but rather to bring into question John Bogle's view of managerial capitalism and its harmful impact on the U.S. economy. How sustainable was the value that Jack Welch created? Today, the answer is much different than when he retired.

CREATIVE DESTRUCTION VERSUS DESTRUCTIVE DESTRUCTION

Typically, the concept of creative destruction is viewed within a definition of technology alone, but it can take form in many ways:

- New markets of products
- New equipment
- New sources of labor and raw materials
- New methods of organization and approaches to management
- New methods of communication, processes, and technologies
- New financial instruments

Creative destruction is best embodied by the saying "out of destruction, a new spirit of creativity arises." This is a path of improvement through failure, the need to create something new by tearing something down. The laws of nature understand this concept, because evolution has taken on these characteristics. Evolution itself can only be successful when change is in balance, not in chaos. An environment of continuous change, of unending chaos, can never lead to evolution. The laws of change in U.S. business back in the early days of the 21st century began to bring forth stability after the chaos of the Great Depression. Tom

Peters and other management gurus of the 1980s proposed a much different concept of management, and we've seen where it has taken us. It has led all corporate managers to the concept of destructive destruction, an environment of change that is constant chaos, constant flux.

Destructive destruction is a concept in today's postclassical management thinking that began in the 1970s, through the beginnings of the deregulation movement between the private and public sectors. I am not a fan of too much regulation, but when regulations were stripped from our business environment, as they were in the 1970s and 1980s, there was little understanding of what the repercussions would be. I consider Mr. Tom Peters to be the father of the discipline of destructive destruction for today's version of postclassical management. His first book, *In Search of Excellence,* written in 1982, was actually a 700-page PowerPoint presentation at first (he was a management consultant for McKinsey), which he condensed, in book format, into eight common themes that are important for a successful corporation:

1. A bias for action, active decision making—"getting on with it."
2. Close to the customer—learning from the people served by the business.
3. Autonomy and entrepreneurship— fostering innovation and nurturing "champions."
4. Productivity through people—treating rank-and-file employees as a source of quality.
5. Hands-on, value-driven management philosophy that guides everyday practice—management showing its commitment.
6. Stick to the knitting—stay with the business that you know.
7. Simple form, lean staff—some of the best companies have minimal HQ staff.
8. Simultaneous loose-tight properties—autonomy in shop-floor activities plus centralized values.

Despite this book's overwhelming success, one-third of the 43 "excellent companies were in financial difficulty within five years of the Peters and Waterman surveys."[13] Consider Peters's response to the approach that was used to determine his original list of 62 excellent companies:

[In] Search [of Excellence] started out as a study of 62 companies. How did we come up with them? We went around to McKinsey's partners and to a bunch of other smart people who were deeply involved and seriously engaged in the world of business and asked, Who's cool? Who's doing cool work? Where is there great stuff going on? And which companies genuinely get it? That very direct approach generated a list of 62 companies, which led to interviews with the people at those companies. Then, because McKinsey is McKinsey, we felt that we had to come up with some quantitative measures of performance. Those measures dropped the list from 62 to 43 companies.

General Electric, for example, was on the list of 62 companies but didn't make the cut to 43—which shows you how "stupid" raw insight is and how "smart" tough-minded metrics can be.[14]

Ouch. Not only was one of the top-selling management books of all time snickered at for including companies that had financial problems a short period later, but the list was generated with a bogus methodology ("Who's Cool?", "McKinsey is McKinsey"), and then Peters admitted (in a 2001 interview with *Fast Company* magazine) that some of the data were "faked data."

Six years after *In Search of Excellence*, Tom Peters came out with another book, very similar in its basic themes, titled *Thriving on Chaos: Handbook for a Management Revolution.* With this book, Peters would really establish himself as the founder of the destructive destruction revolution in management in the 1980s. In it, Peters offered the solution to our business problems, with an unstructured business environment. He started the book with the saying, "If it ain't broke, you haven't looked hard enough . . . fix it anyway." This reminds me of my days as a management consultant when I was obsessed with my role as a disorganization manager, believing that the complacent organization men couldn't do anything right and that I just needed to find their problems.

Before you consider me to be overly critical of one of the most famous gurus of U.S. management, think a minute about the message of an organizational environment in which everything needs to change constantly and anything that isn't changing is broken (even if it's not). This is the business environment of my early management days, the challenge of "you can't do it all at once, but you must," of taking on the next change before the preceding initiative has even been finished (no time for completion if you're in a continuous cycle of change). Today's continuous improvement embodies this motive—to make change happen continuously and to dig up the roots of anything that is preventing you (as the manager) from making this happen.

This is obviously a much different concept than Deming's definition of continuous improvement, and I can't imagine Dr. Deming ever saying "you can't do it all at once, but you must." Such was and is the life of today's postclassical management manager in the destructive destruction world. Not from destruction comes creation, no, there's no time for that. From destruction comes commoditization and compartmentalization, the chunking of people and processes that can be changed in manageable bites. Destructive destruction is like changing the change before it has time to change.

Without the accounting method of activity-based costing, destructive destruction would not be possible at all. Activity-based costing means that costs are assigned to activities in order to determine the cost of a particular activity to the overall product or service that ultimately reaches the customer. Certainly, such a financial accounting method has been useful to U.S. corporations. It has been a rather dangerous tool as well: by enabling the assignment of costs to a certain activity within an overall process, it has been easier to determine whether that activity should be handled more cheaply, outsourced, or even eliminated through consolidation or reengineering. The cost, rather than the value of that activity or cost, is understood, bringing to mind the saying that we "understand the cost of everything, and the value of nothing."

Destructive destruction really started to take off when pieces and parts could be ripped from out of a product life-cycle process for cost savings without completely understanding the hidden impact on the economic value of that activity or process. MNCs pick apart elements of their operations and decide where to source those activities, purely on the basis of price (not cost or value). The U.S. manufacturing industry has been practically eradicated as a function of picking apart the pieces of the product life cycle without expecting any loss of value as a result. Management thinkers believe that moving away from manufacturing blue-collar work is creative destruction, when, in actuality, it is becoming destructive destruction, both to the MNC and to the U.S. manufacturing sector. The MNC is learning today that cutting costs in one element of the supply chain without an understanding of the impact on the entire product life cycle can be a strategy wrought with errors.

PRODUCT LIFE-CYCLE MANAGEMENT AS A FRAMEWORK FOR MANAGEMENT

One of the keys to the future of a management discipline in the United States will be an understanding of this critical concept of Product Life-Cycle Management (PLM). When the United States was growing in its economic strength, PLM was understood within U.S. operations. Henry Ford was an engineer who understood how engineering (today's R&D included) must be tied to manufacturing; he was perhaps the first to think of a modern corporation as a system and to conceive an operation in terms of PLM. The United States covets R&D jobs today but doesn't see the need for manufacturing. This is a critical flaw in our lack of management understanding and in the mode of management thinking that allows the cost to be understood "part by part." Understanding the usefulness of PLM within a company is synonymous with optimizing the variables of labor, capital, and technology within a management equation.

You can't blame globalization for the breakdown in PLM integrity in a MNC, but it must be suggested that a corporate manager viewing PLM differently will likely view globalization differently as well. The conceptual functions of a PLM are as follows:

- Conceive
- Design
- Realize
- Service

During the days of the development of the United States, strong U.S. corporations considered the end-to-end discipline of how a product was conceived—all the way through distribution and its use. Today, the chaos and constant change of destructive destruction allows for none of this. Furthermore, with functions of the company being broken down by activity-based costing accounting, the essence of PLM loses its integrity, whereas globalization and chaos rule the day, putting the U.S. economy in the favor of emerging ones. The classical management discipline can solve this problem for both private corporations and the public sector.

THE TECHNOLOGY ANXIETY WITHIN MANAGEMENT

The last element of today's postmanagement discipline is that of technology anxiety. The conventional thinking in business today typically associates technology as a tool that is overused in its applications, and this is true. In manufacturing and logistics, automation has taken production to the point of facilities using few or even no hourly workers. In the service sector, there is process center automation (including Business Process Outsourcing, or BPO), as well as "Do It Yourself" technologies that can eliminate the need for a workforce. These are all well-known tools, being utilized everywhere.

Furthermore, technology is not only being used to eliminate the need for workers at local factories, processing centers, and retail operations—it is also being used to proliferate the use of offshoring to lower-cost segments of the population. These ideas can lead to productivity when done correctly. But what about IT—the technology designed for managers? So far, there has been an inability for most Fortune 500 corporations to achieve a positive correlation between money spent on IT and sustainable productivity and/or profits. This statement of fact from research isn't sufficient for IT companies to stop parading claims of enormous paybacks on their products, of the use of IT to make life better in Corporate America. At the onset, IT companies have sought to penetrate the world of top management, to make a claim for how IT can transform their respective companies: today, their targets are much less inspirational.

The first true IT system at a large corporation was its cost-accounting system, typically in an Enterprise Resource Planning (ERP) tool, such as SAP (top ERP tool). In many cases, the use of cost accounting in Corporate America gave visibility to some of the silly strategies that could never be justified when viewed properly. However, when also using cost-accounting principles through destructive destruction, corporate managers found the information useful in their cost-cutting schemes. But more was needed by managers, and more was promised by the IT departments. Data warehouses, balanced scorecards, Web portals, and so on were imagined as silver bullets to turn data strategically into information for use, particularly for its management staff.

The problem was that the IT providers and the marketplace couldn't understand why their wonderful tools weren't providing productivity and value, and, therefore, they proclaimed proudly that they were. What they didn't understand (or want to understand) is that the problem in their technologies was a fatal flaw that they couldn't fix on their own: that the death of management was the problem, through technology anxiety.

Peter Drucker noted just a few years before his death that information architecture needs to begin with the data that management need to pursue the company's strategy.[15] How right he was, and how many corporate managers and IT professionals have missed this point. IT, which I define is the practical application of turning data into information, is owned by the IT departments of large corporations. This isn't the fault of IT per se (although much is always blamed on IT), but rather the fault of management. Corporate management is to blame because of their fear of IT as a solution for management. No, this isn't some conspiracy or anything like that, but rather corporate management's irrational path away from analytical solutions and optimizations and closer to maximization through the principle of postclassical management capitalism.

To understand why most corporate managers are afraid of IT initiatives, you must first understand "Buffington's Law" regarding IT initiatives: the success and failure of an IT project is 90 percent a function of business process (including management) and 10 percent a function of technology. This has been proven to me through many IT initiatives in my career, in very different companies. Buffington's Law scares both IT companies and corporate managers alike for the same reason: the IT company wants the customer to believe that the technology is the cure, and corporate leaders want to use a "silver bullet" to make their current problems go away. In many cases, IT initiatives haven't achieved the expected payback on the investment because a lack of understanding of business process is what dooms the investment, not a poor decision in the use of technology. And this poor implementation of Buffington's Law keeps corporate leaders shy of IT investments, when in fact it's just what they need.

With IT investments failing 90 percent of the time because of poor business process, corporate leaders have to look in the mirror and face their own and their company's shortcomings, as opposed to blaming technology and technology companies.

And as a result, IT is often seen as a necessary evil (as opposed to a strategic advantage) for the formulation and management of the structured data, versus a strategic tool seeking to formalize more a greater percentage of the data accessible within the company's product life-cycle process. IT becomes about e-mail systems, and the 5 percent of the company's data that are formalized into an IT system, versus a strategic capture of as much as 90 percent of the data around the organization (customer, supplier, wholesaler, employee, investor, retailer, etc.). Certainly, the whole discipline of IT has been a sad disappointment over the past 20 years, thanks to technology anxiety, which is fostered by today's version of management.

A lack of use of strategic IT in large U.S. business operations also perpetuates the layers of management in these organizations that are used as management relay systems. Instead of data turning into information from all of the environments of the organization (internal and external) being driven from a fairly objective IT information infrastructure, it remains a function of these endless layers of management relay systems, each layer putting its own personal interpretation on the data. Consider Peter Drucker's interpretation of this management relay system:

> Many times, we quickly discover that most management levels manage nothing. Instead, they merely amplify the faint signals emanating from the top and bottom of the corporate infrastructure. I imagine that most CEO's have heard the first law of information theory: every relay doubles the noise and cuts the message in half. The same holds true for most management level, which neither manage people nor make decisions. They serve only as relays. When we build information as a structural element, we don't need such levels.[16]

Today's average corporation has three information systems: one is organized around its formal data stream, which accounts for about 5 percent of the organization's possible information. The second is of the accounting system, which is typically overly complex and of marginal value. Neither of these is a strategic tool, nor is it likely that many of today's disciples of management would even understand how to turn data into information and, subsequently, into strategic actions. The third system is the hierarchy of professional managers and professional staff. The death of management has rendered the possibilities of IT business value useless through its own deficiencies and, in the process, has relegated to managers the role of simply being faint signals of relay systems.

ARE WE REALLY MANAGERS TODAY?

Are U.S. managers focused on innovation and new brand development and implementation, or are we looking for easy-out, quick-hit solutions to achieve our financial numbers? Do U.S. managers understand the importance of the supply chain via the product life-cycle process, or are we commoditizing it, breaking it into pieces in short-term cost-cutting measures? The best way to fuel R&D within U.S. operations used to be within an improvement in productivity in the supply chain. But when R&D has no connection to a supply chain through the commoditization of manufacturing and other key strategic processes, is it possible to innovate through R&D? Sadly, in the United States, the answer is, increasingly, no. Emerging markets have been whipping the United States, not primarily because of a largely mercantile and unfair trade environment, but largely as a result of an environment that has appealed to the decision-making process of the corporate manager, for better or worse.

Classical managers once achieved profitability in their businesses and also balanced the surplus benefits within labor, capital, and technology within the public and private sectors. Today, managers are using these profits to buy back shares of the company's stock and pay off the massive corporate debt that has been accumulated (sometimes from the frenzy of mergers and acquisitions activity). Capital investment continues to fall, because many CEOs don't want to wait for the pay-back period when they are being rewarded on a year-by-year basis. This is a death knell for U.S. manufacturing.

Yet more economists and leaders are turning the corner and asserting as well that today's principles aren't consistent with what management should be. The former chief economist of Morgan Stanley, Stephen Roach, used to be an "advocate of downsizing," but now he has his doubts. Roach believes that U.S. businesses have achieved the productivity that they were looking for in the 1990s, but perhaps in not the best way of doing it. As a result of reengineering, outsourcing, and reinventing corporations, shareholders have done well, but not workers, as Roach articulates:

> I think at the end of the day, Wall Street and the workers are in it together. Because if corporate leaders figure out competitive strategies that also give workers an equitable reward, then I think the productivity gains that have first been uncovered through restructuring will be sustained, and earnings performance will ultimately end up exceeding investor expectations over the longer haul.

> There may be a short period, though, a transitional period where if workers get more, earnings will get hit on a short-term basis and the markets will respond. That's inevitable. Markets go up and down. It's been a one-way bull market for a long, long time.[17]

It is certainly a transformation in thinking worth noting when one of the most important U.S. economists, who was previously a proponent of downsizing, has changed positions to talk about how dangerous it is to our economy for a lack of balance not to be provided by corporate managers. In February 2007, Federal Reserve chairman Ben Bernanke, hardly a liberal, noted the growing income inequality in the United States and of the need for the economics profession to understand why. But perhaps the United States is out of big ideas.

This brings us to Bill Dunk, a management consultant who reads 600 to 700 annual reports each year (a candidate for the show, "America's Dirtiest Jobs"). Mr. Dunk believes that today's corporate leaders are not driven by new ideas, but rather by the same tired reductions in force, operational closures, and other cost-cutting schemes as mentioned in this chapter. Dunk should know, because he has to read the same tired management speeches, year in year out, of how the company will achieve surplus value.

For many, the ideas of Tom Peters, Hammer and Champy, Jim Collins and Stephen Covey haven't served their intended purposes for U.S. business. The only new ideas that we're left with in business today are the ideas of escape from Corporate America, to a world away from the destructive destruction that you have just read about. Timothy Ferriss's *Four Hour Workweek: Escape 9-5, Live Anywhere, and Join the New Rich* is a best-selling business book. Is this any wonder? At least it's a business book with new ideas, even if those ideas are detrimental to U.S. business (can we all really be rich and escape Corporate

America?). Perhaps in today's business book market, it takes this sort of wild-eyed scheme to sell business books, given the lack of new ideas, as Theodore Kinni of *The Business Reader Review* laments:

> The business book, one of publishing's most lucrative niches just a couple of years ago and a dependable source of new ideas, is a fast shrinking genre. These days, when I phone my agent about a new idea, he asks me how many copies of the proposed book I plan to buy. "That's the first question editors are asking me," he says, chuckling in response to my indignant sputtering. Apparently the litmus test of a business book proposal these days is often whether or not the author is willing to buy a few thousand copies of the finished product, thus virtually guaranteeing that a publisher will recoup its costs.[18]

Perhaps there isn't anything left to write about. There are no new ideas, either in the boardroom or in the mind of the business guru. The next business book that you may read could be one of pure fantasy, about a four-hour workweek, or a free book to you, courtesy of a desperate writer (buying his or her own book?). Should we give up, assuming that 600 boring, standard, unimaginative annual reports are what we should expect in the future? What about a business book market with no new ideas? Perhaps, but hopefully not. No more management gurus. No more disorganization manager or destructive destruction. But if not these, then what?

The Lost Art of Management and Productivity

We know that productivity is critical to our economic vitality and plays a key role in raising living standards for all Americans, but there are a lot of things about productivity that are still the subject of study and debate. That is why we have convened this conference. For example, we do not understand all the factors that drive productivity. Our first panel will examine whether productivity gains can accurately be characterized as miracles. If so, what caused these gains and what impact have they had on our economy?

Opening remarks by Elaine Chao, Secretary of Labor, to the "Productivity in the 21st Century" conference on October 23, 2002

The productivity revolution of the late 1990s changed forever the way U.S. businesses operate. Driven by technology and overseas competition, companies radically altered how they manage purchasing policies, inventories, production processes, and, perhaps most important, labor. The U.S. workforce has become much more flexible, allowing businesses to respond faster to changes in demand, to the benefit of businesses and workers.

James C. Cooper, *Business Week,* August 25, 2008, right before the financial collapse.

WHAT IS REAL PRODUCTIVITY ANYWAY?

The mother of all buzzwords in business and economics today is the word productivity. Read the *Economic Report of the President* (2008), and you'll read some predictable, contradictory, and confusing explanations regarding what's happening with respect to productivity. A statement such as "productivity growth appears to be supported by factors that are more difficult to measure" is a typical line that is uttered by economists and pundits to explain how productivity has been surging in the 21st century.

When the last notable conference on productivity, "Productivity in the 21st Century"—with Alan Greenspan as one of the honored speakers—was held in 2002, it was clear that there was no magic understanding of whether or even how productivity was driving the prolonged economic and market growth that was happening, even with so many experts in attendance. Secretary Chao wondered whether productivity gains can be viewed as miracles, which seemed to tie to Greenspan's pondering later in the conference: "if the recent surge in measured productivity is not a statistical mirage or if it is not expunged by data revisions, then we need to ask about its possible causes."[1] With so many of the noted experts in the field confused over such an important topic, is it any wonder that our economy is in such a state of disrepair?

Certainly, much of the economic growth engine in the late 20th and early 21st century in the United States has been attributed to this miraculous yet misunderstood factor of productivity, as a catalyst for surplus value in U.S. business operations. The turning point of this new economy productivity might have been in May 1997, when the Federal Reserve was faced with a difficult decision regarding interest rates. Alan Greenspan, the staunch industrial conservative economist, converted himself and the Federal Reserve in support of this new age of economic limitlessness, largely as a result of the Greenspan Put. President Clinton became Greenspan's partner in this new economic thinking, stating, "I believe it's possible to have more sustained and higher growth without inflation than we previously thought."[2] All of this new economy growth was happening in ways that weren't easy to measure but that "felt right." Thus, the problem must be in the measurement techniques, not in the actual results. Twelve years later, we still don't understand the measurement of productivity, although, with the collapse of our financial markets, it appears safe to call the miracle more of a mirage.

In this chapter, I explain why productivity is a lost art, why it's considered either unexplainable and/or a miracle, and why it correlates directly to management being a dead discipline. I have given the "Productivity Is a Lost Art" speech on numerous occasions during book tours and general presentations, and there are always detractors who debate this statement, although not as much recently! One such detractor, an editor from a major metropolitan newspaper, wrote to me to say the following:

> One big problem with your argument: productivity rises year by year due largely to technology. This has had huge ramifications for the economy, as noted many times by Alan Greenspan during his Fed tenure.

Across the board in research, conferences, and the media, there was a conventional view that productivity was rising, but it wasn't exactly clear as to why. When a person from an audience asks me, "Why do you suppose productivity is a lost art when statistics state otherwise?" I answer, "Because the statistics are wrong." I also ask the audience if there is anyone who understands how the government and businesses measure productivity; there are few who attempt to try and nobody who really can answer the question accurately. Certainly, there is an astounding difference of opinion among the experts on even how to define and measure the term: the U.S. government wishes to consider labor productivity as the clear definition, but some economists believe that multifactor productivity is more accurate, and a third group believes that both definitions are misleading. One thing is for certain—the importance of productivity to the future of the U.S. economy, as noted by R. Glenn Hubbard at the previously cited 2002 conference:

> There is no single policy issue more important for the future of the country than understanding the determinants of increasing productivity growth.[3]

It's true, but first we must understand what productivity really is. This is the problem: how can productivity improve in the United States when our policy makers and business leaders aren't quite sure how to define and measure it? There is somewhat of a chicken-and-egg conundrum between management and productivity in U.S. operations: without a clear measurement of productivity set forth, there is really no use for the discipline of classical management. Today's study of productivity is just that: economists wandering around, trying to explain by way of econometrics what's happening in our economy and not quite being able to do so. It's the theoretical construct of a quantitative model that is impressive in its complexity but that means very little when one is trying to understand our real economy and to find solutions.

First, a basic primer is needed on the term productivity and other related terms in economics. If the purpose of economic activity is the satisfaction of human needs, productivity is a ratio to measure how well an organization (in this case) converts input resources (labor and capital or materials) into goods and services. The goal of a company is to produce surplus value in a production process, and productivity is the method of doing so through the optimal use of the inputs (labor and capital) to achieve the highest surplus value. The surplus value calculation is the only valid method for understanding how the profitability of a company and productivity are tied to one another—it is the key to understanding what I mean by classical management.

Therefore, to understand productivity, corporate managers must understand how to create greater surplus value through the input variables of capital and labor, respectively. But there's another variable as well that is important to business: technological change (including innovation and invention). In economics terms, technology can be depicted mathematically in the production function as the relationship between inputs and outputs. With an invention, technological change can improve productivity by using a lower amount of labor than before.

Therefore, the corporate manager can achieve greater productivity through a mix of technological change, labor, and capital.

Certainly, technological change was been a huge variable to the increases of productivity in the United States over the past century, aided directly by classical management. From the 19th century came such significant inventions as electricity and the internal combustion engine, which continued to spur productivity in the U.S. as late as the 1970s. Although electricity started off as little more than a scientific curiosity in the late 19th century, it would take decades into the 20th century for the U.S. infrastructure to become electrified. The internal combustion engine as well may have been made practical for personal and commercial use in the late 19th century, but it took decades in the 20th century for autos to be available to the masses and four decades later to have a national highway system and retail supermarket shopping to enable suburban life. These magnificent innovations led to practical inventions, which prompted technological change and productivity in the 20th century such as the United States has ever seen.

However, an econometric equation cannot measure the difference in technological change beyond the theoretical. What's important for real economics is the understanding of a multiplier effect of technology on society through the practical use of some inventions. Furthermore, because such benefits are from applied uses rather than purely from the invention itself, classical management as a force in the use of technology is poorly measured.

TODAY'S PRODUCTIVITY MEASUREMENTS: REAL OR IMAGINED?

Productivity measurements tell this story. The average productivity rate of 1.75 percent in the late 19th century and early 20th century jumped to 3.75 percent in the decade following World War I and then returned to a pace of 1.75 percent. After World War II, productivity rose again to 2.75 percent, only to fall to 1.5 percent within the period of the mid 1970s to the mid-1990s.[4] Calculated productivity surged again to 2.5 percent per year from 1995 to 2000, a much higher rate than the 1.4 percent of the average of the 20 years prior. Since 2000, calculated productivity has shown to increase to even higher levels (an average of 4.1 percent between 2001 and 2004), raising questions of whether this increase is real or a result of poor measurement. For 2008, non-farm productivity grew by 2.8% percent according to the government statistics, an unbelievable result given the virtual financial collapse of U.S. economy just one quarter later! The latest surge in productivity is even more unbelievable, given that the economists and pundits can't explain what it is attributed to and that the econometric measurement approaches are changing. The new economy was a productive era for the United States, yet few really understood why, other than through econometric measurements!

Even though econometric productivity measurements took off in the mid-1990s, there was an anomaly at the U.S. corporation regarding wages and productivity. In the past, economics concluded that wage increases would always

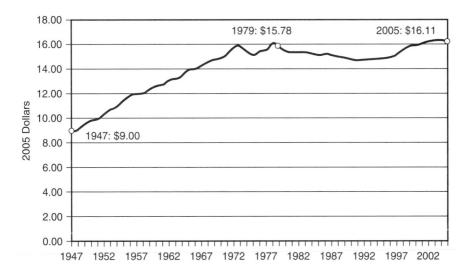

Figure 6.1 Average Hourly Earnings of Production and Non-supervisory Workers, 1947–2005

follow a productivity increase. In the 1990s, this wasn't the case: productivity increased while wages remained flat to falling, as is evident in Figure 6.1. Economists like Alan Greenspan attributed this improvement to the Information-Communication-Technology (ICT) revolution and globalization, which were both perceived to be misunderstood by statistical measurement. Although a large percentage of the productivity gains during the 1990s are attributable by the popular media to ICT, most noted researchers suggest that this wasn't the case. As Roach, Brynjolffson, and Strassmann, among many noted economists, state, the productivity gain appeared to be more from the production and distribution of computing and telecommunication services, rather than the utilization of these devices at the corporation.

And even computer manufacturing gains attributed to productivity in the U.S. economy are questionable, given that the U.S. economy gets credit for total manufacturing (in productivity), when much of the manufacturing process happens overseas. This doesn't mean that business value isn't possible from the implementation of IT, but rather that there isn't any documented evidence that it has been achieved at most corporations, and at material levels that would have an impact on national productivity results.

Productivity was measured in such a strange way at corporations that practically the purchase of a PC alone would constitute productivity growth, no matter how inept the company was in using this tool to improve surplus value. The distribution of these productivity benefits didn't appropriately filter into business processes or to the workers, as is clear when the economists of the day called the improvement in business conditions a jobless recovery, whatever that is supposed to mean!

Although the productivity growth from 1995 to 2000 at least had a targeted explanation, the productivity growth from 2001 to 2004 was much more of a mystery. In the last months of 2001, the Federal Reserve chairman wasn't discussing productivity or technology, but rather globalization:

> We keep forecasting stabilization but there has been no evidence of it anywhere . . . We currently are observing the obverse of the extraordinary accelerations that occurred in world economies during the latter part of the 1990s as a consequence of increased globalization—a development now seen as a two-edged sword.[5]

The last five years of the 20th century had an average calculated productivity growth of almost 3 percent, the fastest since World War II. Now Alan Greenspan was raising the stakes and sharing the credit for this growth between technology and the increasingly global marketplace, a new world. From a traditional economic sense, it is rather clear that technological progress can increase real productivity, but can productivity be driven solely through the globalization of the labor market? Globalization pressures in manufacturing and offshoring helped drive some of these divergences between labor wages and productivity growth, but it isn't clear how globalization by itself can drive productivity.

Contrary to any rules of logic, calculated productivity actually increased from 2001 to 2004 by an average of 4.1 percent! Today, there's a plethora of suspected reasons as to what happened: a real estate bubble, corporate accounting tricks, globalization, incentive-based stock options, and poor productivity measurement techniques. But there have been few, if any, who have attributed this productivity statistical growth to any sort of capital deepening (increased capital investment per worker), technological change associated with IT and human capital, business-process reengineering, or other such factors: solutions associated with classical management.

The intangible capital investment in organizations and business processes to make the PCs, telecommunications, and Internet take off hasn't yet happened to that same extent as electricity or the engine, and this is clearly a missing element of the role that classical management should have played in this story line. Instead of this optimization of labor, capital, and technology, U.S. corporate management took another path for the use of technology in business operations: a reduction of labor costs through temporary workers and offshoring.

The coincidence of astronomical U.S. productivity growth in the 1990s and 2000s with the surge in outsourcing and offshoring is conspicuous indeed. Economic theory supports the notion that the U.S. population's standard of living will rise alongside productivity growth, but these large productivity gains have not benefited workers in the form of higher wages, which seems counterintuitive. The significant percentage of manufacturing jobs (nominal) lost in the United States (25 percent since 1991) and the decline or flattening of wages are well documented, and globalization is one of the prime factors for this. In the measurement, when a manufacturer outsources work, labor productivity increases directly because the outsourced or offshored labor used to produce the product is no longer employed in the manufacturing sector and therefore isn't counted in the denominator of the labor productivity equation.

Attempts are made by the U.S. government to capture these data of the outsourced labor, but measurement techniques are admittedly poor. Recent government reports have raised similar concerns that data understate offshoring activities of U.S. companies because of the difficulty of measuring the prices and quantities of imported inputs accurately.[6] And in private industry, the story gets much worse, because productivity and cost savings are interchangeable and supported as such in productivity statistics.

Cost savings do not match with conventional economic wisdom of what constitutes productivity, and yet it gets measured as such. This has done more damage to the proper use of the disciplines of management and productivity than any other phenomenon in recent history, and it begins to explain to the reader how damaging such policy stances and statistics have been to the long-term viability of the U.S. economy.

The terrible irony is that U.S. operations have been viewed by Wall Street as resiliently productive for utilizing the cheap foreign labor of offshore operations; at the same time, such actions have had an adverse impact on the long-term competitiveness of the U.S. economy and the living standards of its workers in ways that are still not well understood. Furthermore, it should be questioned as to whether these actions are even productive to the companies themselves in the short-run, suggesting that Wall Street has had it dangerously wrong for some time now. The current state of the financial market correction seems to be a powerful indication of that point.

COOKING THE PRODUCTIVITY BOOKS?

Today's corporate manager has options for achieving productivity, as it is measured today. It can be achieved through smarter, more efficient U.S. workers, from an investment in capital equipment, and/or from the use of cheap foreign labor. Perhaps these corporate managers have it right after all—capital investments have a delayed effect on achieving benefits and are difficult to get approved. Capital investments also require an additional investment step of intangible capital to retrain the workers, improve business processes, and provide the necessary skills to the workforce. Because all of these steps are so difficult and time-consuming, why shouldn't the manager just take an easy-out and simply outsource labor for pseudoproductivity gains? If you are a corporate manager and your finance department requires a draconian, lengthy approval process for capital (putting your job at risk if you mess it up) and if accounting principles favor quicker-hit, less-capital solutions, and if your workforce is rebelling against detailed, grueling process-improvement exercises—why not take the easier out-sourcing approach to productivity? The research findings suggest that this is what's happening in our corporations today:[7]

1. An apparent understatement of the contribution of outsourcing to the staffing sector in previous productivity statistics.
2. Findings that services offshoring, which is likely to be significantly under-estimated and associated with significant labor cost savings, accounts for a surprisingly large share of recent manufacturing multifactor productiv-ity growth.
3. The small high-tech sector, which pioneered domestically, accounted for about one-third of multifactor productivity growth in the United States in the late 1990s.

The research findings overwhelmingly suggest that the mismeasurement and labor cost savings associated from outsourcing and offshoring have adversely influenced manufacturing, in particular, and aggregate productivity growth. This obviously is a death blow to the discipline of classical management, which relies heavily on capital and intangible investments and a commitment to process-improvement approaches, all to optimize labor, capital, and technology for the betterment of the corporation and the U.S. economy.

Once again, this bastardization of the term productivity has been supported by the financial community, which is the primary culprit indicted in the confusion of the terms cost savings and productivity. Through the use of accounting gim-micks, surplus value is increased, capital investments decline, and stock prices rise as a function of these productivity improvements.

U.S. capital expenditures increased in the 1990s, only to fall in the 2000s. During this same period, IT accounted for 45 percent of the increase in produc-tivity for all of manufacturing during this decade, and, in this industry, labor pro-ductivity increased by 961 percent for semiconductors and by 1,495 percent for computers, both of which are industries that were largely offshored.[8]

The small, outsourced IT industry being accountable for such a large per-centage of our total productivity gains (during a period of lower capital invest-ment) suggests what many noted economists mentioned about IT business value being more of a function of the production of this equipment than the utilization of it. If the manufacturing of IT investments is stripped from the productivity in using them, capital investments fell in the 2000s, which is a strange statistic indeed, given the high increase in the productivity rate of the 21st century thus far. This is a strange correlation to historical precedent, particularly when it is announced that IT has spurred this productivity revolution. Instead, these dis-crepancies are indicative of the changing of the definition of the term productivity to coincide with how MNCs are using the worldwide labor market to improve finan-cial results.

Once the new rules are set, it doesn't take much for today's corporate managers, who are motivated by financial incentives, to figure it out. Contrary to the perceptions of the popular media, trick-and-treat management isn't primarily an act of greedy corporate managers in action, although it certainly has been an act of self-interest for us all. There's not really much trickery going on here, just a bastardization of what productivity and management were designed to be, supported by accounting rules and analysts' reports. It's a question of corporate managers playing by the rules, but by a rule set that is bad for the U.S. economy and for our business operations.

Clearly, today's achievement of productivity at U.S. corporations has been more attributable to the use of temporary workforces, offshoring to foreign operations, and financial engineering than to the utilization and fulfillment of capital investments, ingenuous approaches to reengineering business processes to improve labor output, or other methods of classical management.

Most of today's methods to improve productivity haven't frequently assisted the U.S. workforce, the workforces of the destination sources of outsourcing (China, India, etc.), or even the overall viability of the company's product life-cycle process. Through the classical management era of the 20th century, there was a strong correlation between labor gains and productivity growth. This is how economics and management are supposed to work in conjunction with one another.

As is shown in Figure 6.2, there appears to be a perfect correlation between wages and productivity, but we must look below the surface to understand truly

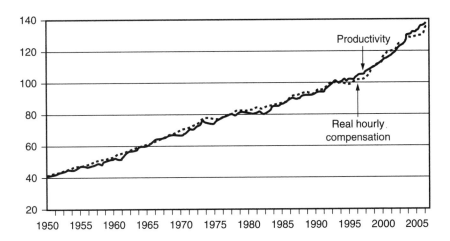

Figure 6.2 Productivity and Real Compensation Grow Together Index 1992–100

Note: These data cover allall persons (including supervisory and proprietors) in the nonfarm business sector. The real product wage is hourly compensation detected by the price index for nonfarm output. Shaded areas denote recessions.

why these statistics are not valid. Today there is a growing labor inequality in the United States that is a direct function of globalization, as even Ben Bernanke has stated. The changing nature of the definition of the term productivity and the difference between the terms of wages and compensation allow the data in Figure 6.2 to mislead us.

PRODUCTIVITY FOR WHOM?

Frequently, when the term productivity is discussed in the popular media or even in academic circles, the discussion more often than not relates to its quantitative measurement, without even discussing the importance of the income distribution process of surplus value (productivity achieved). This is one of the great missing links in this productivity discussion: whether it matters or not how the surplus value from a corporation is allocated to its stakeholders. As was proven through the astounding progress made by the United States in the 20th century, income distribution does matter, and when classical management enabled the middle class to drive and multiply economic growth through an improving relationship between the worker and consumer (á la Henry Ford's vision), our economy took off.

The question of income distribution gets a little more complicated, because the private sector is essentially stateless and is expected to be callous toward multiplying economic growth within any economy, even though this is a fatal assumption. The MNC and the corporate manager have more at stake with the productivity and prosperity of their labor and consumer markets than what they believe to be true today. A solution is discussed in chapter seven that help improve the productivity and prosperity of their labor and consumer markets will grow their businesses in the 21st century, whereas those that exploit them will lose business.

Today, it's just the opposite: a case can be made that companies that have exploited labor and consumer markets in the United States and China (for example) have achieved better financial performance over the past few decades as a function of globalization. With respect to our financial accounting system, these results haven't measured corporate economic value or even the value of the operation to society. It's just a measured accounting value. However, to paraphrase the CEO of Costco, "it's not philanthropic, but just good business to do so." Productivity may not be redefined in aggregate as this, but it's my conclusion that companies that choose to optimize both the labor and consumer markets, versus exploiting them, will see greater business growth in the 21st century. What we've seen over the past 20 years has been productivity generated from a flawed financial and accounting system only.

The business process in economics consists of the production process and the income distribution process of a company. For all intents and purposes, this is the definition of the role of the classical manager at the large MNC. After all, seeking to increase the surplus value of the company (production process) and to know how to optimize the distribution of that (my definition of management's role) is really what a good corporate manager must do. Yet, as indicated throughout this book, a good corporate manager is sometimes unable to focus on this, given the existing business environment that requires him or her to focus on different priorities: the monetary process for how a company finances the business and the market value process that determines how investors value the company.

In conventional economic terms (and in classical management), the business process should be the driver of value, whereas the monetary and market value processes should support it, but today, it's in reverse. In the 1930s through early 1950s, this was the case, but, after a while, competition waned and complacency took over, and the business process of U.S. operations was rendered less important. A focus on productivity was traded for a focus on administration through the 1970s, and, starting in the 1980s, there was a focus on disruption and chaos over the true definition of creative destruction.

Through this evolution, productivity measurement supported the wrong actions for corporate managers to undertake, and, therefore, productivity was not truly sought. In a nutshell, this describes qualitatively what many workers and even managers in the United States already feel: a "Twilight Zone" real world where productivity statistics are measured as strong, but true market fundamentals are less than favorable. Real labor wages in the United States have fallen for much of the population, even though statistics (such as those shown in Figure 6.2) suggest otherwise. Physical and intangible investments have dwindled since the 1990s, net of the manufacturing of IT investments. True productivity as a function of tying investments (such as IT) to business processes (versus just productivity through purchasing computers) is weak and overstated.

And, perhaps most important, we are blindly offshoring so much of the product life-cycle management of goods and services of the U.S. production process that we are literally handcuffed and can't do much at all to improve real productivity. We're back to the chicken-and-egg conundrum regarding productivity and management: can corporate managers go after real productivity without a real productivity measurement, and can a real productivity measurement thrive within U.S. business operations without a real discipline of management?

THE DANGERS OF THEORETICAL PRODUCTIVITY

Let's start with the lack of a real productivity measurement in place today. When we hear the term productivity in U.S. economic statistics, it almost always means labor productivity, as a default. Labor productivity is measured as a ratio of output per labor hour, assuming that other factors, such as capital investment, are shown in labor improvements, which is a stretch to assume. Although this measurement is relatively simple to calculate, it has clear limitations that make it of limited value in analysis. Increases in labor may reflect the worker's ability to produce more, the existence of technological improvements, or even accounting games (labor being outsourced, therefore no longer accounted for as labor, but services)— there are no distinctions drawn in the measurement.

Therefore, labor productivity becomes problematic because productivity increases may be construed with substitutions for labor, such as the use of outsourcing and offshoring. Measuring outsourcing as a gain versus a substitution for conventional labor is perhaps the greatest measurement problem.

Measuring the effectiveness of labor in a corporation may have been more useful in the past, when the definition of labor was more conventional. It is becoming increasingly nebulous with the changing nature of the labor force— from traditional to third-party employment (domestic outsourcing, temporary labor, foreign offshoring). As a greater percentage of a corporation's workforce becomes unconventional, the measurement of labor productivity becomes less reliable.

An alternative measurement technique to using labor productivity is the use of multifactor productivity (MFP) in measuring productivity. MFP measures both the efficiency of capital and labor, versus just labor on its own. This allows for a more refined understanding of what is and isn't driving productivity (labor, capital, and even technology), but it leads to a more complex academic exercise, making MFP not something that is easily understood by noneconomists (such as corporate managers, thus rendering it useless beyond theoretical constructs). But using different measurement techniques changes the productivity result: in using MFP, the Organization for Economic Co-Operation and Development (OECD) found U.S. productivity gains from 1996 to 2004 of 1.2 percent to be much lower than the official government result.[9] In fact, as is shown in Figure 6.3; the U.S. productivity miracle becomes much less impressive and more reflective of our current state economy.

This once again supports the view that the productivity gains associated with IT spending in the late 20th to early 21st century may not have been as originally advertised, given the influence of other factors. U.S. labor clearly enjoyed improvements as a function of the large-scale purchasing of PCs, telecommunications, and

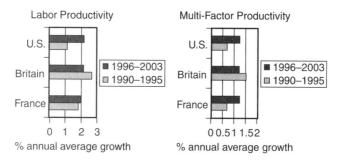

Figure 6.3 Different Methodologies in Measuring Productivity

services, but perhaps not as great a benefit when the overall capital investment costs and the lack of investment in intangible expenditures (investment in people) are taken into consideration. MFP sniffs this out perhaps better than labor productivity, but there are questions as to the accuracy level of both in real-life corporate environments. Needless to say, the measurement of productivity in corporations and in the U.S. economy needs clarification to support a move toward an improvement in results and overall competitiveness in the global economy.

CORPORATIONS: DO THEY UNDERSTAND REAL PRODUCTIVITY?

One of the biggest problems with measuring productivity in corporate operations is the inability to understand the factors that drive or profit from its growth. On the capital improvement side, companies are more willing to invest in capital spending for physical assets (computers, heavy equipment, new factories, etc.) than to make the investment necessary to transform these physical assets as productive tools for increasing the surplus value of the company. The difference is the need for an investment in intangible factors, which is often the key for achieving the benefits from the physical investment. This distinction of what may be construed as an intangible investment is very difficult to measure using current productivity measurements, and therefore, corporations don't understand it as a contributing factor, even though it is crucial to the physical technology rollout.

Without an appropriate measurement of productivity, many companies believe that a purely physical capital investment is their sole path to productivity, particularly in light of slower capital spending (meaning that less capital is available). Strong manufacturing organizations have succeeded when a capital investment is installed, along with an investment in strong business practices to achieve productivity.

From a labor standpoint, many economists are biased into believing that very little improvement can be driven from labor without a capital investment, but this shouldn't be the case, by definition. During the bloated corpocracy days of the 1950s through the 1970s, there was a dangerously bureaucratic definition of productivity tied to administration and organization. There was not an understanding of how the labor factor must also improve without a capital investment in order to increase the surplus value of the corporation, because this approach doesn't translate well into an econometric formula. With the 1980s came the days of reengineering, which were really more a function of destructive destruction driven by the disorganization managers than improvements for how business processes should be optimized, including an infusion of capital investment.

Today, there is no measurement tool for corporations to allow them to understand how productivity can be derived through business-process reengineering, versus creating a state of constant change and chaos. Likewise, most corporate managers have no idea how to drive productivity, versus being in the camp of either the complacent organization man or the disruptive disorganization manager. It's scarcely an issue that appears in the mathematical models of the macroeconomist or in the daily routines of the corporate manager. One thing is for sure: efforts such as business-process reengineering cannot be easily measured (if at all) using standard measurements of productivity such as labor productivity and MFP. Therefore, true efforts to improve business processes are often ignored, given the difficulties of measurement and of their implementation.

Simply put, both the labor productivity and MFP measurements are of little practical use to the U.S. business operation in understanding productivity and competitiveness in the marketplace. Measuring productivity using labor productivity isn't at all consistent with how corporations make productivity decisions. If a manufacturing company is seeking expansion of its production process, as one option, it can build a highly automated plant and look for a highly educated workforce to work in this plant. The other option (keeping this example simplified to two options) is for the company to outsource operations to a low-wage, low-technology operation, run by a third party, often offshore.

It's fairly obvious that a decision based on labor productivity pro forma would automatically conclude that the choice to make is that of the highly automated facility, supported by a highly educated workforce, other things being equal. Yet, as we all know today, CFOs of MNCs aren't keen on approving large capital expenditures to achieve productivity in the model of Henry Ford and his River Rouge plant. Instead, a much lower capital expenditure—in a foreign plant, using low labor rates—defines productivity for a growing number of MNCs. And the U.S. financial accounting system has been in full support.

MFP isn't the silver bullet in calculating productivity, even if it is a better technique than the labor productivity definition. In manufacturing, MFP is typically measured using KLEMS: capital (K), labor (L), energy (E), materials (M), and purchased business services (S). One of the problems with using MFP is that it is especially difficult to measure, particularly in comparison to labor productivity. But perhaps an even greater problem with using this technique is the fundamental issue of what this productivity index measures. Outsourced labor isn't considered labor anymore, but instead it masquerades as a purchased business service. So, even though MFP is a more effective and aggregate economic approach to measuring productivity, the use of outsourcing for the labor function really distorts the productivity measurement of the company.

Of great concern in the measurement of outsourcing labor in the productivity determination is how these data are captured, because the measurement is not based on direct evidence, but rather on data collected from Business Expenses Survey (BES), which is administered to companies in the wholesale, retail, and services sectors. This survey is conducted twice per decade; the last survey was conducted in 2002. According to the Census Web site, 2007 BES data won't be published until March 2009, essentially making the data obsolete before they even hit the streets!

Companies that complete this survey are asked to report their expenditures on contract labor, defined as "persons who are not on your payroll but are supplied through a contract with another company to perform specific jobs." It is assumed that the companies that answer this survey complete the survey properly, including all workers who fit this category. Therefore, the data being used to construct KLEMS productivity statistics are old (six years old) and of a questionable degree of reliability and validity, given that these data are accumulated as a function of a survey of a company that may or may not be answering the survey properly. There is no direct evidence placed into this data of outsourcing activity. As we know, in today's dynamic, fast-changing global economy, six years is an eternity. So much for the validity of even using MFP analysis to understand productivity and the degree to which it is affected by worker improvements, capital initiatives, or even outsourcing techniques for short-term cost reduction.

HOW BAD PRODUCTIVITY DECISIONS ARE MADE

Consider an example of how productivity in the manufacturing sector can be shown to improve as a function of outsourcing. If a piece of sophisticated equipment is being manufactured by an MNC based in the United States, the company may want to determine whether it is more productive to develop and produce this product in the United States or in China. Although the cost of R&D engineering in China is assumed to be 20 percent of that in the United States, it is also assumed that Chinese engineers take twice the number of hours to develop the product than U.S. engineers or require a significant intangible capital investment in training (leading to quality issues if not done). If true economic techniques are in place to understand the number of hours spent to develop this product, the company's productivity would decline if shipping the work process to China led to an increased number of hours needed to perform the task relative to design, technology, and quality, plus other logistical factors.

Furthermore, there is no way to measure the impact on the product life cycle and on the marketing of separating pieces of the supply chain. However, MFP can be used and the Chinese labor can then be measured as a separate input, weighed by its cost share. As a result, MFP actually rises—not only from an economics standpoint but from a financial accounting standpoint, because the process of outsourcing to China appears to be the cost-beneficial approach, considering the cost of labor as a bigger factor, potentially, than other factors such as customer service, logistics, and quality (not even considering the impact on U.S. labor markets). The question is whether this analysis leads to the correct decision for the corporation in how productivity is measured today.

There are endless examples of how both government economics and corporate statistics support this paradigm shift in how to measure productivity improperly. Consider a large consumer products company (which shall remain nameless) that manufactures billions of dollars' worth of a staple product that retails for $3. This product is a very light product (both the product and the packaging) and can be produced without the use of much human labor. This seems to be the perfect product for the company to optimize manufacturing in the United States, right?

First, the large percentage of its market share is in the United States, with a small but growing market presence currently in Asia. Second, with it being a lightweight product, there are questions as to whether—from the standpoint of an overall supply chain (planning, manufacturing, inventory, ordering, shipping, etc.)—it makes sense in terms of cost to produce the product in Asia or South America and ship it to the United States. Third, with it being a highly automated manufacturing process, there are questions as to whether South America and Asia can achieve this company's expected level of quality to the customer. The company being discussed has a long history of customer satisfaction regarding the quality of its product.

From this standpoint, all of the stars appear to be aligned for the company's management to analyze the variables and to seek improvements within a U.S. manufacturing and R&D environment (keeping product life-cycle management tightly integrated). You can probably guess what happened next in this example: corporate management and finance did a productivity analysis of the product and decided to move production operations to Asia and South America.

From a corporate standpoint, this decision was doomed from the start, given the nature of the product and the reliance in the product life-cycle process on higher technology manufacturing. In hindsight, it was an obvious mistake in terms of profitability and productivity. Production facilities in the United States were shut down as a result, and senior leadership was unwilling to admit to making a mistake.

This decision had an initial favorable impact on the company's financial statements, given how plant shutdowns and other restructuring costs are able to be taken off income and balance sheets. However, after the initial benefits, the story line has changed: quality has suffered, product image is hurt, and higher-paying jobs have been lost—all of which have direct impact on a company's product life-cycle process and on the U.S. economy. Clearly, a lack of classical management techniques allows a highly esteemed modern corporation to make such a poor decision.

On the services side, the concept of shared services is all the rage today at U.S. corporations and is viewed by some to be, in theory, a diametrically opposite business model from outsourcing. Shared services is conventionally defined as the centralization of a function to an internal service provider that is present in multiple locations in an organization, such as backroom functions of human resources, finance, or information services.

Previously, the main driver of a shared services concept was technology, achieving productivity of some sort through automation, economies of scale, and/or specialization. In a finance department, the use of an Enterprise Resource Planning (ERP) system, scanners, and the streamlining of processes are typically what companies have done within their internal operations. In some cases, companies have gained productivity improvements through an internal shared services concept; in other cases, they have not.

However, increasingly, companies are redefining shared services, not as a realignment of their internal organization, seeking gains through technological change that drives productivity, but rather through outsourcing these functions to overseas operations—where the name of the game is more about lower wages than it is about process improvements and technological enhancements. Many of the large IT service providers (IBM, HP, Accenture, and others) have set up back-room operations in Mumbai or Bangalore, India, in order to process billions of dollars of payables for U.S. operations. In many cases, they are not using cutting-edge methods of payment-processing techniques that would be expected from high-tech companies, relying instead on lower labor costs.

Although this isn't empirically proven, I've come across many executives who have outsourced payment processing overseas and have experienced more problems as a result, as would be expected (lower labor costs, cultural issues, logistics, etc.). I've also come across operations in India that are using outdated technologies instead of keeping work in-house with up-to-date technologies. And, in many cases, the amount of labor to process an accounts payable through an overseas model is less productive when the number of worker-hours involved are factored in but more productive when the outsourced labor is considered to be a variable outside of the labor input.

None of this takes into account rework costs or related costs associated with poor service (such as late payments to suppliers). This is not an anti-offshoring opinion at all, but rather a statement of fact based on the difference between the economic value of outsourcing, the productivity measurement of it, and even the corporate accounting representation of it. As previously mentioned, outsourcing by itself cannot drive productivity, as technology is able to do.

REAL PRODUCTIVITY AND CLASSICAL MANAGEMENT: THE EQUATION FOR SUCCESS

Today's corporate managers don't understand this to be the case, and there is no clear-cut way for corporate managers to measure productivity, no rules of the game defined in management to help them. The company sets its strategic direction, and, in almost every case, a public corporation defers to decisions that increase short-term, accounting surplus value and improve the value of the company on the open market. And most corporate managers wishing to apply the rules of classical management in contrast to this environment are quickly instructed to do otherwise. This isn't a question of one rogue company choosing to circumvent management and the true rules of productivity, but rather the entire system that is in place today, with few exceptions.

So there you have it: the economic techniques in place to measure productivity in the U.S. economy are poorly defined and misunderstood, academic, of little use to business operations, antiquated (using survey techniques, as an example), based on outdated data (measurements twice per decade, despite how quickly the global economy is transforming), and extremely inadequate—whether the choice of measurement for productivity is the labor productivity approach, which is most widely used, or the MFP method, which appears to be slightly more accurate. And what's so amazing is that productivity as a function of the U.S. economy has been lauded as a miracle since the 1990s, without much of a clear explanation as to why—other than that measured numbers have proven it out as such.

The greatest problem is that this current definition of productivity actually hurts worker compensation instead of promoting it, creating a win-loss proposition that can never lead to optimal results. Some suggest that wages and productivity have improved together. One noted example is Martin Feldman's working paper, which concludes that real compensation has kept up with productivity by including compensation for managers versus focusing on hourly wages alone (washing away the impact of income-inequality issues). However, his assumptions are questionable because he included higher benefit costs, not an increase in real wages.

Other economists suggest that real wages shouldn't keep up with productivity growth rates because technological change should have a greater impact on productivity than the worker's contribution. Both of these theories are incongruent with the way in which productivity used to be looked at as a covenant between all parties to share in the surplus value of the company. Productivity cannot be viewed as optimal unless the target is to improve in some sort of balanced manner.

Productivity measurements of today—which distort the data by showing growth figures by measuring the equation inappropriately and which confuse cost reduction with productivity—are not helping matters. The current state of rapid erosion in our economy—which supposedly came from out of nowhere, even though the economic collapse was, in reality, a slow train wreck—supports my conclusions.

There's no way around it: productivity's true measurement cannot exist without classical management, and classical management cannot exist without productivity's true measurement. Today we have neither, and yet we have workers, managers, investors, and consumers asking what's wrong with our economy! Ronald Reagan noted when he was President that economists unsuccessfully try to model what happens in real life, and many of our government agencies and corporations are making decisions in this flawed *Alice in Wonderland* model.

Despite what the statistics are telling us about productivity, it shouldn't be all that difficult to comprehend that our national economy is not as productive as the statistics indicate. Income distribution or surplus value distribution is a factor of productivity as well: the current record level of income inequality, when measured properly, has had an impact on real productivity. A worker isn't more productive simply by making a lower wage, being a temporary worker, or even by losing his or her job to an overseas operation, but the economic statistics suggest that this is the case.

A corporate manager isn't making a very efficient decision to outsource the production of a product to a developing nation if that action disrupts the entire product life-cycle process for the product. We as managers, workers, investors, and consumers must start living in our real world instead of in this *Alice in Wonderland* world where up is down and down is up.

Certainly, the U.S. economic model of the 1950s was a lot simpler, with a larger percentage of our economy being national, not global, with less global competition and involvement, and a regulated environment that restrained many of the constituents (workers, managers, investors, consumers) from expecting too much. The world was much different then, and there weren't a billion entrants from the developing nations all looking for their piece of the American Dream or globalization. But, given the craziness and complexity, shouldn't this lead to our business environment needing the discipline of classical management more instead of less?

Management's rigidity and structure in the post-World War II era wasn't perfect, but it was more cognizant of the true definition of productivity. The policy makers of that time remembered the days of the robber baron, when workers and consumers were left hanging at the expense of the investor or owner. Some innovative management theorists then invented the American Dream, which was perfected by Henry Ford in his wisdom to improve the lot of both the worker and the consumer at the same time. There perhaps is no better example of productivity than one that enables the middle-class income to grow at the same time as it reduces the prices of goods, enables the demand of production to grow, produces a multiplier effect on the economy, and strengthens the company through solid product life-cycle management practices. Today, there is even a greater need for classical management to come to the rescue.

Can the Wal-Mart example be seen in the same light? As a U.S. corporation, Wal-Mart, in effect, broke the mold for management in retail: increase the surplus value of the company solely by having the lowest price. The absolute lowest price has been achieved at Wal-Mart by economies of scale; beating suppliers into submission to lower the price, including the drive to offshoring; superior logistics to reduce supply chain costs; and lower worker wages. There is no question that, in stock market terms, Wal-Mart is one of the greatest retail stories ever, and it has been so successful that it has completely transformed the entire retail industry. With revenue that has grown to more than $300 billion from less than $16 billion a little more than 20 years ago, Wal-Mart has been an unbridled success in terms of what it has offered to its investors and how it has transformed the definition of a consumer in the purest term.

I remember that when I was growing up and I'd visit my grandmother in Baltimore city, we'd have to walk to five different stores just to do her grocery shopping. Today, it still amazes me to walk into a Wal-Mart, Target, or K-Mart and see a family's shopping cart roll by with eggs, a color TV, and men's underwear, all at the lowest price possible! In this purest sense of the term, this is consumers' heaven: a time-saver because they know that they need to go to no place other than Wal-Mart to meet their family's needs. But, of course, you know the rest of the story.

Wal-Mart is not the villain here, even if its business practices don't follow the classical management rule of optimization between consumers, workers, managers, and investors. From the standpoint of today's false productivity, Wal-Mart is the champ, with the highest revenue and a very healthy market position in the United States and internationally. Consumers appear to be happy with its prices and choices, and investors are content with its earnings—so it matters less to the company if workers aren't happy with their compensation and if suppliers feel squeezed in the supply chain. There are fewer places to work, fewer places to shop, and—for suppliers—fewer retailers to distribute your product into. Consumers and investors have demanded more and more Wal-Marts, cheaper and cheaper prices.

A reverse process was created from Henry Ford's welfare capitalism: instead of the welfare of workers enabling consumers and them enabling workers in return, the Wal-Mart model achieved lower prices at the expense of workers, which is now having an adverse impact on the consumer market!

Forget the economists: consumers and investors defined productivity in such terms, validating the ridiculous econometric techniques mentioned in this chapter. Productivity died, and the classical managers weren't there to save it. Consumers lusted for something more than productivity, driven obsessively for more, more, more. We all believed in this economic limitlessness, expecting the benefits to never end, for the shoe to never drop, while we obsessively craved the Wal-Mart experience.

In the year 2008, we were all standing around asking what happened. Corporate managers are continuing this economic limitlessness process, keeping the dream alive for our next stock option or bonus payout. We've traded real productivity for economic limitlessness, ignoring the obvious realities of living in a finite world. And now we look out on the horizon, angrily seeking the scalps of the Chinese, Arabs, and Russians who have been taking advantage of us for so long, at least from the distorted perceptions of a growing percentage of Americans. We still refuse to look into the mirror.

The rest of this book is about solutions, about what is possible in the United States, a country with a vibrant and leading-edge discipline of management and productivity. The fact that classical management and productivity are linked so closely to one another historically is a sign of promise, particularly given how these disciplines have progressed so tightly in the United States' past. Management and productivity are missing elements in attracting MNCs to operate in the United States versus in Asia and other developing areas. Establishing and enabling the best management system in the world would be a huge competitive advantage for our operations, and it would give us an edge at least equal to the advantage that some of these nations have relative to low-cost labor.

In closing this chapter, I want to quote Albert Einstein, who once noted, "if you are out to describe the truth, leave elegance to the tailor." These solutions don't need to be overly complicated to be effective. What is needed is effectiveness, simplicity, and a return to the basics.

Solutions for Restoring Value in the U.S. Economy

"If you change the way you look at things, the things you look at change."

Dr. Wayne Dyer

I didn't quite know what to expect from the audience on a beautiful early spring day in April 2008 at a speaking engagement for my book, *An Easy Out,* at the midtown Manhattan Science, Industry, and Business Library. How many people, within a few miles up Broadway from Wall Street, were interested in hearing about the declining U.S. economic position on a day when the Dow Jones Industrials had closed at 12,619, just a few points off the year's high? Apparently, not as many people as I thought. The people who did attend were typical of the demographics from any other city, although there seemed to be a few bond trader types in the audience, who scoffed at my opening line: "as sunny as the day is today, it's as bad as our economy is." When I spoke of the financial bubble that continued to brew just a few miles up the road, I received some eye rolls and a few nods.

The largely middle-class audience was unsuspecting of what October 2008 would present to them; they were unaware that we were just months away from one of the greatest financial crises in our nation's history. Nothing against my detractors, but intelligence is worth little when it's focused on the wrong problem. The problem that I've focused on in the first six chapters of this book is the role of management and productivity in U.S. corporations and the economy. This is the right place to start. The solutions that I will be proposing are fundamentally the same as those that I discussed in April when your 401(k) was worth 25 percent more, your mortgage and money market funds were stable, and you weren't as worried about your job as you are today. Are economic and business solutions that change with the state of the economy real solutions if the fundamental problem remains the same? If we've learned anything over the past 30 years, it should be that the answer is no.

Even so, the critics are out there and they will refute the idea that management is dead and productivity is a lost art, bristling at any solution that dares to veer away from conventional wisdom and emotional reaction. Einstein's notion that "insanity is doing the same thing over and over again and expecting different results" rings true here. Through the years of my career, I've found that this correlation between management and productivity to be of critical importance to the success of a corporation and an economy, and the same tired remedies of government intervention and financial engineering have been proven deficient over and over again.

From the dawn of the 20th century until the middle of the 20th century, true productivity soared in the U.S. economy at the same time as the classical definition of management was originated, developed, and enabled. Proving this case can be done not only through an identification of the problem but also through an implementation of the solutions. The solutions presented in this chapter will be challenging, but one should be wary if they weren't. After all, cleaning up a slow train wreck takes time and effort, if done properly.

As noted in this book, my hypothesis is that the corporate manager can drive long-term value in U.S. business operations when an environment of classical management is enabled to focus on real productivity. The problem isn't the individual corporate manager, but rather the system of management. Today, we understand that our toxic economic environment was built on economic limitlessness more so than on the personalities of a few greedy, unethical management leaders. For years, we've gotten lost in the symptoms of characters like Ken Lay and Jeffrey Skilling of Enron rather than focusing on the root of the problem. We know that management of today doesn't make sense, even though Tom Peters and other gurus told us that we need to thrive in chaos, not necessarily rationalize it. As Alice said in *Alice in Wonderland*, "I can't explain myself, I'm afraid, Sir, because I'm not myself you see." A corporate manager isn't a manager in the classical sense, you see.

As I write this chapter during the fourth quarter of 2008, we are in the middle of a financial meltdown of our economy unlike anything that any of us have seen in our lifetimes. We are now in the middle of 1970s style stagflation of unstable oil prices, the potential of inflation (if money rates stay so close to a rate of 0 percent), unemployment, and a recession, and the worst may not have even arrived yet. September's Wall Street collapse is indicative of an economy built on financial transactions, a house of cards. If you watch CNBC *Bubblevision,* you'll hear of technical factors and econometric theory that continues to perpetuate the same story, promoting Einstein's definition of insanity. From this chapter, you'll learn of solutions based on real economics (not econometrics) that will be driven by a partnership of workers, managers, investors, and consumers, not solely through bond traders and think-tank analysts. They are solutions of productivity, based on Main Street activity, that of the classical manager.

According to Charles Morris's book, *The Trillion Dollar Meltdown,* the disasters of the 1970s were attributable to three primary roots: the loss of business vision, demographical shifts, and gross economic mismanagement.[1] I believe that the same categories of root causes apply today: the loss of business vision is the lack of a classical management focus and the failure of the private enterprise to enable management and productivity success. Likewise, the gross economic mismanagement is a function of a failed public economic policy that moved our solutions to improve U.S. competitiveness toward Wall Street instead of Main Street, to the central bankers and financial analysts rather than the middle class, middle manager of U.S. operations.

Before I discuss what the solutions need to be for 21st-century management, I'd like to provide a brief synopsis of what can't be considered a solution anymore. One, the role of management can no longer be reduced and replaced with technocratic policy and Wall Street bubble economics, the dream of economic limitlessness. This topic bears repeating, given the fallacious definitions of productivity that are so harmful and prevalent in our economy and corporations today and what appears to be no end in sight of this insanity. Given how painful our current economic conditions are, there will inevitably be a great sense of political expediency connected to solving the problem, which will lead to politicians emotionally looking for the easy-out, the next bubble to exploit, the next big thing that will give the public some hope.

In an article in *Newsweek* on September 1, 2008, economist Robert Samuelson accused both Barack Obama and John McCain of playing fantasy politics in much the same way many of us play fantasy baseball or football. Samuelson's message was that none of the politicians are serving up the difficult solutions that will add up to solving the problems because the voters aren't really interested in buying into it. Even Alan Greenspan, known in this book without affection as the serial bubbler, struggles with policies being promoted by either side of the political fence.

In the past 30 years, we've seen our economic superpower status dissipate in ways that we would have thought unimaginable during the 1970s. Who would have thought in the 1970s that Communist China would eventually be the holders of $1.8 trillion in U.S. debt and a major source of funding for our financial markets? Nobody then could have dreamed of this happening. If we stay on the course of bubble economics or follow the Keynesian technocrats, what will happen in the year 2030 that we can't dream today would ever be possible? Do we want to really find out? What we should not do is to buy into the same old fantasy solutions instead of discussing the sacrifice and heavy doses of unpopular medicine that are necessary. This book prescribes those unpopular yet effective medicines.

The first thing to talk about in terms of solutions is a new set of rules that will enable this 21st-century management in the corporate setting. These rules will redefine what 21st-century management will mean to the corporate manager, consultant, labor union, policy analyst, corporation, and business school. The quote from Alice in Wonderland bears repeating, "I'm not myself, you see," and we managers must understand that we are Alice as well (and not ourselves). We are not managers, because management is dead.

With these new rules, we can become managers again, right in the knick of time for the global economy. Corporate managers who understand and apply these rules will become more successful than their counterparts. MNCs that support managers who apply these rules will have a competitive advantage over their competitors who don't. Consulting firms that build these rules into their business models will be able to promote the right behaviors and practices for their clients, and they will be able to provide value added services that their clients really need. Policy analysts and government municipalities that understand these rules will be able to establish a business environment that will encourage MNCs to locate operations to the United States and provide the right stimulus packages for their constituents (workers and consumers). Labor unions can transform their operating models to take this into consideration and to partner with this 21st-century management, rather than promoting a contentious, nostalgic relationship. And lastly, the sacred ground for these new rules should be our business schools, teaching the next generations of what management is and what its role should be in the U.S. economy.

SOLUTION #1: RULES FOR A NEW DEFINITION OF MANAGEMENT

The new rules of management are as follows:

- Productivity.
  - Redefining productivity in real, not academic or econometric terms.
  - Training managers to understand the new definition of productivity to drive it at the corporation and economy.
  - Managers driving productivity that benefits both the public and private sectors concurrently.
- Economic Limits
  - Managers must work within economic limits, not without them.
  - The greatest economic growth comes from optimizing limits, not ignoring them.
  - Corporations or economies that seek economic limitlessness will be damaged by such assumptions in the future.
- Change
  - Change cannot be defined solely through chaos or disruption.
  - Variables can cause change through disruption (i.e., technology), but change isn't completed without stability (through training, process improvement, etc.).
  - Change is hard work and takes sacrifice.

How many corporate managers really understand the term productivity? Furthermore, is there a clear definition of the term tied to restoring value at the corporation and economy? The answer is negative on both fronts, and, therefore, you really can't blame corporate managers for this problem. The importance of corporate managers understanding the new rules of productivity is of critical importance to our economy, just as it was when Henry Ford understood its true meaning 100 years ago. To understand these new rules, managers must be trained to be systems thinkers, understanding the full story of how economic growth happens. Even though the term systems thinking wasn't in vogue 100 years ago, Henry Ford understood the meaning of this term and that a corporation is to function as an overall business system, not as a list of components.

The concept of systems thinking really defines productivity, because it views certain problems as parts of an overall system, rather than focusing on isolated outcomes, such as defining productivity solely as a function of labor, or on the outsourcing to Asia without understanding the full consequences of doing so to the product life cycle. System thinking mirrors our human environment to that of nature, with our ecosystems being the perfect system, when in harmony. Nature is always looking for perfect harmony in its environment, and, when an element of nature changes, it often changes the entire ecosystem surrounding it. Nature doesn't maximize; it optimizes.

Managers have control over a corporation and economy much as nature has control over the ecosystem. When disturbances occur, nature seeks harmony through changes throughout the system: too much of any singular disturbance ruins the ecosystem. Productivity is just that—harmony across the entire economic system (individual corporation or economy, public and private sectors)—and, when done properly, it adapts accordingly to achieve this harmony. When this occurs, real productivity and surplus value occur, optimizing the wealth across all stakeholders. This isn't a utopia, but rather an economic condition that was proven possible in our past.

SOLUTION #2: A NEW MODEL FOR THE DISCIPLINE OF ECONOMICS

This solution will provide the framework for the corporate manager, corporation, and other stakeholders for why this definition of productivity must be understood and implemented. Unfortunately, today's corporate managers have no incentive to be systems thinkers. Until they learn how to become systems thinkers and have an incentive to think that way, the definition of productivity will be inefficient and misguiding.

Corporate managers must begin to understand that their primary goal is to increase the company's surplus value via productivity, and the best way of achieving this is through being systems thinkers: balancing labor, capital, and technology through their role. It will not occur through relying on the academic econometric measurement tools of our statisticians, but rather in real-life situations that managers deal with every day. For this to happen, our corporate managers must learn and practice these rules.

There are examples of this happening in business today: Costco, Nucor Steel, and Coors Brewing Company are examples of productivity through this systems view of the product life-cycle process. If more Main Street corporate managers understood real productivity, Wall Street econometricians wouldn't be pressured to promote financially engineered solutions and government policy analysts would support a different approach.

One such Main Street systems thinker is Warren Buffett. Buffett's view on the markets and the economy is consistent with systems thinking: he noted that the market isn't efficient and that the financial industry is making money through increasing transactions without adding any value to the economy ("financial weapons of mass destruction" in Buffett terminology). Buffett's mentor was Benjamin Graham, a famous economist and investor, who once said that an investment is most intelligent when it is most businesslike and that investors must look at stocks as though they were businesses.

These statements seem rather simple and deductive, but such logic appears to be largely missing today. Central bankers, financial analysts, economists, and inefficient managers have defined productivity much differently than Warren Buffett, and the results have spoken for themselves. Today, Buffett still draws more than 20,000 attendees for his shareholder's conference, and the audience hangs on his every word, promoting real productivity through systems thinking. Only through looking at a stock as a business—optimizing labor, capital, and technology—has Warren Buffett seen productivity differently than others, which has contributed to his reputation as the Oracle of Omaha. As a manager, Buffett has understood productivity in ways that others, such Alan Greenspan, have not.

Defining the new rules of productivity returns corporate managers to being responsible for growth and innovation. However, for this to happen, the new rules of productivity must be understood by Wall Street and by government econometricians as well. Therefore, redefining productivity in more practical terms for use in Corporate America (how to optimize labor, capital, and technology and ensure that all constituents share in the increases to surplus) is one piece, but the other is also in the econometric definitions being used and promoted by policy analysts and statisticians as well.

The econometricians and policy analysts must understand how their definitions and applications of productivity have led us to the present economic collapse. Then, they must become a part of the real change that's needed: to redefine and evangelize this true definition of productivity, in both academic and corporate settings of economics, to improve U.S. business operations and the U.S. economy in its competitiveness in the global economy. Corporate managers, government economists, policy analysts, consultants, and business school professors must be trained to understand this new definition of productivity, rising like a Phoenix out of the ashes of the old approach that led us down our current path. If we don't educate and train business professionals in what happened, what's the chance of it not happening again?

The same logic applies today within corporate and consulting settings relative to the concept of economic limitlessness. With production methods having improved dramatically in the 19th and 20th centuries, economics increasingly was known as the dismal science, for having the audacity to suggest, as Thomas Malthus did in the late 18th to early 19th century, that the population would grow geometrically whereas the food supply and utilization of natural resources would only grow arithmetically, leading to a Malthusian catastrophe. Many social and economic experts believed that the Industrial Revolution, in effect, disproved the theory of the Malthusian catastrophe as a possibility, and, through technological innovations, we have been fooled to believe that economics is the social science of unlimited growth and thus unlimited revenue and profit.

Today's definition, through the use of econometrics, is that production resources and natural resources will not only enable corporations to continue to grow, but require them to (market dictum), and for the consumers to continue to want to consume more. U.S. workers and consumers have been the benefactors of economic limitlessness—until today, when the bubble burst. The role of the true economist had disappeared, and Malthus is thought of as a heretic to capitalism. In Malthus's day, there were about a billion people on the earth, and today there are more than 6.6 billion. According to Angus Maddison's statistics, there will be more than 8 billion people in 2030, all living with expectations based on the American Dream—but still within the same landmass, with fewer natural resource possibilities.

It was thought that the success of the Industrial Revolution effectively killed the purpose of economists, because there was no need for constraints and optimization when economic limitlessness was possible and even preferable. Econometricians arose—not to put limits on economics but rather to develop complex models for how unlimited growth would be possible. Economics and management both died together. Today, we must reincarnate the ideas of management and economics together through the understanding of limits, not limitlessness.

We must replace economic limitlessness with economic limits, not necessarily defined in dastardly terms as a Malthusian catastrophe, but defined within simpler economic (not econometric) terms. Our economists, technocrats, and policy makers must understand and be trained within these new rules of economic limits if we expect that MNCs will practice them through the optimization of labor, capital, and technology in order to achieve greater surplus value goals for their stakeholders than before.

New economic models must tie productivity to limits within the economy, leading to surplus growth for the stakeholders (both public and private). And, if this is the case, there will again be a need for the classical manager within the corporation in a role other than as a professional administrator or disorganization manager. And it is my hypothesis that this will lead to greater profit growth for the corporation, not less. It is my prediction that managers, corporate organizations, and economies that understand that optimizing limits will lead to growth, not the opposite, will prosper while others won't. This will be a major paradigm shift for business in the 21st century!

The definition of change must also be understood by the 21st-century manager. When I was working on my undergraduate degree in the mid 1980s, the futurist who spoke corporate change to me was Alvin Toffler. His books, *Future Shock, The Third Wave,* and *Powershift,* were some of the first books written to discuss what many people call the new economy. He inspired Mikhail Gorbachev, was ranked with Bill Gates and Peter Drucker as the most influential business leader of his time, and was noted by *People's Daily* as one of the top 50 foreigners who had shaped modern China! His brand of change considered not just the technological, but also the societal element of change as well. As Albert Einstein noted, "technological change is like an axe in the hands of a pathological criminal."[2] Toffler's influence on management and change was that the transformation started off as very disruptive and unrelenting but that it needed to become stable and had also to take into account the psyche of the individual and society in order to be accepted.

This was a different philosophy from that of many of the theorists who followed Toffler, who believed that change should remain disruptive and only be focused on the private sector. A state of constant change is the axe in the hands of the criminal, as Einstein warned us. Mary Shelley's epic novel, *Frankenstein,* was first published in 1818 and showed us how the Industrial Revolution could lead to the monster being the master, a bastardization of technological change. The post-industrial wave, Alvin Toffler's third wave, was unleashed on us starting in the 1970s, and we have yet to bring this monster under real control. Today, we have no control over the monster running our business environment. It is on us, and we are it, just as was the case during Mary Shelley's era.

As in a parent–child relationship, managers must nurture change, not perpetuate it and agitate on its behalf again and again. Today, the opposite is still in vogue, and managers perpetuate and agitate for change as a sign of being adaptive and conventional. Through my two decades of management involvement in business schools, academia, consulting, and corporations, I have worked hard to stabilize pockets of chaos to implement change, and, when I have been able to do so, I have achieved enormous benefits.

In a corporation, change must be done through people, and people shouldn't be agitated and disrupted, but rather led through opportunities. As difficult as it can be, the 21st-century manager must be in place to stabilize, not wreak havoc over the business environment. Good managers have a knack for how to do this, and it will be a skill of critical importance in our global economy. Therefore, change must be taught to managers as a tool to stabilize, not disrupt. As in nature, too much disruption leads to damage, not growth. Today, managers are captured and controlled by chaos and disruption; in the future, it needs to be the other way around. Change must eventually lead to stabilization for growth and innovation to occur.

SOLUTION #3: A BUSINESS CASE: IMPROVING THE PLIGHT OF WORKERS AND CONSUMERS

I sincerely believe that most corporations want to put its workers first, which they all state to be the case on their Web sites and via other media. The following are a few statements under the "Careers/Employment" section of the Web sites of two retail competitors:

> Welcome to **Company A** careers. As our associates can attest, working for **Company A** is the chance to be a part of a company unlike any other in the world. It's more than a job; it's a place to develop your skills and build a career with competitive pay and health benefits for you and your family. To work for **Company A** is to be welcomed into a diverse family, where the individual contributions of every associate are respected and valued. Above all, it's an opportunity to join a team who is helping the world live better every day.

> If you are an ambitious, energetic person who enjoys a fast-paced team environment laced with challenges and opportunities, you've come to the right place. Our successful employees are service-oriented people with integrity and commitment toward a common goal – excellence in every area of their personal and business lives. Read on to discover how to pursue employment opportunities with us. **Company B** offers great jobs, great pay, great benefits and a great place to work.

Can you guess who these two large retailers are? Or, more important, can you guess which of these large retailers has a well-recognized reputation for being a worker-friendly employer versus the company that has a reputation for being an unfriendly one? Probably not. **Company A** is Wal-Mart, the company demonized as worker-unfriendly and **Company B** is Costco, the company praised as worker-friendly. Perhaps both of these great companies aspire to have worker-friendly environments, but, in application, they have much different results. Both Wal-Mart and Costco have been profitable and growing companies, as shown in Figure 7.1. Wal-Mart may be the world's largest retailer, but Costco's growth and relationship with Wall Street may actually be superior, as is indicated by the following statistics.

The information shown in Figure 7.1 delivers a mixed message story to Wall Street regarding the performance of these two retailers. By looking solely at the white columns, Wal-Mart is the runaway champion of retail—the biggest, most

	Revenue	Return on Assets	Return On Equity	Operating Margin	Earnings Growth	P-E Ratio
Wal-Mart	397 billion	9.0%	20.8%	5.8%	16.8%	15.5%
Costco	70.3 billion	6.1%	14.3%	2.8%	31.7%	20.8%

Figure 7.1 Wal-Mart Versus Costco Financial Comparison

celebrated retail story of all time. Wal-Mart's story is well documented—through squeezing suppliers ("making them more efficient") and keeping labor costs low—but this is what Wall Street demands from the company, correct? Well, maybe not, as indicated by the grey boxes in Figure 7.1.

With a lower operating margin than Wal-Mart, Costco is still showing greater earnings growth, largely through a stronger growth in customer loyalty and new business. This has led the investment community placing a premium on Costco's stock in comparison to Wal-Mart's, with Costco's Price-Earnings ratio 25 percent higher than Wal-Mart's. This is the untold story: that real productivity can be rewarded by Wall Street analysts if management has an effective product life-cycle management strategy to benefit all stakeholders.

The story line of Costco's development is the business case for management that is mentioned in Solution #3 and an example of today's 21st-century management, as follows:

1. Worker's pay: Costco's average pay of $17 per hour is 42 percent higher, on average, than Wal-Mart's.
2. Employee benefits: Costco's employees paid 4 percent of their health care costs until pressured by Wall Street, and it was raised to 8 percent. Retail average is 25 percent, with Wal-Mart employees paying 34 percent plus deductible (with 48 percent of employees being covered versus 82 percent of Costco's).
3. Worker productivity: Costco's revenue per employee is five times higher than Wal-Mart's, and its turnover for the first year is 20 percent, much lower than Wal-Mart's 50 percent. Worker turnover for Wal-Mart employees is 50 percent versus Costco's 24 percent.[3]
4. CEO pay: Jim Sinegal, CEO of Costco, had a salary of $350,000 in 2007, with stock options increasing his compensation to $2.1 million. Contrast this compensation to that of Lee Scott, former CEO of Wal-Mart, with a total salary of $29.7 million in 2007. In 2006, Sinegal didn't even get a bonus because the company had missed its financial targets, an unheard of statement for one of the largest U.S. corporations.
5. Board of Directors: Charlie Munger, Warren Buffett's long-time Berkshire Hathaway partner, has been a director at Costco for 10 years. "Retailing isn't rocket science. Costco has figured out the big, simple things and executed with total fanaticism," Munger noted in 2007.[4]
6. Profit margins: For the good of the consumer, Costco has a rule that no branded item can have a margin greater than 14 percent, and no private label item more than 15 percent. This is in contrast to the average markup for a supermarket of 25 percent and for a department store of 50 percent. Wal-Mart doesn't have the same rule as Costco on its markups, and it's done to maximize its operating margin versus an optimization for all stakeholders in its product life cycle.

Costco's story is the prototypical business case statement for 21st-century management: a balance of the surplus value between consumers, workers, investors, and management. But this story is atypical today:

> "From the perspective of investors, Costco's benefits are overly generous," says Bill Dreher, retailing analyst with Deutsche Bank Securities Inc. "Public companies need to care for shareholders first. Costco runs its business like it is a private company." Mr. Dreher says the unusually high wages and benefits contribute to investor concerns that profit margins at Costco aren't as high as they should be.

> "The last thing I want people to believe is that I don't care about the shareholder," says Jim Sinegal, Costco's president and chief executive since 1993. "But I happen to believe that in order to reward the shareholder in the long term, you have to please your customers and workers."[5]

Costco is a remarkable story of 21st-century management, much like that of Henry Ford and his company 100 years ago. In 1908, Henry Ford was called a traitor by his colleagues and one who misapplied biblical principles, as quoted in chapter one. Today, Jim Sinegal has been castigated by some Wall Street analysts, who sound eerily similar to those robber barons of yesteryear, who carried the same ill grievances against optimization. Sinegal is a man who has spent 50 years in retail, and he understands the importance of business principles over financial engineering ones. Sinegal once noted that Wall Street will make money today and tomorrow, but he wants to build a company that will be here 50 or 60 years from now. This is the same viewpoint that Henry Ford expressed 100 years ago. It is a much different from the conventional wisdom in U.S. business today, as is evident in an internal Wal-Mart memo written by M. Susan Chamber, executive vice president of benefits:

> Given the impact of tenure on wages and benefits, the cost of an Associate with 7 years of tenure is almost 55 percent more than the cost of an Associate with 1 year of tenure, yet there is no difference in his or her productivity. Moreover, because we pay an Associate more in salary and benefit as his or her tenure increases, we are pricing that Associate out of the labor market, increasing the likelihood that he or she will stay with Wal-Mart.[6]

The term "Walmartization" is the antithesis of Solution #3, whereas the Costco model is the example of the solution. Walmartization has become the business model cliché of addition through subtraction (achieving business growth through cost reductions rather than investments), whether it is through retail or Corporate America. Research on Wal-Mart's impact on employment is inconclusive regarding whether or not it adds or subtracts jobs to our economy, but it is clear that it has had a negative impact on wages.[7]

But Wal-Mart isn't the villain here. Rather, Costco is the model; the former is more the rule and the latter more the exception. When companies cut wages and benefits for the sake of profitability, as Wal-Mart has done, it may appear to be a financially wise move, in the short-run, but it must be viewed suspiciously in the long-term. Is it possible for more corporate managers to aspire to become Jim Sinegal instead of Lee Scott? It is possible, but only if the system of management enables them to do so, which, today, it does not.

Corporate leaders take note: not only is Solution #3 a possibility for you and your company, the future welfare of your corporation depends on it. For instance, consider the case of my employer, the Coors Brewing Company, the third-largest brewing company in the United States and the operators of the world's largest brewery (at the time of this writing under a pending merger with Miller Brewing Company). In this world's largest facility, there is a highly tenured workforce that is seen as a blessing, not a financial curse. Certainly, having a more tenured workforce can be seen as a curse on Wall Street because of labor and benefit costs, but not so for Coors in Golden, Colorado. Over the past two years, production capacity at this older brewery increased significantly through process-improvement efforts driven by the workforce. Through a mutual sense of respect and benefit between the workforce and management, such accomplishments were made possible, and they have enabled Coors manufacturing to support the company's sales and marketing goals and initiatives to achieve record levels of growth.

This is in contrast to another large manufacturer in Colorado, the Swift meat-packing plant, in Greeley, Colorado, which was raided and charged with using illegal workers and is now shipping in legal, low-paid workers from Somalia and still having labor difficulties (by not respecting the cultural mores of its work-force). As documented in the book, *Fast Food Nation,* this Swift plant has continued to find productivity improvements, much as Wal-Mart has: to seek to improve bottom-line results through the commodization of labor costs. This is in contrast to the Coors Brewing Company, which has achieved true productivity through a tenured workforce of 25-, 30-, and 35-year employees.

It is a business case of improving the plight of the workers instead of commoditizing them. Production workers must be understood as a component of the product life cycle, rather than as a commodity to be minimized. Doing so has proven to be a practical and profitable policy for workers, stockholders, managers, and even consumers. It is an example of the principles of 1908 that enabled our economy to grow alongside our corporations. It is my theory that it will also be a practical and profitable policy of the future.

Nucor Steel is another example of how Solution #3 works in business today. As shown in Figure 7.2, the United States is no longer a giant manufacturer in the steel industry. China is responsible for one-third of all steel production in the world and the United States is responsible for less than 10 percent of the world market (the United States is also the largest importer of steel). Today, the U.S. steel sector is but a shadow of a once-proud tradition; U.S. labor unions are accusing foreign steel producers of dumping excess steel capacity into the U.S. market, putting serious pressure on U.S. manufacturers. At the beginning of the 21st century, more than 20 steel companies were forced into bankruptcy and 25,000

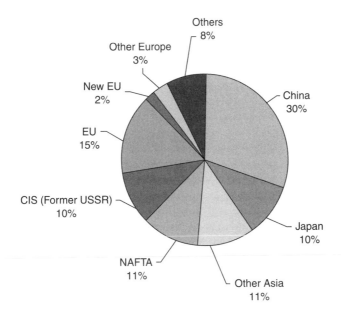

Figure 7.2 World Steel Production

Source: Wiki-Invest, 2008

workers lost their jobs, according to the United Steelworkers of America (USWA); this was on top of massive manufacturing losses that had occurred over the prior two decades in a competitive global environment.

Today, even amid the debris in the industry of a failed relationship between the labor unions, workers, management, consumers, and shareholders, Nucor Steel has emerged as a hope within a virtually hopeless environment. Operating in a much different environment from that of U.S. Steel (Andrew Carnegie's old company, which used to produce two-thirds of all U.S. steel and now handles less than 10 percent), Nucor Steel has a business model that truly optimizes labor, capital, and technology as an example of 21st-century management. Nucor is the largest steel producer in the United States, with sales of more than $6.2 billion annually. It is also the nation's largest recycler, recycling more than 14 million tons of scrap steel annually.

For a company facing bankruptcy in 1964 amid a tough industry, how did Nucor Steel survive and thrive? For one, Nucor is a nonunion operation, believing that unions in the steel industry have been a destructive force in terms of productivity and progress. This doesn't mean that Nucor has done any union-busting in its operations, because it hasn't had to. Instead, Nucor has never laid off an employee because of a work stoppage; workers are paid incentive bonuses, which can be 80 to 150 percent of an employee's base pay, executive compensation is lower than at its competitors, and the company has a policy of egalitarian benefits that is almost beyond belief—such as senior executives who do not qualify for certain benefits that lower-level employees have.

Beyond putting the worker first (including listing the names of all 18,000 workers on the cover of its annual statement), Nucor has been a technological leader in the United States, being the first company to use electric arc furnaces for melting recycled steel. Not only have these new production technologies enabled a massive degree of car recycling (10 million cars in 2007), it has also reduced the energy use for these manufacturing facilities, the space needed required to build a steel mill, and the capital associated with such a project. And such efforts have paid off with Wall Street, as is evident by looking at Nucor's stock price over the past five years. Costco, Coors, and Nucor all have the same pattern of 21st-century management optimization, and, as a result, Wall Street has noticed and rewarded these companies.

Manufacturing operations have been at risk in the United States for decades now, and a lot of companies from our past are no longer in business today. Revere Copper Products is one of the oldest, if not the oldest, manufacturing companies in the United States, founded in 1801 by Paul Revere himself. Today, Revere Copper is not only a successful manufacturer of copper and alloy products amid a competitive global environment, it is privately owned, with its only shareholders being its employees. It is a manufacturing company that not only succeeds in a competitive market via strong business principles, but also by improving the fate of its workers through employee ownership. Success in manufacturing is possible in the United States in a business case that values the employee, a classical management concept! U.S. corporations, take note of the blueprint for success in the future global economy!

SOLUTION #4: MANAGERS OWNING PRODUCT LIFE-CYCLE MANAGEMENT

As mentioned under Solution #1, productivity must be redefined in systems thinking terms rather than compartmentalization, as it is today. In 1990, the whole concept of the product life-cycle management unintentionally took a turn for the worse when Gary Hamel and C. K. Prahalad published *The Core Competence of the Corporation*. Of similar background and profile to Tom Peters, Hamel, a consulting type (he founded Strategos, a famous consulting firm) who made millions and, with Prahalad, inspired managers and corporations to focus on what they are good at and to outsource what they aren't good at, allowing the company to concentrate on its strengths.

Indirectly, the popularity of these ideas triggered a chain of events that pronounced the decoupling of the product lifecycle process, which then led to the sum of the parts being greater than the whole. In this world that was so crazy about core competency, there was less need for an integrated product life-cycle process, in the style of Henry Ford or General Motors in the early 20th century, and more need for an approach to decoupling and cost-reducing areas that used a method of addition through subtraction.

In particular, manufacturing became a prime opportunity for offshoring; managers believed that the ideation, R&D, product design, specifications, logistics, and other aspects of the product life cycle could remain intact when such a big piece of the overall puzzle was shipped away, in some cases to an operation with a 12-hour time difference, a much different culture, and a lower-paid, less-educated workforce without an integrated strategy. Offshoring can be a successful endeavor, but the continuation of offshoring without an accompanying understanding of the overall value proposition of an intact product life-cycle process can be problematic. Irrational outsourcing has often been the result of a continuation of poor management practices.

This is not solely a matter of public policy, but also of private, corporate common sense. Keeping manufacturing tied to R&D and to other aspects of the product life-cycle process can provide a very effective business practice, tied to top-line growth. As an example of how separation of the life cycle can become problematic, consider the Mattel toy recall that was so heavily covered by the media in August 2007. Toys produced in China were found to contain traces of lead paint, and magnets were discovered to be a choking hazard for small children. This became a media sensation for pundits and politicians who wanted to politicize the event, with China portrayed as uncaring regarding the safety of our children, as President-elect Barack Obama said in December 2007:

> "I would stop the import of all toys from China. Now I have to say, that's about 80 percent of toys that are being imported right now," he said, but he did not provide details on how such a ban would be carried out.[8]

A missing element of the story wasn't being publicized; as the owner of the product, it is the responsibility of the Mattel Corporation to have discovered the poor and unsafe design of the product, not the factory in China. In the Mattel case, as in quite a few of these product quality issues, the most important concern isn't the efficiency and quality levels of the production facilities located overseas, but rather the separation of the manufacturing portion of the cycle from the rest of the product life-cycle process. In an effort to save face, Mattel Corporation issued a public apology to China's safety chief, Li Changjang, as reporters and lawyers looked on:

> "Mattel takes full responsibility for these recalls and apologizes personally to you, the Chinese people, and all of our customers who received the toys," Thomas A. Debrowski, Mattel's executive vice president for worldwide operations, told Li.[9]

In its role as the manufacturing center of the world, China manufactures a product's consistency as close to specification as possible, but it often doesn't design it. Computer programmers in India shouldn't always be to blame for software code that doesn't work—when the functional and technical software specifications are often developed in the United States, and those documents are "thrown over the wall" for Indian programmers to code and, many times, even test. These are typically failures in business process through and through and all too often blamed on the offshore producers.

Unfortunately, by the time that corporate managers realize the errors of their ways, it is too late to do anything about it. These unfortunate decisions are made by managers who are chasing an outdated and shallow definition of productivity, which leads to a loss of economic surplus value in the end. The product life-cycle management process is the soul of the company, and too few managers today really understand this concept as a beginning-to-end business practice.

Today's 21st-century managers must understand the importance of product life-cycle management for their corporation as a function of good marketing and innovation. They may outsource a compartment of the product life-cycle process—but only after they understand the full impact on the entire life-cycle process and on all stakeholders—and keep these processes virtually intact through improved management discipline, regardless of whether a third party is involved.

Manufacturing in China or Mexico isn't the problem per se; the problem is insufficient classical management. Management needs to ensure that the separation of manufacturing doesn't have an adverse impact on the overall product life-cycle process. Typically, it's systems thinking that leads to productivity and sales, not compartmentalization. Sales and innovation cannot happen within it.

Corporations must be able to source production and processes all over the world, but with strong processes, management, and end-to-end life-cycle integrity. Corporate managers who respect the product life-cycle process do just that, whereas today's managers, who view a corporate operation as a myriad of siloed processes, don't. The good corporate leaders, like Warren Buffett, respect the product life cycle of a corporation, but there are many others who believe that the dismantling and relocating of processes and operations is simply a sign of smart globalization.

It is my hypothesis that well-respected sales and marketing executives of the future must recognize increasing sales as a function of a stable, end-to-end product life-cycle process versus a disjointed one, yet many U.S. companies today don't understand this. Future business growth in all sectors will connect with this concept of product life-cycle management, more so than in the past.

Not only is dismantling the product life cycle into compartments a productivity strain on the corporation, it is detrimental to the U.S. economy as well. As China grows its manufacturing responsibilities for the world, it gains an entrée into other aspects of the product life-cycle process, most importantly, R&D. As all nations understand and as noted in the discussion on the space race between the Soviets and the Americans, R&D are key elements of any economy and corporation. Foreign companies have only been in China for a little over a decade now, and, even in such a short time, China is gaining prowess in this critical element of corporate activity. R&D increased by 23 percent in 2006, primarily driven by private companies (71 percent), but also by the government and universities. By 2007, China had established 1,160 R&D centers, an amazing acceleration of activity in a short time![10]

Despite some challenges that could slow down this R&D growth in the future (human resource and intellectual property rights, standards), China and India will become emerging markets for R&D, no matter how the U.S. business environment responds to global challenges. However, when the business strategy compartmentalizes aspects of the product life cycle, as is happening, the process of moving responsibilities overseas will only be exacerbated, for a variety of reasons (including cheaper labor, even in the R&D centers). U.S. corporate managers must take note of this for the betterment of their corporations and national business environments.

And will the United States ever have again, as Franklin Delano Roosevelt noted, an "arsenal of democracy," with manufacturing being so unimportant in our current economy? Corporate managers must understand product life-cycle management to restore the principles of management, in the honor of Henry Ford and W. Edwards Deming.

SOLUTION #5: REAL USE OF INFORMATION TECHNOLOGIES AS A BUSINESS SOLUTION

I have given speeches about the topic of the business value of IT now for more than 10 years, tying the poor correlation of IT business value with the poor utilization and execution of this tool by corporate management. Today, little has changed: too many corporate executives consider IT to be solely for use in data processing, enterprise resource management, and other tactical types of uses, little of which has direct meaning to them. The use of IT in accounts payable, payroll, inventory management, and other types of tactical processes has resulted in improvements in measured productivity through technological change (automation in many cases), but also through offshoring to lower-cost labor markets.

A computer originally was a person who solved equations, perhaps with a calculator. Are we moving "back to the future" with some of these labor ploys (favoring lower labor costs over better technologies)? The use of automation to solve business-process challenges (optimization through technology) is a true example of productivity, but outsourcing is more a displacement of the workforce (if done primarily through the use of labor over technology). U.S. corporations are becoming uninterested in taking the "difficult-in" (as opposed to the easy-out), by achieving productivity through the use of IT, and they are instead falling back on offshoring as the easy-out.

Job opportunities in the United States are being lost or are unexplored as a function of this phenomenon as well. At least in conventional management thinking (and you know how much credibility that term receives in this book!), IT has matured in its return on investment to the corporation, offering at least marginal returns of late. But this means that, by achieving only a marginal return on investment and then offshoring, U.S. corporations and managers are essentially forgoing growth opportunities in the IT sector—through the misdiagnosis of productivity, assuming that lower labor cost is sufficient. This affects productivity, for both the company and the U.S. economy.

The new 21st-century manager won't see it this way. This new type of manager believes strongly that information is critical to his or her ability to optimize labor, capital, and technology in order to improve the distribution and growth of surplus value to workers, consumers, investors, and the managers themselves. This manager doesn't believe that IT should be used solely by technicians, or overhead departments to automate tactical processes and operations, but should be employed by the top corporate leaders themselves (as Peter Drucker suggested), particularly in sales growth and marketing (innovation as much as in cost reduction), assisting in the retention of the integrity of the product life-cycle process.

This goal can only be realized by taking the following 10 important steps, in order, and without taking shortcuts (such as jumping right to a technology solution):

1. Foster an understanding by the corporation's top leaders of how the knowledge and formalization of the corporation's information sources will increase the surplus value of the corporation and distinguish the company as a market leader. Explain that information sources are not the same as the company's information system.

2. Hold the top leadership of the company responsible for this paradigm shift in redefining information and to be held responsible for strategic decisions driven by information rather than by data or experience (in more cases). This is an adoption of the new 21st-century approach to management.

3. Develop hiring policies and profiles for 21st-century managers, who can drive productivity through the capture and development of formalized information: a new 21st-century manager.

4. Map all of the information sources for the corporation, from one end of the product life cycle to the other. Define information so as to link the product life cycle as one end-to-end strategy.

5. Complete a model of how all of these information sources integrate with each other within the corporate system. This is detailed, tedious work, but critical to the success of utilizing IT to grow surplus value in a competitive global economy.

6. Analyze the current state: which of these information sources are currently being formalized and which aren't? Note the difference between information and data on this one. Most companies today have less than 5 percent of their information sources formalized.

7. Determine the business value of this current state of information sources. How can they be improved? Tie these answers to using the product life cycle in developing one end-to-end strategy for growth.

8. For the remaining information sources that aren't formalized, determine the business value of formalizing them.
9. Explain the business case for formalizing the information sources, linking them together for an overall information management approach for the corporation, training the managers of the corporation to become 21st-century managers, and transforming the corporation and culture to these new principles.
10. Make it happen within the corporation. Explain how these information sources will improve the surplus value of the company and optimize the variables of labor, capital, and technology. Sell the win-win proposition across stakeholders. Provide incentives to these new managers for taking the right behaviors.

Solution #1 focused on redefining the rules for productivity and management—rules that everyone involved with corporations in the United States (corporate employees, consultants, unions, academicians, policy analysts, Wall Street, government regulators, etc.) must understand. Solution #2 presents a new economic model, and Solution #3 is the business case that must express the mind-set that management must be a function of optimizing the surplus value for workers, consumers, investors and managers, and the companies that are doing this today were introduced. Solution #4 discusses how strategies of the company must be viewed from a systems view—versus the Wall Street financial engineering mentality of compartmentalization, the chopping up of functions for cost reduction rather than keeping the life cycle whole for sales growth. Solution #5 transforms corporate management from a cult of personality leader (like a Jack Welch)—who casts his personal, subjective, shadow mightily over the organization—to an information-based culture, with the corporate leaders basing more decisions on data, rationalizing decisions on the overall product life cycle, optimizing the surplus value across all stakeholders.

In the 1950s, when classical management started to fall apart, the organizations were sterile and lifeless, but organized and stable. Once deregulation happened and the consultants had sold us all on the importance of chaos, the structures fell apart and it was seen as leadership for managers to invoke their own creative wills on the organization, as if they were deities to all of the stakeholders. And these leaders were paid like deities, compared to the CEOs of the 1950s, who were just slightly higher-paid managers.

Today's technologies can obtain an amazing percentage of the corporation's available information, so why aren't more corporate managers taking advantage of these them? It is simply because of the lack of a new 21st-century management mind-set that views information as the rational option but one that limits the subjectivity of the top leaders of the corporation. Running a corporate organization with managers who utilize the harnessed 75 percent of the corporation's information sources (as an example) versus cult of personality managers who choose to harness only 5 percent of the information sources is a complete paradigm shift for corporate managers of today. But it is certainly an innovative approach for bringing management back to life in a 21st-century manner.

As effective as Henry Ford was in understanding the needs of the worker and consumer, imagine how much more effective he would have been with the use of Radio Frequency Identification (RFID), databases, the Internet, ERP systems, and other IT investments that can be used in U.S. business operations that are tied to strong processes and information definitions.

Certainly, this can be achieved in any nation, by any corporation, but the U.S. business environment has a unique opportunity to excel in these areas, particularly in comparison to the upstart developing nations that continue to attract more operational centers from the United States through lower wages. The time has come for the discipline of management to become the productivity driver it once was, but updated using the latest technologies to enable classical management. With the tapping of information through the enabling technologies on the market and having a proper public policy that supports economic liberalism for our economic environment, this can happen today. It will, without a doubt, improve the competitiveness of U.S. corporate managers and business operations. This is an idea that adds value across both the private and public sectors of the U.S. economy.

SOLUTION #6: AN EFFECTIVE PRIVATE-PUBLIC SECTOR PARTNERSHIP

Solution #1 defines the new rules of productivity that, if achieved, will improve the welfare of both public and private sector entities. This is not primarily an act of social philanthropy, but rather a multiplier that is created between the private and public sectors to improve the competitiveness and productivity of an economy and a corporation. In the past two decades, corporations have been able to profit through improving the financial results of the corporate entity, at the expense of the public sector. As a result, today's business leaders can't fathom that it is even possible as an option to make decisions that are mutually beneficial to both the corporation and the native economy.

Therefore, the onus today rests on the native country to provide a compelling case for why a private corporation should want to partner with it, rather than using it for one-sided purposes. If the U.S. economy is as productive as the econometric statistics indicate, why are so many corporate operations moving overseas to China, India, Brazil, and Mexico, among others? An easy-out excuse is to pin the explanation on lower wages that are tied to measured productivity, suggesting that a corporation would exit a productive national market in favor of one that solely offers a lower wage rate. The truth of the matter is that the United States is no longer a competitive environment for manufacturing relative to the global economy, and this is a function of factors beyond labor rates. Fixing this problem is where the public sector fits in, making the United States a productive global environment.

Today, the focus of our public sector government should be to partner with the private sector to grow the U.S. economy instead of hindering it or promoting false growth inspired by financial engineering or emotionally charged bailouts. In 2008, when the U.S. government started the year by running a $350 billion annual budget deficit (but closed it through nearly $1 trillion in deficit) without investing in sufficient funds to make the U.S. economy more competitive, the federal government wasn't playing a useful role in economic matters. Although so many economists contend that a public deficit wouldn't have an adverse impact on the economy and is a useful approach for stimulating the economy, it hasn't been proven as an effective macroeconomic strategy over the past 40 years.

The 2010 federal budget deficit dwarfs over the red ink of past years at an estimate of $1.75 trillion. This outdated neo-Keynesian approach of growing the economy through consumption rather than investment is a major strategic flaw for our economic collapse of today. The verdict of how all of this spending will assist in the productivity improvements of the private sector and its balance to the public sector remains to be seen.

A different, albeit less popular, approach is to reduce the federal deficit and to stimulate the economy through investment, not consumption. Figure 7.3 is a breakdown of federal spending for 2009, which provides a telling tale. Other than health care entitlements (Medicare, Medicaid), Social Security, and Defense, the next largest category of expenditure is the payment on the federal debt (8.50 percent of total). The amount of money spent on paying the federal deficit will be greater than the amount spent on the Departments of Health & Human Services, Education, Veteran Affairs, Housing & Urban Development, State, and Agriculture combined! Today's federal budget woes pale in comparison to what's facing us in the future. As the Government Accountability Office (GAO) notes, unless something changes, all tax dollars in 2040 will be spent on nondiscretionary spending of retirement, health care, and interest on the debt. Today's deficit is over 12% of our total economy, the largest percentage since World War II! Clearly, this isn't a stable sign for creating a sustainable partnership between the public and private sectors.

Today, the Japanese, Chinese, British, and oil exporters are funding our deficits, but we cannot expect this to last forever. During 30 of the past 35 years, the United States has run a budget deficit (it's hasn't been since 1961 that the debt has been reduced), and we're seeing the signs of the impact that this is having both on our private and public sectors' ability to compete in a global economy. As our federal government reduces tax rates, while discretionary and mandatory funding increases (4.9 percent and 6.2 percent, in 2009, respectively), our trade deficit escalates. This is because 70 percent of our oil is imported and we purchase more and more from other nations, whereas the Chinese are saving and sacrificing for their collective futures.

Most important, this consumption-based approach is starving our public sector from investing in the growth necessary for the U.S. economy to be competitive in the attraction of MNCs. We have no economic policy for growth, no rallying cry such as that from the Sputnik scare, and little investment to attract businesses to the United States for manufacturing. Without a publicly driven national strategy for true economic growth, our economy will not attract MNCs

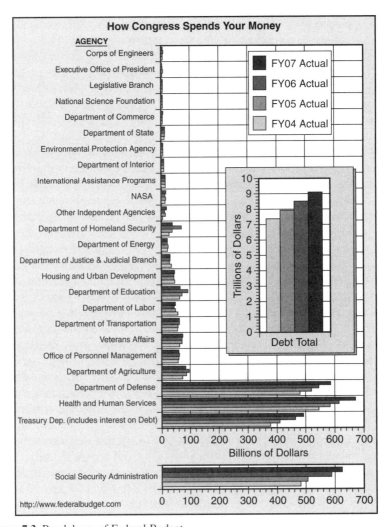

Figure 7.3 Breakdown of Federal Budget

for job creation and the newly trained 21st-century manager (Solution #1) will be of little use in making the national economy thrive.

Out of every 12 dollars of tax revenue collected by the federal government, one dollar goes to the debt payment and is a missed opportunity to invest in a public-private partnership of competitiveness in order to achieve productivity through a concept of the government spurring business growth through investment. Areas of our economy that are conducive to a public-private partnership are public-technological infrastructure, infrastructure for manufacturing growth, education reform, and R&D and incentives for emerging-sector growth.

In the case of infrastructure, we need support from the public sector for legacy infrastructure (bridges, roads, rails, ports, electrical grids, levees, airports, etc.), as well as new technology infrastructure (RFID access points, wireless, broadband, etc.). As I noted two years ago in *An Easy Out,* the public infrastructure nightmare is well documented. Updated for 2008, the current cost to upgrade the public infrastructure in the United States over a 5-year period is $1.6 trillion, according to the American Society of Civil Engineers (ASCE).[11]

These legacy infrastructure costs are definitely the responsibility of the public sector, and MNCs evaluate the state of a nation's infrastructure when making sourcing decisions. New technology infrastructure is an investment in the future as well, providing more developed nations, such as the United States, with a competitive advantage in comparison to developing nations (as noted in Solution #5). With an emerging half trillion dollars in federal budget deficit year over year, the amount of money that Americans are spending on interest payments comes close to covering the investment needed for both legacy and new technology infrastructure; instead, the entire Department of Transportation budget for FY 2009 is $11.5 billion, hardly what is needed to fix our crumbling transportation infrastructure.

According to Thomas Friedman, the United States should be nation-building— in the United States itself. The U.S. underinvestment in infrastructure is not only creating very dangerous situations (such as the bridge collapse in Minnesota a few years back), but it is holding back our economic potential as a function as well. While China, India, Brazil, and Russia are drastically improving theirs, ours is weakening—along with our competitiveness position.

Economists assert that an investment in a nation's infrastructure has a greater positive multiplier on economic growth than do stimulus rebate checks, yet that payout is costing us $170 billion in FY 2009. Dollars budgeted for transportation infrastructure are less than 10 percent of that, and high-technology infrastructure investment isn't even on the radar screen.

Even in the public sector, our focus is on short-term, immediate band-aids versus longer-term solutions that come with sacrifice. Sacrifice and investment are the policy that we need today from our government, if there were only a politician willing to take this very unpopular stance. If only the public knew of the importance of a public-private partnership for private sector job creation, perhaps our politicians would act on it!

Should the public sector invest in our nation's infrastructure to improve manufacturing? As in the following discussion of Solution #8, the answer is *yes.* The same applies to investments needed for our educational system and in emerging sectors of the economy. If spent efficiently (and I know that this is a big "if"), such investments should have a much greater multiplier effect on the national economy than rebate checks to the citizens or bailouts to failing corporations (that used to call themselves MNCs!). Competitiveness has different definitions today: corporation versus corporation and national economy versus national economy. Investment in national economy through public-private partnerships leads to economic growth, just as the corporation that invests in its future will grow as well. Given our deficit situation, Americans must sacrifice to allow this to happen, and such sacrifices will pay off for our nation in the long-term. There is no other viable solution to our economic problems.

SOLUTION #7: BALANCE BETWEEN REGULATION AND DEREGULATION

As discussed in this book, the United States had a highly regulated economy in the middle of the 20th century, and today it faces what many would consider to be a largely deregulated one. The lack of effective regulatory control has been problematic, and the see-saw back and forth of an ineffective regulated and deregulated government approach tells quite the tale. The heavy regulation of the mid-20th century created situations such as portrayed in William Whyte's *Organization Man,* a narrative about an administrator (not a manager) who couldn't work his way through a paper bag unless his boss was on the other side of it telling him what to do.

Too quickly (or so it seems), the disorganization manager (my term) came onto the scene—where chaos means change and constantly changing things means progress, with the discipline of management not really having a fighting chance. Policy wonks and ideologues in Washington debate the general theories of regulation and deregulation, but not many of these policy leaders truly understand the impact that such policy changes have on individual managers in their private sector roles.

Policy changes become an ideology without an understanding of practical implementation problems when the role of the corporate manager is not factored in or understood. The balance between policies of deregulation and regulation must be understood within the management function of optimizing labor, capital, and technology, and, if not, it becomes a rather academic and ideological discussion, without understanding of the ramifications of such decisions.

We should have learned how dangerous this practice was through the deregulation ideology from the late 1970s and early 1980s. This is not to say that the "Reagan Revolution" deregulation was a bad idea. Rather, it's to note that, when dramatic policy changes are considered, an assessment of how such policies affect the private sector is more important than the development of the policy itself. Much as when technology is introduced to a corporation, stability must be ensured through training and by adopting better business processes.

When regulation or deregulation takes place, a sufficient amount of human and intangible capital must transform chaos into stability. This takes on an especially relevant note today, in the light of the public's crazed demand for increased government intervention and regulation because of the ghastly financial collapse in the Fall of 2008.

SOLUTION #8: IMPORTANCE OF MANUFACTURING

Let us not forget the critical errors that were made in the 1970s to transform our national economy from a smokestack economy to a paper-intensive FIRE economy (Finance, Insurance, Real Estate). The truth that Americans are beginning to learn today is that this FIRE economy that has been promoted over the past 30 years is a system in which participants trade pieces of paper but are not involved in any productive activity, for the most part. With Americans manufacturing a declining percentage of goods for the world and much less of what we consume, we must begin to question this strategy for our nation. Therefore, there should be perhaps no greater policy initiative from our government to undertake than a national program of investment and policy to promote the importance of a strong manufacturing base to the U.S. economy. In contrast to chapter four, which documented the castles being built in the air through financial engineering, this chapter emphasizes a rejuvenation of industrialization, which must occur quickly.

Many Americans are unable to wrap their heads around our nation becoming a manufacturing power again because we have been told for decades that migrating away from it is a sign of societal progress. Images of the rust belt are conjured or of dying manufacturing entities, such as the auto industry, hanging on by their fingernails and begging for government bailouts. At the end of 2008, the Treasury Department was focused on providing financial assistance packages to the U.S. auto industry, sending a message to the public that manufacturing wasn't viable anymore without a government handout.

Furthermore, instead of using public investments in the development of emerging manufacturing companies and industries residing and incubating in the United States, the public sector prevents creative destruction from focusing capital to competitive and emerging markets and companies in lieu of these bailouts; tens of billions of dollars to be allocated to the management of the Big Three, who deny that the leadership is the problem, and to the benefit to the labor unions, who profess that no concessions should be made by workers who earn more than $70 per hour.

Private capital markets with innovative ideas cannot compete with billion-dollar tax breaks and bailouts of the dinosaurs of industry. Most dangerous of all, the American public stereotypes manufacturing as these moribund companies in uncompetitive sectors of our economy, rather than as innovative and competitive companies in emerging sectors that can be our future.

Most Americans aren't rallying around manufacturing because they envision it as the smokestack relics of our past, rather than as the future hope of a real new economy: biotechnology, energy, food, health care, and so on. For a national program of investment and policy to occur, our public sector must rally private sector interests around the right emerging opportunities, forcing creative destruction to occur. In the place of General Motors and Chrysler will be the manufacturing sectors of America's future, if done properly. Let the newly trained 21st-century management drive manufacturing rather than politicians and government economists who are resuscitating the failing relics of our past.

Today, manufacturing represents only 10 percent of our total employment and a declining percentage as well, and it is not seen to be of strategic importance to our future. Yet there are beacons of hope in the steel industry (Nucor Steel), consumer products (Coors Brewing), and other areas that can shine the light brightly, as our national policy focuses on the manufacturing of the future. Today, there are more manufacturing companies that are successful in the United States than is known by most Americans, and this suggests that manufacturing is not only possible, but preferable.

Even fewer Americans understand how significant the opportunities are in the next generation of manufacturing, such as energy, health care, biotechnology, and IT. But consider how much public funding has gone in the past few decades to either moribund manufacturing entities or the FIRE economy rather than emerging manufacturing opportunities. Is our public-private focus on the correct method to build a sustainable economy? If alternative energy vehicles are critical to our national security, why isn't our public-private partnership investing more in alternative fueling-station infrastructure? If health care is an overwhelming drain on our nation's productivity, where's the investment between public-private partnerships in biotechnology? If IT is are critical to a competitive economy, why has the investment from the U.S. public-private partnership paled in comparison to that of nations such as South Korea and India? The examples and the opportunities are enormous, whereas our national response is depressing and underwhelming.

Perhaps the idea of manufacturing enterprise zones (MEZs) is the most intriguing idea of all for the deployment of a new manufacturing-based economy in the United States. Instead of creating an environment of draconian business-operating rules, through protectionism and mercantilism, or accounting rules and financial systems that promote sending work to other nations, why can't our technocrats establish MEZs for business growth and job creation? Policies of establishing MEZs, allowing for tax breaks, an improved regulatory environment, optimal labor laws, and improved physical infrastructure will reverse the trend and bring manufacturing jobs back into the United States.

If you believe this is a fantasy, ask yourself this simple question: when was the last time that a politician in the United States proposed a strategy to be pro-manufacturing and actually did something about it? There is no question that a manufacturing business case can be supported that enables better-paying jobs in the United States (with affordable health care) and is competitive with the major manufacturing nations for many (not all) goods from a total cost perspective.

If a MNC is simply looking for lower labor rates, a U.S. operation will never be competitive. But if total cost and value are measured and policies are in place to optimize, it is possible. An MEZ area can be a laboratory for the United States to prove to our nation that manufacturing leads to production and productivity, rather than to more bubbles and financially engineered paper shuffling.

Our public-private partnerships must also promote an understanding and a policy around supporting manufacturing and the entire product life-cycle process of a corporation. During the 19th and early 20th centuries, Britain sought to be the financial arm of a crown of colonies, with the subjects having manufacturing and extraction production capabilities in servitude to the Queen or King. By having the manufacturing operations, the colonial lands wanted more of the product life cycle and more of their own political independence from Britain.

History bears repeating today, as China gains greater strength through manufacturing to seek R&D, product development, and so on. Manufacturing jobs not only pay more to U.S. workers than most low-end service jobs, but the creation of a manufacturing base also supports the entire product life-cycle process, stabilizing our economy as well. Policy makers and economists must better understand how MNCs make decisions, understanding that system thinking leads to greater productivity through retaining more parts of the product life-cycle process. National policies and investments must focus on this rather than on enabling the commodization of elements or on focusing on stale sectors or nonproductive ones (such as FIRE) that create little sustainable value.

Lastly, classical management has little relevance to a FIRE-based economy, because such industries are more transactional than they are productive. Classical management died when the focus of our economy strayed away from manufacturing and toward financial engineering. By definition, the theory of classical management is tied to manufacturing in the optimization of labor, capital, and technology.

A rejuvenation of a national policy toward manufacturing will lead to investment and a redefinition of management to its classical days, updated to become 21st-century management. Instead of white-collar jobs leaving the United States to support outsourcing overseas, classical management will cause jobs to flock to the United States because of this magical potential that's possible for a public-private sector balance enabled by economic liberalism. All factors considered, a national program supporting manufacturing (over FIRE) will ignite 21st-century management and reignite our economy toward productivity, attracting MNCs to set up business operations in our land. It's a strategy of the utmost importance!

SOLUTION #9: THE IMPORTANCE OF PUBLIC EDUCATION

What happened in the U.S. public education system basically followed a similar pattern as did our corporations and the fate of classical management. Through the 1960s and the 1970s, the decline of U.S. education became obvious through failed ideologies and practices, much as it did in the business environment of the time. But, in 1983, Ronald Reagan's National Commission on Excellence in Education published *A Nation at Risk,* which was a landmark event in the history of U.S. education. It concluded, for the first time, that U.S. schools were failing miserably. Secretary of Education T. H. Bell noted that the U.S. educational system was failing to meet the need for a competitive workforce (sound familiar?). Some of the findings from this study were jaw dropping: 13 percent of all 17-year-olds were classified as illiterate and the U.S. ranking in many categories against the world was never first or second but last place seven times.

The year 1983 was a landmark year for me as well: I graduated from public education (high school), and, despite my educational accomplishments later in life, I was nothing better than a "C" student through my high school years, forcing me to contemplate the effectiveness of the public education system.

It is the twenty-fifth anniversary of this landmark study and its call for reform, so how have we done? Check out *Strong American Schools'* report card of our progress since then on the twenty-fifth anniversary of this initial report:

> While the national conversation about education would never be the same, stunningly few of the Commission's recommendations actually have been enacted. Now is not the time for more educational research or reports or commissions. We have enough commonsense ideas, backed by decades of research, to significantly improve American schools. The missing ingredient isn't even educational at all. It's political. Too often, state and local leaders have tried to enact reforms of the kind recommended in *A Nation at Risk* only to be stymied by organized special interests and political inertia. Without vigorous national leadership to improve education, states and local school systems simply cannot overcome the obstacles to making the big changes necessary to significantly improve our nation's K-12 schools.[12]

Much as with our business environment in the United States, the problem with our educational system is environmental, not related to the individual per se. As shown in Figure 7.4, the U.S. educational system is better funded than that of other nations but deficient in its results. From 1951 to 1991, the annual expenditure per student in U.S. public schools went from $1,189 to $5,237, an increase of 350 percent! Teachers' pay has risen as well (45 percent in real wages from 1961 to 1991), while SAT scores fell by 41 points from 1972 to 1991.[13]

Figure 7.5 presents the story that U.S. class sizes are lower than the norm, particularly in comparison to those Asian nations that are outperforming the United States on a regular basis. Almost in any measurement of cost and benefit, the U.S. public school system continues to decline, particularly in comparison to our foreign competitors. Chester Finn, a former Reagan administration official noted, "surely college ought to transport one's intellect well beyond factual knowledge and cultural literacy. But it's hard to add a second story to a house that lacks a solid foundation.

Our K-12 public education system is responsible for providing that solid foundation for the U.S. workforce in order to compete against the emerging powers of Asia and elsewhere. The problem with our underlying educational framework was found to be flawed 25 years ago, much as in the 1980s, when our business environment was flawed by a lack of competition and heavy regulation. In business, reform led to deregulation, which led to bubble growth, which led to

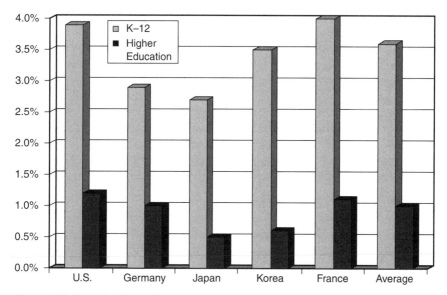

Figure 7.4 Education Expenditure as a Percentage of GDP

collapse. In education, reform was even less effective, and it has led to our nation losing its competitive position relative to emerging Asian economies.

In the early days of his presidency, President Bush took a different tone to reform, noting that testing is crucial to "determine whether or not children are learning."[14] Beginning in third grade, students are tested every year, and schools

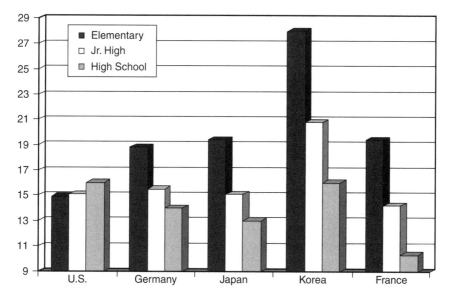

Figure 7.5 Average Class Size, by Level

and teachers are evaluated based on results. Americans looked at this approach as competition, and competition is good, but it neglectfully ignored much of the underlying problem that was identified 25 years ago in *A Nation at Risk*.

Simply stated, today's public school districts are run by administrators, much as corporations were run in the 1950s. They are run by a cadre of interlocking bureaucracies that prohibits or maybe just slows innovation and the optimization of investment (capital), teachers (labor), and technologies. Kevin Marlatt, a nationally renowned public school administrator, has struggled: implementing innovative solutions for learning and skill development in inner-city Denver, going up against tenured teachers, administrators, and unions. In his struggles to reform the system, he noted to me:

> Too often the structures, policies, rules of practices and alliances take on a life of their own and demand service in their own right. They begin to have the appearance of "Angels" full of light demanding attention, sacrifice and praise. Thus the bureaucracies of education become the "served," and "revered" rather than servants designed to support the true mission an object of public education, the deep learning of students. These Angelic bureaucracies will never sacrifice and like all "Angels" must always demand praise and allegiance to the status quo. A challenge to these "Angels" is an attack on orthodoxy.

But all of the blame, or even most of it, shouldn't be placed on the school systems. The middle-class culture of contentment that was forming (as described by Carroll Quigley) in the 1950s continues today: parents may be unwilling to invest the amount of time in their children that is necessary for them to be a success either at school or in their future endeavors. Presidential candidate Barack Obama tells the story of his single mother waking him up at 4:30 a.m. to study before the day began. How many parents today are willing to do much more than the minimum required from the schools and other institutions?

Nearly 40 percent of Americans ages 55 to 64 have a bachelor's degree or an associate's degree, making us first in the world in this age range. For 25- to 34-year-olds, it remains 40 percent, but we are tenth in the world, behind many of our top competitors.[15] Our culture today isn't an education culture, and we've hit the snooze button from the alarm that went off 25 years ago, and we've gone back to sleep.

SOLUTION #10: 21ST-CENTURY MANAGEMENT IN MBA PROGRAMS

In the early 1980s when I was graduated from high school, the fledging U.S. school system received a warning sign, which it basically refused to act on. At the same time, our policy makers were beginning to liberate business from the constraints of overregulation, but without knowing the impact of doing so. I made my way through an undergraduate degree in Industrial Psychology and then on to an

MBA program, immediately becoming immersed in the issue of competitiveness and productivity relative to an emerging Japan. Leaving this world, I entered Corporate America and was immediately at the disposal of "Pink Slip Norm," and then I went on to consecutive bubble economies of dot-com and the housing growth periods.

Today, as I sit back and review these 25 years, I wonder who can really stop this perpetuation of a lack of management. It can't be the corporate managers, who are too busy fighting the battle in a highly competitive world economy. How about the consultants? They are certainly smart enough, but experience teaches us that, for the most part, they are no longer the solid independent thinkers that they were but have turned into a cottage industry. What about the policy makers? Typically, the independent policy analysts have a bias toward government or macroeconomic policy as the solution, such as using monetary policy, trade sanctions, or even Keynesian economics to stimulate the economy (no balance between private and public sector policy). Solutions proposing government or government policy as a solution have failed miserably and probably are the prime reason for why we are in this mess in the first place. Alan Greenspan is the prototypical genius one day and then a pariah much later on. This sort of thinking no longer applies in the 21st-century economy.

The answer to this problem is simple; the incubator for 21st-century management must be the U.S. MBA program. As mentioned earlier chapter, the role for today's MBA program is to perpetuate what business leaders shouldn't be doing, versus what they should. The academic setting is complicit in the problem, with Ken Lay being an example in a case study of excellence in 1999 and a case study in failure just five years later.

Higher-learning institutions should be a forum of discourse of uncovering the underlying problems within the business environment and drawing on solutions that challenge the notion of conventional wisdom. William Whyte's *Organization Man* highlighted an unhealthy relationship in the United States between its corporations and academia, with academia focused on social skills, group dynamics, and belongingness rather than teaching students to think for themselves.

Today, how different is the university setting at the typical MBA program in the United States? Perhaps the approach to pedagogy is more dynamic and engaging, but is the result much different? Instead of academia bringing innovation to the corporation, it is often the other way around. In working with many universities across the nation through many associations, I have found that the corporate leader is frequently asked to discuss the topic of management, instead of academia kick-starting dialogue from a different point of view. When today's corporate manager of chaos is the instructor, as opposed to the business school professor, there is a problem in these existing relationships.

Today's MBA program should redefine itself as a forum for improving the competitiveness of U.S. business operations through management, versus perpetuating the chaotic, win-lose international economy in today's mad dash. MBA programs rarely discuss the definition of productivity and don't even provide anything more than the most generic definitions of management. How about the business case of management; that is, making an economic case for how corporations can succeed through optimizing labor, capital, and technology for the benefit of all stakeholders? Not very often is this discussed, even relative to how destructive a Wal-Mart can be to our economy.

In my years of experience in being involved directly with corporations and academia, I've not seen a focus on the importance of product life-cycle management or the proper management implementation and use of IT. On the public-sector side and in terms of responsibility to the private sector, MBA programs should teach students how public sectors should enable business growth—rather than legislate, regulate, or deregulate it, as has been the failures of the most recent decades. In the past two decades, MBA programs have flowered praise over the path of the dot-com and the venture capitalist, ignoring and even chiding the role of manufacturing in the U.S. economy. These are all examples of the failures of our institutions to lead the charge, to set course on a different economic direction.

Today, that opportunity exists again for our MBA programs, with the focus on 21st-century management. In doing so, MBA programs can establish real partnerships between themselves and corporations that are looking for new directions to take. With a new direction in place, these MBA programs will gain the reputation both from the private sector and the potential student prospects of what management should be. Not only is this a powerful marketing medium, it's a legitimate focus point for higher learning.

Today, many universities have research facilities focused on emerging markets, such as energy and biotechnology. What about a research facility focused on 21st-century management? Perhaps not as ballyhooed, but nonetheless any less important, is the need for our nation to develop a new generation of top management that can be a competitive advantage for U.S. business operations, to bring jobs and consumer products to our markets.

These are the solutions that I'm proposing to overcome a lack of a management discipline in our business environment today. Yes, management's absence is happening all over the globe, but it is particularly painful in the United States, given that this is its birthplace and where it became powerful, driving our economy to unprecedented heights. There you have it: seven chapters describing how management is dead, how and why it died, and what must be done today to counteract this large void in our nation's economic engine. Now it's up to you, the reader, to do something about it.

Conclusion: The Few Becoming a Trend

"In the struggle for survival, the fittest win out at the expense of their rivals because they succeed at adapting themselves best to their environment"

Charles Darwin

This opening quote best describes the essence of today's management problem: managers will adapt to their environment, whether it's a healthy one or not. For the past 40 to 50 years, the role of the corporate manager has adapted to becoming an administrator, during the days of the regulated bloated corpocracy, and the cult-of-personality individualist, during the days of the deregulated casino economy. More often than not, successful managers have been judged not by principles of classical management, but rather through the benchmarks of fulfilling suboptimal objectives. Every once in a while, someone such as Jim Sinegal of Costco or Dan DiMicco of Nucor Steel has come along in the form of classical management, but these are exceptions and not rules, by any stretch of the imagination. Those who expect our corporate leaders to behave as Henry Ford did in 1908 don't understand how our business environment makes this prohibitive, following the rules of evolution.

The position of this book is that management has died as a function of this sickly business environment in the United States for more than half a century. Chapter seven provides the remedies needed to bring this social science discipline back to life. In this book, I've intentionally taken the reader through the past of our economic transition in order to track what has happened and to follow the rise and fall of management to the rise and fall of our business competitiveness. The good news to this story is that U.S. corporations and our public policy analysts should be as open-minded as ever to consider these different perspectives, given what's happening in our economy today.

Jim Sinegal, who is highlighted in this book, is the founder of Costco, yet he spends 200 days per year visiting Costco operations, answers his own phone, and schedules his own appointments. He is not leading Costco through layers of management or Wall Street coercion, but through understanding the fundamentals of the business rather than the neat and tidy view of a company from a largely removed corner office. When Sinegal notes that "pay good wages, and you'll get good people and good productivity," he truly understands the meaning of management. This is the framework from the era of Henry Ford, when management was originated 100 years ago.

In contrast, many of the principles of Wal-Mart's business model represent the antithesis of what 21st-century management needs to be about. The failures of our business model today can be explained in terms of a lack of real productivity and in terms of a lack of real management. It can be described as simply as that, linked together.

Speaking of contrasts, when steelmaking in the United States is supposed to be nothing if not dead, a company such as Nucor Steel has a management approach as refreshing as it is an oddity. The approach includes managers being compensated with 75 to 90 percent of the market average (making the difference on incentives, if performance merits this), modest pay disparities in place between hourly and management staffs, and a level of factory worker engagement rarely seen in any industry. There are stories of legend: factory workers going the extra mile, acting as walking advertisements for the company, as **the way** it used to be, proud to say they work for Nucor. This is unusual and very difficult to sustain, given the financial environment of the U.S. economy, but not impossible. It's a story of what is possible if we choose to look at the problem at bit differently and act on it. Manufacturing in the United States needs to be our future, not our past.

At the Coors Brewing Company, the leadership of the company understands that the quality and vitality of our products depend on a healthy and engaged workforce, particularly in the production workforce. Just as at Costco and Nucor, the phrase "people first" isn't just a slogan, but rather a way of operation. Safety is the most important factor in how the business is run, and then comes how the people are treated and compensated. If these two factors are handled well by management, service and productivity follow. Such is a part of a company's culture versus something that is a cliché for human relations. It's a story of a foundation—where 21st-century management can start and then become the solution for our need for global competitiveness.

More good news is that the companies that have been highlighted in this book are from some of the troubled sectors of the economy: manufacturing and retailing. So many headlines are made over Wal-Mart's average hourly wage of just over $10 per hour, and, along with the average work week of 34 hours, the pay for this worker is almost $18,000, well below what is required for a two-person family. But very little is made over Costco providing a decent livable wage and offering affordable benefits, despite being in the same sector as Wal-Mart! Conventional wisdom suggests that U.S. operations shouldn't even think about the steel industry at all. There's nothing that management can do to change this trend. And yet there are examples of extraordinary companies and their management that inspire us, that explain to us what 21st-century management can be all about. Too much has been made of how management and industry have failed the public trust, and not enough energy has been focused on examples of how this can be turned around: the gain of productivity from Main Street instead of Wall Street.

The rebirth of management should happen right now, stemming from what was born 100 years ago and as a reaction to our recent financial collapse. Henry Ford had a vision, and the public and private sector turned this into an institution and culture within our business environment through the World Wars and into the middle of the 20th century. Can a new crop of 21st-century visionaries provide our future, with the support of business schools to drive change? They must. As Oliver Wendell Holmes once said, "To reach a port we must sail, sometimes with the wind, and sometimes against it. But we must not drift or lie at anchor." It's the last hope for the American Dream for the middle class. It's time for us to move ahead and make it happen now!

For more on what you can do to inspire and drive 21st-century management, please go to www.jackbuffington.net. Thank you for making a difference!

Notes

CHAPTER ONE

1. *The Executive Life*. 1956. New York: Doubleday.

2. "Indiana to Beijing," 2008. *Wall Street Journal*, May 6.

3. Wikipedia, "Ford Model T." Available online at http://en.wikipedia.org/wiki/Ford_Model_T.

4. Wikipedia, "Ford Model T." Available online at http://en.wikipedia.org/wiki/Ford_Model_T.

5. Time Life Books. 1998. *End of Innocence: 1910–1920, Our American Century.* Alexandria, VA: Time-Life Books, 115.

6. Georgano, G. N. 1990. *Cars, 1886–1930*. New York: Crescent Books.

7. Frank, Thomas. 2008. "Our Great Economic U-Turn," *Wall Street Journal*, May 14.

8. Brown, Sherrod. 2008. "Don't Call Me a Protectionist," *Wall Street Journal*, April 23.

9. "Hot and Bothered," *The Economist*, June 26, 2008.

10. Wikipedia, "Management Consulting." Available online at http://en.wikipedia.org/wiki/Management_consulting.

11. Drucker, Peter F. 1989. *The New Realities: In Government and Politics, in Economics and Business, in Society and World View*. New York: Harper & Row.

12. Gantt, Henry L. 1903. "A Graphical Daily Balance in Manufacture," *Transactions of the American Society of Mechanical Engineers*, Volume XXIV, pages 1322–1336.

13. Moore, Stephen, and Simon, Julian L. 1999. *The Greatest Century That Ever Was*. Cato Policy Analysis, 1. Available online at http://www.cato.org/pubs/pas/pa364.pdf.

14. Moore, Stephen, and Simon, Julian L. 1999. *The Greatest Century That Ever Was*. Cato Policy Analysis, 3. Available online at http://www.cato.org/pubs/pas/pa364.pdf.

CHAPTER TWO

1. Smith, Adam, Edwin Cannan, and Max Lerner. 1937. *An Inquiry into the Nature and Causes of the Wealth of Nations*. New York: Modern Library.

2. Woog, Adam. 1999. *A Cultural History of the United States: The 1900's*. San Diego, CA: Lucent Books, 33.

3. *Achievements in Public Health, 1900–1999*. Centers for Disease Control and Prevention. Available online at http://www.cdc.gov/mmwr/preview/mmwrhtml/mm4822a1. htm#fig1.

4. London, Jack. 1990. "War of the Classes: A Class Struggle." Available online at http://london.sonoma.edu/Writings/WarOfTheClasses/struggle.html.

5. Beatty, Jack. 2007. *Age of Betrayal: The Triumph of Money in America, 1865–1900*. New York: Alfred A. Knopf, 54.

6. Greenwood, Janette Thomas. 2000. *The Gilded Age: A History in Documents*. New York: Oxford Press, 20.

7. Beatty, *Age of Betrayal,* 22–23.

8. Beatty, *Age of Betrayal,* 349.

9. Carnegie, Andrew 2008. Available at http://www.bgsu.edu/departments/acs/1890s/carnegie/carnegie.html.

10. Chernow, Ron. 1998. *Titan: The Life of John D. Rockefeller, Sr*. New York: Random House.

11. Drucker, Peter. 1993. *Post-Capitalist Society*. New York: Harper Business, 49.

12. Robinson, Dilys. 2005. "Thinkers for the 21st Century," *Training Journal* (February): 30.

13. Montgomery, David. 1989. *The Fall of the House of Labor: The Workplace, the State, and American Labor Activism, 1865–1925*. London: Cambridge University Press, 251.

14. Drucker, *Post-Capitalist Society,* 34.

15. Montgomery, *The Fall of the House of Labor,* 254.

16. Mankiw, Gregory. 2007. "How to Avoid Recession? Let the Fed Work," *Wall Street Journal* (December), 23.

17. MIT Entreprenuership Center, 2004. *Alfred Sloan, Inventor of the Modern Corporation*. Available online at http://www.inventhelp.com/Alfred-Sloans-Concept-of-the-Corporation.asp.

18. Madison, Angus. 2008. "Statistics on World Population, GDP and Per Capita GDP, 1-2006 A.D." GGDC Faculty of Economics. Available online at http://www.ggdc.net/Maddison/.

19. Deming, W. Edwards. 2000. *Out of Crisis*. Boston: The MIT Press, 2.

20. Magnier, Mark. October 25, 1999. "The Fifty People Who Influenced Business This Century," *LA Times, U-8*. Available online at http://deming.org/index.cfm?content=651.

21. Deming, *Out of Crisis,* 3.

22. Deming, *Out of Crisis,* 3.

23. Robert Reich. 2007. *Supercapitalism: The Transformation of Business, Democracy, and Everyday Life*. New York: Alfred A. Knopf, 7.

24. Whyte, William. 1956. *The Organization Man,* Philadelphia: University of Pennsylvania Press, Introduction.

25. Morris, Charles R. 2008. *The Trillion Dollar Meltdown: Easy Money, High Rollers, and the Great Credit Crash*. New York: Public Affairs, 3.

CHAPTER THREE

1. Dickson, Paul. 2008. PBS Nova. "A Blow to the Nation." Available online at http://www.pbs.org/wgbh/nova/sputnik/nation.html.

2. Ramsey Nancy. October 4, 2007. "10 Questions about Sputnik." Available online at http://www.cbsnews.com/blogs/2007/10/04/couricandco/entry3329489.shtml.

3. Miyoshi, Masao. 1991. *Off Center: Power and Culture Relations between Japan and the United States.* Cambridge: Harvard University Press, 64.

4. "The Times and Japan-Bashing." 2007. Available online at http://opinion.latimes.com/opinionla/2007/10/cold-copy-the-t.html.

5. "Power Struggles," *The Economist,* May 29, 2008.

6. Mahbubani, Kishore. October 11, 2008. The New Asian Hemisphere. Available online at http://www.mahbubani.net/.

7. Amadeo, Kimberly. 2007. The U.S. Trade Deficit. Available online at http://useconomy.about.com/od/tradepolicy/p/Trade_Deficit.htm.

8. Fallows, James. 2008. "The $1.4 Trillion Question," *The Atlantic Monthly,* January/February, 38.

9. "The $1.4 Trillion Question," 98.

10. Reich, Robert B. 2007. *Supercapitalism: The Transformation of Business, Democracy, and Everyday Life.* New York: Alfred A. Knopf, 125.

11. Sorman, Guy, and Puri, Asha. 2008. *The Empire of Lies: The Truth about China in the Twenty-First Century.* New York: Encounter Books, x.

12. Steingart, Gabor. 2008. *The War for Wealth The True Story of Globalization, or Why the Flat World Is Broken.* New York: McGraw-Hill.

13. Sorman and Puri, *The Empire of Lies,* 107.

14. Chuanheng, Lu. 2008. "No Legal Recourse for Poor Chinese Workers." UPIAsia.com, January 31. Available online at http://www.upiasia.com/Society_Culture/2008/01/31/no_legal_recourse_for_poor_chinese_workers/3942/.

15. Woetzel, Jonathan, and Devan, Janamitra. 2008. "Growing Pains," *Wall Street Journal,* April 14.

16. Buhl, David. 2007. "Banking in China," University of St. Gallen, December 22. Available online at http://www.glorad.org/hsg/dbic/reports/16%20Banking%20in%20China%20-%20Buehl.pdf.

17. Setser, Brad. 2008. "What to Do with a Half a Trillion a Year? Understanding the Changes in Management of China's Foreign Assets," cfr.org, January 15. Available online at http://www.cfr.org/content/publications/attachments/Setser%20China%20Paper.pdf.

18. Steingart, *The War for Wealth.*

19. Batson, Andrew. 2008. "China Announces Major Stimulus Plan," *Wall Street Journal,* November 10.

20. The Economist Intelligence Unit. 2008. "China's Economy," *The Economist,* March 18. "Sweet and Sour Pork," *The Economist,* May 13, 2008.

21. "The Middle Kingdom Middle Class," McKinsey Quarterly Chart Focus Newsletter. Available online at http://www.mckinseyquarterly.com/newsletters/chartfocus/2007_06.htm.

22. Karabell, Zachary. 2007. "Watch out for the China Bashers," *Wall Street Journal,* September 5.

23. Altman, Daniel. 2006. "Managing Globalization: China as Economic Bogeyman May Be Wrong Strategy for Washington," *International Herald Tribune,* December 12.

24. Mankiw, Gregory. 2008. "Beyond the Noise on Free Trade," *New York Times,* March 16. Available online at http://www.nytimes.com/2008/03/16/business/16view.html? ex=1363320000&en=4d785d6a6f56fead&ei=5124&partner=permalink&exprod=perma-link.

25. Sun, John. 2008. "Does Made in China Still Make Sense?" *China Magazine,* May/June, 36.

CHAPTER FOUR

1. Moore, Stephen, and Simon, Julian L. 1999. "The Greatest Century That Ever Was," *Policy Analysis,* December 15, 1.

2. Quigley, Carroll. 1966. *Tragedy and Hope.* Macmillan, New York, 1243.

3. Shiller, Robert. July/August 2008 "Infectious Exuberance," *The Atlantic Monthly,* 19.

4. Morris, Charles R. 2008. *The Trillion Dollar Meltdown: Easy Money, High Rollers, and The Great Credit Crash.* New York: PublicAffairs, 2.

5. Morris, *The Trillion Dollar Meltdown.*

6. Quigley, *Tragedy and Hope,* 1243.

7. Truthandpolitics.org. 2004. "Relative Size of Public Spending, 1940-2003." Available online at http://www.truthandpolitics.org/outlays-per-gdp.php.

8. Morris, *The Trillion Dollar Meltdown,* 14.

9. Cooper, James C. 2008. "Services: A Heavyweight in a Hard Fight." *Business Week,* May 19.

10. Phillips, Kevin. 2008. *Bad* Money. New York: Penguin Group, 40.

11. Fromson, Brett D., July 28, 2008. "Being Alan Greenspan," ABC News. Available online at http://abcnews.go.com/Business/story?id=88536&page=1.

12. Fromson, "Being Alan Greenspan."

13. Sheehan, Fred. . July 20, 2007. "Alan, We Hardly Knew Ye." Available online at www.safehaven.com.

14. Mandel, Michael. 2008. "The Fed's Revolution," *Business Week,* March 31.

15. Wikipedia, "Charles Keating." Available online at http://en.wikipedia.org/wiki/Charles_Keating.

16. Fleckenstein, William A., and Sheehan, Frederick. 2008. *Greenspan's Bubbles: The Age of Ignorance at the Federal Reserve.* New York: McGraw-Hill, 34.

17. Reich, Robert. 2007. *Supercapitalism: The Transformation of Business, Democracy, and Everyday Life.* New York: Alfred A. Knopf, 60.

18. Fleckenstein and Sheehan, *Greenspan's Bubbles.*

19. Federal Reserve Board. 2004. "Remarks by Governor Edward M. Gramlich, May 21, 2004." Available online at http://www.federalreserve.gov/boarddocs/speeches/2004/20040521/default.htm.

20. Phillips, *Bad Money,* 34.

21. "Corporate Profits and Population, Capital Flow Analysis." Available online at http://www.capital-flow-analysis.com/investment-essays/profits_population2.html.

22. Wikipedia, "Boskin Commission." Available online at http://en.wikipedia.org/wiki/Boskin_Commission.

CHAPTER FIVE

1. Dilbert.com, The Characters. 2008. *United Feature Syndicate, Inc.* Available online at http://www.dilbert.com/.

2. Whyte, William Hollingsworth. 1956. *The Organization Man.* New York: Simon and Schuster, 14.

3. Reason, Tim. 2002. "Meet the New Boss," *CFO Magazine,* January 1. Available online at http://www.cfo.com/printable/article.cfm/3002766/.

4. Reich, Robert. 2007. *Supercapitalism: The Transformation of Business, Democracy, and Everyday Life.* New York: Alfred A. Knopf,, 36.

5. Steingart, Gabor. 2008. *The War for Wealth The True Story of Globalization, or Why the Flat World Is Broken.* New York: McGraw-Hill, 137.

6. Google IPO Prospectus. 2004. Available online at https://www.ipo.google.com/data/prospectus.html.

7. Graham, John. R., Harvey, Campbell. R., and Shivaram. Rajgopal. 2005. "The Economic Implications of Corporate Financial Reporting." *Journal of Accounting and Economics.*

8. Akers, Michael D., Giacomino, Don E., and Bellovary, Jodi L. August 2007. "Earnings Management and Its Implications," *The CPA Journal.* Available online at http://www.nysscpa.org/cpajournal/2007/807/essentials/p64.htm.

9. Beck. Rachel. "All Business: Cost Cutting Nightmare." 2008. ABC News. Available online at http://www.newsvine.com/_news/2008/01/11/1220069-all-business-cost-cutting-nightmare

10. Henkoff, Ronald." 1990. Cost Cutting: How to Do It Right." *Fortune,* April 9.

11. Bogle, John. 2003. "What Went Wrong in Corporate America?" February 24. Available online at http://www.vanguard.com/bogle_site/sp20030224.html

12. Reich, *Supercapitalism,* 113.

13. Byrne, John, December 3, 2001. "The Real Confessions of Tom Peters." Business Week Online. Online available at http://www.businessweek.com/magazine/content/01_49/b3760040.htm

14. Drucker, Peter. 2002. *Managing in the Next Society,* St. Martin's Press, New York, 8.

15. Drucker, 33.

16. "Interview with Stephen Roach, Morgan Stanley's Chief Economist," *Frontline.* Online available at http://www.pbs.org/wgbh/pages/frontline/america/interviews/roach.html

17. Kinni, Theodore. March/April 2003. "Have We Run Out of Big Ideas?" The Conference Board. Available online at http://www.conference-board.org/articles/atb_article.cfm?id=180.

CHAPTER SIX

1. United States Department of Labor. "Productivity in the 21st Century." 2002. Department of Labor Productivity Conference, October 23, 2002, 105. Available online at http://www.dol.gov/21CW/prod-book.pdf.

2. Foust, Dean. 1997. "Alan Greenspan's Brave New World," *Business Week,* July 14. Available online at http://www.businessweek.com/1997/28/b35351.htm.

3. "Productivity in the 21st Century," 8.

4. "Productivity in the 21st Century," 110.

5. Fleckenstein, William A., and Sheehan, Frederick. 2008. *Greenspan's Bubbles: The Age of Ignorance at the Federal Reserve.* New York: McGraw-Hill, 126.

6. Yellen, Janet. 2006. "Economic Inequality in the United States," *FRBSF Economic Letters,* No. 2006-33-34, San Francisco: Federal Reserve Bank of SF.

7. Government Accountability Office (GAO). 2004. *Current Government Data Provide Limited Insight into Offshoring of Services.* GAO-04-932. Washington D.C.: Government Accountability Office.

8. Houseman, Susan. 2007. "Outsourcing, Offshoring, and Productivity Measurements in US Manufacturing," *W. E. Upjohn Institute for Employment Research* (April), 23.

9. Houseman, "Outsourcing," 4.

CHAPTER SEVEN

1. Morris, Charles R. 2008. *The Trillion Dollar Meltdown: Easy Money, High Rollers, and the Great Credit Crash.* New York: PublicAffairs, 2.

2. Albert Einstein quote. 2008. Available online at http://www.wisdomquotes.com/cat_changegrowth.html.

3. Featherstone, Liza. 2008. "Wage against the Machine," *Slate Magazine,* June 28. Available online at http://www.slate.com/id/2194332/.

4. MSN Money. February 16, 2007. "Costco: The Anti-Wal-Mart." Available online at http://articles.moneycentral.msn.com/Investing/Extra/CostcoTheAntiWalMart.aspx?page=all.

5. Eigsti, Roger. 2008 "Costco Pays Workers Too Much?" Ethix. Available online at http://www.ethix.org/article.php3?id=219.

6. "Reviewing and Revising Wal-Mart's Benefit Strategy." 2008 Wal-Mart Watch. Available online at http://walmartwatch.com/img/sitestream/docs/Susan_Chambers_Memo_to_Wal-Mart_Board.pdf.

7. Wirtz, Ronald, January, 2008."The Research Literature on Wal-Mart: Some Frowns, Some Smiley Faces." Minneapolis Federal Reserve. Available online at http://www.minneapolisfed.org/publications_papers/pub_display.cfm?id=1122.

8. Falcone, Michael, December 19, 2007. "Obama: Stop Chinese Toy Imports." *The New York Times Daily Blog.* Available online at http://thecaucus.blogs.nytimes.com/2007/12/19/obama-stop-chinese-toy-imports/?apage=2.

9. MSNBC. September 21, 2007. "Mattel Apologizes to China over Recalls." Available online at http://www.msnbc.msn.com/id/20903731/.

10. Thorpe, Evan. 2008, "Bringing R&D to China, *China Business Review.* Available online at http://www.chinabusinessreview.com/public/0803/thorpe.html#fig1.

11. American Society of Civil Engineers. "Report Card for America's Infrastructure." 2005. American Society of Civil Engineers. Available online at http://www.asce.org/reportcard/2005/index.cfm.

12. Strong American Schools. "A Stagnant Nation: Why American Students Are Still At Risk," 2008. ED in 08. Available online at http://www.edin08.com/uploadedFiles/Issues/Issues_Pages/EDin08_Stagnant_Nation.pdf.

13. James, David. 2008. "Will Testing Solve Our Schools' Problems?" *Journal of College Admission.* FindArticles.com. 29 Oct. Available online at http://findarticles.com/p/articles/mi_qa3955/is_200207/ai_n9122072.

14. James, "Will Testing Solve Our Schools' Problems?"

15. Malveaux, Julianne. 2008. "Time to Address Our Education Crisis, Too," *USA Today,* 10/24/08, 11A.

Bibliography

1. Akers, Michael D., Giacomino, Don E., and Bellovary, Jodi L. 2007. "Earnings Management and Its Implications." *The CPA Journal,* August.

2. Altman, Daniel. 2006. "Managing Globalization: China as Economic Bogeyman May Be Wrong Strategy for Washington." *International Herald Tribune,* December 12.

3. Barshefsky, Charlene, and Gressner, Edward. 2005. "Revolutionary China, Complacent America." *Wall Street Journal,* September 15.

4. Beatty, Jack. 2007. *Age of Betrayal: The Triumph of Money in America, 1865–1900.* New York: Alfred A. Knopf, 22–23.

5. Bernstein, William J. 2008. *A Splendid Exchange: How Trade Shaped The World.* New York: Atlantic Monthly Press.

6. Berry, Wendell. 2008. "Faustian Economics." *Harper's Magazine,* May.

7. Bogle, John C. 2005. *The Battle for the Soul of Capitalism.* New Haven: Yale University Press.

8. Bogle, John C. 2005. "The Ownership of Corporate America: Rights and Responsibilities." *Vanguard,* April 11.

9. Bogle, John. 2006. "Whose Capital Is It? Putting Owners Back in Control." *Business Economics* 41 (2): 47–52.

10. Brown, Sherrod. 2008. "Don't Call Me a Protectionist." *Wall Street Journal,* April 23.

11. Buhl, David. 2007. "Banking in China." University of St. Gallen, December 22. Available online at http://www.glorad.org/hsg/dbic/reports/16%20Banking%20in%20China%20-%20Buehl.pdf.

12. Buffington, Jack. 2007. *An Easy Out: Corporate America's Addiction to Outsourcing.* Westport, CN: Praeger.

13. Champy, James. 1995. *Reengineering Management: The Mandate for New Leadership.* New York: HarperBusiness.

14. Chandrasekhar, C. P., and Ghosh, Jayati. 2005. "The Chinese Bogeyman in US Clothing." Networkideas.org, April 26. Available online at http://www.networkideas.org/themes/trade/apr2005/tp26_US_Clothing.htm

15. Chang, Ha-Joon. 2008. *Bad Samaritans: The Myth of Free Trade and the Secret History of Capitalism.* New York: Bloomsbury Press.

16. Chernow, Ron. 1998. *Titan: The Life of John D. Rockefeller, Sr.* New York: Random House.

17. China Banking Regulatory Commission. 2006. *Banks and Enterprise Privatization in China.* Beijing: CBRC.

18. Chuanheng, Lu. 2008. "No Legal Recourse for Poor Chinese Workers.' UPIAsia.com, January 31. Available online at http://www.upiasia.com/Society_Culture/2008/01/31/no_legal_recourse_for_poor_chinese_workers/3942/.

19. Clark, Gregory. 2007. "A Farewell to Alms: A Brief Economic History of the World." In *The Princeton Economic History of the Western World.* Princeton, NJ: Princeton University Press.

20. "Clipping the Dragon's Wings." *The Economist,* December 19. 2007.

21. Collins, James C. 2001. *Good to Great: Why Some Companies Make the Leap— And Others Don't.* New York: HarperBusiness.

22. Cooper, James C. 2008. "Services: A Heavyweight in a Hard Fight." *Business Week,* May 19.

23. Covey, Stephen R. 1990. *The Seven Habits if Highly Effective People: Restoring the Character Ethic.* New York: Fireside Book.

24. Crothall, Geoffrey. 2008. "Worker's Rights in China." *Wall Street Journal,* May 1.

25. Deming, W. Edwards. 2000. *Out of Crisis.* Cambridge, MA: The MIT Press.

26. Dickson, Paul. 2001. *Sputnik: The Shock of the Century.* New York: Walker Publications.

27. Dorgan, Byron L. 2006. *Take This Job and Ship It: How Corporate Greed and Brain-Dead Politics Are Selling Out America.* New York: Thomas Dunne Books/St. Martin's Press.

28. Driskill, Robert. 2008. "Why Do Economists Make Such Dismal Arguments about Trade?" *Foreign Policy Magazine,* May.

29. Drucker, Peter. 2002. *Managing in the Next Society.* New York: St. Martin's Press.

30. Drucker, Peter. 1993. *Post-Capitalist Society.* New York: Harper Business, 49.

31. Drucker, Peter F. 1989. *The New Realities: In Government and Politics, in Economics and Business, in Society and World View.* New York: Harper & Row.

32. Edersheim, Elizabeth Haas, and Peter F. Drucker. 2007. *The Definitive Drucker.* New York: McGraw-Hill.

33. Ehrenreich, Barbara. 2001. *Nickel and Dimed: On (Not) Getting by in America.* New York: Metropolitan Books.

34. Emmott, Bill. 2008. *Rivals: How the Power Struggle between China, India and Japan Will Shape Our Next Decade.* Orlando, FL: Harcourt.

35. Engardio, Pete. 2006. *Chindia.* New York: McGraw-Hill.

36. Fallows, James. 2008. "The $1.4 Trillion Question." *The Atlantic,* January/February, 35–48.

37. Fallows, James. 2007. "China Makes, The World Takes." *The Atlantic,* July/August, 47–60.

38. Fallows, James. 2008. "The $1.4 Trillion Question." *The Atlantic,* January/February, 38.

39. Fishman, Ted C. 2005. *China, Inc.: How the Rise of the Next Superpower Challenges America and the World*. New York: Scribner.

40. Fleckenstein, William A., and Sheehanm Frederick. 2008. *Greenspan's bubbles: The Age of Ignorance at the Federal Reserve*. New York: McGraw-Hill.

41. Florida, Richard. 2008. "The Rise of the Mega Region." *The Wall Street Journal*, April 12, A8.

42. Foust, Dean. 1997. "Alan Greenspan's Brave New World." *Business Week*, July 14. Available online at http://www.businessweek.com/1997/28/b35351.htm.

43. Frank, Thomas. 2008. "Our Great Economic U-Turn." *Wall Street Journal*. May 14, 2008.

44. Friedman, Thomas L. 2005. *The World Is Flat: A Brief History of the Twenty-First Century*. New York: Farrar, Straus and Giroux.

45. "From Mao to the Mall." *The Economist*, February 14. 2008.

46. Galbraith, John Kenneth. 1967. *The New Industrial State*. Boston: Houghton Mifflin.

47. Gordon, Bernard K. 2006. "Asia's Trade Blocs." *The Wall Street Journal*, November 17.

48. Graham, John R., Harvey, Campbell. R., and Rajgopal, Shivaram. 2005. "The Economic Implications of Corporate Financial Reporting." *Journal of Accounting and Economics*.

49. Greenwood, Janette Thomas. 2000. *The Gilded Age: A History in Documents*. New York: Oxford Press.

50. Gross, Daniel. 2006. "FIRST—The Productivity Watch—The Nirvana of High Growth and Low Inflation May Be Over." *Fortune* 154 (5): 28.

51. Hadi, Mohammed. 2008. "A Rising in the East." *The Wall Street Journal*, February 20.

52. Haft, Jeremy. 2008. "Another China Trade Opportunity." *The Wall Street Journal*, May 19, A13.

53. Hakkio, Craig S. 1995. "The U.S. Current Account: The Other Deficit." *Economic Review*, Third Quarter.

54. Hale, David. 2008. "Brave New Economy." *The Wall Street Journal*, February 22.

55. Harris, Michael D. S., Herron, David, and Iwanicki, Stasia. 2008. *The Business Value of IT: Managing Risks, Optimizing Performance, and Measuring Results*. Boca Raton, FL: CRC Press.

56. Helprin, Mark. 2008. "The Challenge from China." *The Wall Street Journal*, May 13, A17.

57. Henkoff, Ronald. 1990. "Cost Cutting: How to Do It Right." *Fortune*, April 9.

58. Hindley, Brian, and Erixon, Fredrik. "Dumping Protectionism." *The Wall Street Journal*, November 1.

59. Houseman, Susan. April 2007. *Outsourcing, Offshoring, and Productivity Measurements in US Manufacturing*. W.E. Upjohn Institute for Employment Research. Available online at http://www.upjohninst.org/publications/wp/06130wp.html

60. Karabell, Zachary. 2008. "Who Stole the American Spirit?" *The Wall Street Journal*, May 14, A21.

61. Karabell, Zachary. 2007. "Watch Out for the China Bashers." *The Wall Street Journal*, September 5.

62. Khanna, Tarun. 2007. *Billions of Entrepreneurs: How China and India Are Reshaping Their Futures—and Yours*. Boston, MA: Harvard Business School Press.

63. Lapham, Lewis H. 2008. "Estate Sale." *Harper's Magazine,* May.

64. Laszlo, Ervin. 1972. *The Systems View of the World; The Natural Philosophy of the New Developments in the Sciences.* New York: G. Braziller.

65. Mahbubani, Kishore. 2008. "The Case against the West." *Foreign Affairs,* May/June.

66. Malone, Michael S. 2008. "Taking on the World." *The Wall Street Journal,* April 5, A9.

67. Malpass, David. 2007. "Global Boom." *The Wall Street Journal,* April 9.

68. Mandel, Michael. 2008. "Multinationals: Are They Good for America?" *Business Week,* March 10, 41–45.

69. Mankiw, Gregory. 2008. "Beyond the Noise on Free Trade." *New York Times,*
70. March 17, 2008.

71. Moore, Stephen, and Simon, Julian L. 1999. "The Greatest Century That Ever Was." *Cato Policy Analysis,* 1. Available online at http://www.cato.org/pubs/pas/pa364.pdf.

72. Morris, Charles R. 2008. *The Trillion Dollar Meltdown: Easy Money, High Rollers, and the Great Credit Crash.* New York: PublicAffairs.

73. Pesek, William. 2007. "The Dollar's Tarnished Crown." *International Herald Tribune,* November 18.

74. Peters, Thomas J. 1992. *Liberation Management: Necessary Disorganization for the Nanosecond Nineties.* New York: A. A. Knopf.

75. Peters, Thomas J. 1987. *Thriving on Chaos: Handbook for a Management Revolution.* New York: Knopf.

76. Peters, Thomas J., and Waterman, Robert H. 1982. *In Search of Excellence: Lessons from America's Best-Run Companies.* New York: Harper & Row.

77. Pettis, Michael. 2008. "What's Causing China's Inflation?" *The Wall Street Journal,* Asian Edition, April 17.

78. Phillips, Kevin. 2008. *Bad Money: Reckless Finance, Failed Politics, and the Global Crisis of American Capitalism.* New York: Viking.

79. Porter, Michael E. 1985. *Competitive Advantage: Creating and Sustaining Superior Performance.* New York: Free Press.

80. "Productivity in the 21st Century." 2002. Department of Labor Productivity Conference, October 23, 105. Available online at http://www.dol.gov/21CW/prod-book.pdf.

81. Quigley, Carroll. 1966. *Tragedy and Hope: A History of the World in Our Time.* New York: Macmillan.

82. Ranson, David. 2007. "Protectionism and the Falling Dollar." *The Wall Street Journal,* October 30.

83. Reich, Robert. 2007. *Supercapitalism: The Transformation of Business, Democracy, and Everyday Life.* New York: Alfred A. Knopf.

84. Roach, Stephen S. 2008. "China and Core Inflation." *The Wall Street Journal,* April 1.

85. Roach, Stephen S. 1998. "No Productivity Boom for Workers." *Issues in Science and Technology* 14 (4): 49–56.

86. Roberts, Dexter. 2008. "China's Factory Blues." *Business Week,* April 7.

87. Rodgers, T. J. 2002. *Corporate Accounting: Congress and FASB Ignore Business Realities.* Cato Institute briefing papers, no. 77. Washington, D.C.: Cato Institute.

88. Setser, Brad. 2008. "What to Do with a Half a Trillion a Year? Understanding the Changes in Management of China's Foreign Assets." cfr.org, January 15, Available online at http://www.cfr.org/content/publications/attachments/Setser%20China% 20Paper.pdf.

89. Shih, Victor. 2008. "China's Credit Boom." *The Wall Street Journal,* Asia Edition, February 21.

90. Shiller, Robert J. 2000. *Irrational Exuberance.* Princeton, NJ: Princeton University Press.

91. Sloan, Alfred P. 1964. *My Years with General Motors.* Garden City, NY: Doubleday.

92. Smith, Adam, Cannan, Edwin, and Lerner, Max. 1937. *An Inquiry into the Nature and Causes of the Wealth of Nations.* New York: Modern Library.

93. Sorman, Guy, and Puri, Asha. 2008. *The Empire of Lies: The Truth about China in the Twenty-First Century.* New York: Encounter Books.

94. Steingart, Gabor. 2008. *The War for Wealth: The True Story if Globalization or Why the Flat World Is Broken.* New York: McGraw-Hill.

95. Strassmann, Paul A. 2004. "Six Rules for Finding IT Value." *Cutter IT Journal* 17 (8): 5–9.

96. Strassmann, Paul A. 1998. "Outsourcing IT—Techies: You Don't Understand Them, You Don't Like Them, They Cost a Fortune—and Here's Why You Should Keep Them In-House." *Across the Board* 35 (5): 23.

97. Strassmann, Paul A. 1985. *Information Payoff: The Transformation of Work in the Electronic Age.* New York: Free Press.

98. Strassmann, Paul A. 1990. *The Business Value of Computers.* New Canaan, CN: Information Economics Press.

99. Sun, John. 2008. "Does 'Made in China' Still Make Sense?" *CHaINA Magazine,* May/June.

100. Sweet and Sour Pork." *The Economist,* May 13, 2008.

101. "The Middle Kingdom Middle Class." *McKinsey Quarterly Chart Focus Newsletter.* 2007 Available online at http://www.mckinseyquarterly.com/newsletters/chartfocus/2007_06.htm.

102. Taylor, Frederick Winslow. 1967. *The Principles of Scientific Management.* New York: Norton.

103. Thorniley, Daniel. 2005. "Global Corporate Strategy in 2006-08." *Economist Intelligence Unit,* November.

104. Toffler, Alvin. 1980. *The Third Wave.* New York: Morrow.

105. Tollefson, Erik. 2008. "Seeing Red." *The Economist,* May 1.

106. Waldman, Cliff. 2008. "America's Educational Performance: Implications for Global Competitiveness."Manufacturing Alliance, May 13.

107. "Washington Masks Deficits Using Accounting Tricks." *USA Today,* July 15, 2002. Available online at http://www.usatoday.com/news/opinion/2002/07/16/nceditf.htm

108. Welch, Jack, and Byrne, John A. 2001. *Jack: Straight from the Gut.* New York: Warner Books.

109. Whyte, William Hollingsworth. 1956. *The Organization Man.* New York: Simon and Schuster.

110. Wilby, Bill. 2008. "The Dollar and the Market Mess." *The Wall Street Journal,* January 23.

111. Woetzel, Jonathan, and Devan, Janamitra. 2008. "Growing Pains." *The Wall Street Journal,* April 14.

112. Yellen, Janet. 2006. "Economic Inequality in the United States," *FRBSF Economic Letters,* No. 2006-33-34, San Francisco: Federal Reserve Bank of SF.

113. Zakaria, Fareed. 2008. *The Post-American World.* New York: W.W. Norton.

Index